A MANIA FOR MAGNIFICENCE

A MANIA FOR MAGNIFICENCE

LOUIS KRONENBERGER

AN ATLANTIC MONTHLY PRESS BOOK
LITTLE, BROWN AND COMPANY
BOSTON · TORONTO

LIBRARY OF CONGRESS CATALOG CARD NO. 79–186965

FIRST EDITION

T05/72

"Whatever Became of Personal Ethics?," "A Taste of Money," and "Fashions in Vulgarity" from *The Cart and the Horse* copyright © 1957, 1958, 1961, 1962, 1963, 1964 by Louis Kronenberger. Reprinted by permission of the publisher, Alfred A. Knopf, Incorporated.

"The Rise of Gibbon and the Fall of Rome" from *The Republic of Letters* copyright © 1947, 1949, 1952, 1954, 1955 by Louis Kronenberger. Reprinted by permission of the publisher, Alfred A. Knopf, Incorporated.

"Horace Walpole's Letters" and "The Letters — and Life — of Henry Adams" from *The Polished Surface* copyright © 1965, 1966, 1967, 1969 by Louis Kronenberger. Reprinted by permission of the publisher, Alfred A. Knopf, Incorporated.

"America and Art" from *Company Manners,* copyright 1951, 1953, 1954 by Louis Kronenberger. Reprinted by permission of the publisher, The Bobbs-Merrill Company, Inc.

"Wit and Humor" from *Quality: Its Image in the Arts,* edited by Louis Kronenberger. Copyright © 1969 by Balance House. Reprinted by permission of Atheneum Publishers and Marshall Lee.

ATLANTIC–LITTLE, BROWN BOOKS
ARE PUBLISHED BY
LITTLE, BROWN AND COMPANY
IN ASSOCIATION WITH
THE ATLANTIC MONTHLY PRESS

*Published simultaneously in Canada
by Little, Brown & Company (Canada) Limited*

PRINTED IN THE UNITED STATES OF AMERICA

To
Julie and John Kronenberger
and
Liza and George Wanklyn

FOREWORD

It was while looking for a title to this book that the title of one of its essays seemed applicable to a fair number of others. This hadn't come about by accident, for all the essays dealt with facets — social, economic, artistic, technological — of *culture*, whether on broad terms or in terms of a single person. That a number of these essays have something in common does not turn it into a rigid theme. Since the mania is for many kinds of magnificence, what we have is not so much a theme as variations on one.

The idea of "magnificence" perhaps calls for comment. Consider the word itself, a word that nobody slurs over or hurries past. Yet, though there are few grander words in the language, there are a number that speak more of greatness. Magnificence isn't quite the word for extolling supreme merit, or at all a word that mates with virtue or honor or humanity at its noblest. It bespeaks size more than stature — something physically vast or splendid, tending toward the man-made, the materialistic, the visual; or, on occasion, mated with something trivial or small. It is at its smallest in a magnificent compliment or liar or hoax; it is at its least man-made in a magnificent view or a magnificent thunderstorm. It is at its most man-made in a magnificent palace or coronation, and the word is perhaps most at home in lordly, worldly, wealthy surroundings — a magnificent tiara or yacht.

Thus magnificence seems in great part allied with money. It can be built, it can be bought; and those who most aspire to it can confuse it with mere expensiveness or excessiveness or undue display. I suppose people can be called magnificent; indeed two or three of the very rich *have* been — Suleiman the Magnificent; Lorenzo the Magnificent; Morgan the Magnificent. In any case the word, if associated in most of its connotations with affluence, seems connected with magnanimity or humaneness in none of them. It

can, to be sure, include munificence, as in a magnificent contribution or bequest, such as created Vanderbilt and Stanford Universities and the Carnegie Institute — the largess of men who, far
from humane could be heartless, far from magnanimous could be
ruthless, and whose magnificent contributions can be matched
by their magnificent coups and grabs.

Yet, though lacking in virtue and nobility, magnificence can have
great scope, amplitude, eminence, and can derive from notable
projects or ambitions that are often close to mania. Thus the title
of this book can be applied not just to the Louis XIVs and Prince
Regents and various industrial potentates, but to a letter writer so
magnificent in amplitude as Horace Walpole, to a diarist so magnificent in scope as Greville, to a historian so magnificent in span
as Gibbon. At the other extreme Harold Nicolson has close to a
mania, while lacking the mastery, for grandee living.

Perhaps by now you wonder about my own predilection for magnificence. A personal mania for it I think I can disclaim, but a vi-
carious one I may well have, from my great enjoyment of the
urbane, brilliant, worldly aspects of culture. And I would think my
approach to the material in this book is as much my reason for writing about it as is the material itself, for it much less calls for a
black-or-white or yes-or-no approach than for a mixed or moot or
skeptical or ironic or ambivalent one.

But let me shift ground to remark that though almost all these
essays were written after 1960, they treat of almost every period for
the last three centuries. One of the very few "periods" of the past
three centuries that they don't treat of is the last seven or eight
years. Yet these, if too few years to constitute a period, have done
the work of something far more than one. Such early-1960s essays
as "Whatever Became of Personal Ethics?" "A Taste of Money,"
and "Fashions in Vulgarity" treat of matters that today cannot but
seem very secondary when set against the overwhelming subject
matter of the late-1960s: Vietnam, blacks, drugs, slums, pollution,
crime. These things have swept to one side much that earlier confronted and troubled us; they are like great ideological epidemics
that require, and will not easily find, large sociological remedies;

and to a considerable extent they dominate our reading and our talk.

Yet it would be the merest cant to suppose that they dominate our egos or ambitions or actions. They may have quite usurped the limelight while darkening the sky, but except as they directly affect or endanger us, we go on for the most part much as usual. This doesn't apply to the young, who *started out* differently; but elsewhere liberalistic social morality is quite often still maintained at the expense of personal ethics — except where liberalism can no longer cope with the problems it once did. No longer, for one example, is it simply the blacks' civil rights or their nonviolent demands that such liberalism must deal with today. As for egos and ambitions and pleasures, they haven't changed, except for the worse. Thus where in the early 1960s the Metropolitan Museum paid over two million for a less than great Rembrandt and exhibited it to gaping crowds attracted not by the picture but by the price, in the late 1960s Boston's Museum of Fine Arts boastfully exhibited a Raphael which the Italian government has accused them of smuggling. And consider the prices fetched today, whether for a masterpiece or the merest preliminary sketch; and in an era of frightfully menacing inflation where, one must ask, is there a worse inflated market — with the museums never once protesting it?

But much else persists elsewhere. Thus far, that colossal mania, the conquest of uninhabitable space, hasn't solved the problem of a single bestially overcrowded slum. Telegraph Avenue may for a while have obscured Madison Avenue, where it today is moribund and Madison Avenue very much alive. On a smaller scale, the mania for magnificent gourmet food in lordly restaurants grows ever more intense, with people exulting rather than exploding over a dinner for four costing $350. As for the like mania in wine, it perhaps suffices that a single very cobwebbed bottle of Lafite Rothschild was sold for around $5000. But possibly the most revealing of all the manias is the increasingly large number of firms that *stress* in their advertisements how very expensive their products are.

Just so, I don't feel that the facets of social culture I scrutinized less than ten years ago are really buried under the weight of the sociological crises that have arisen since. Instead they both stare straight out at us in the newspapers: blacks, drugs, crimes, Vietnam in the headlines; jewels, gourmet restaurants, swank parties, self-promotion in the ads and the gossip columns and the feature stories. What alone would prevent the complete polarization of these two groups is that on occasion the drugs may cost even more than the dinners.

CONTENTS

I

STYLE, IN LIFE AND LETTERS

1

WIT AND HUMOR

Wit and humor are one of those long-linked pairs that suggest a very close — a kind of brother-and-sister — blood relationship; yet, if viewed that way, they must also be assumed to exhibit distinct family differences, in both temperament and attitude toward life. As pairs go, they are perhaps better thought of as something like salt and pepper. In any case, both of them are able to flourish in various forms, and to exhibit merit in a way that protests our simply lumping them together as "comedy" or "laughter." For comedy and laughter are chiefly occupied with the nature of the beast, where our concern is whether or not it is a thoroughbred. Furthermore, why we laugh has been a chief analytical pursuit from Aristotle to Freud, and it has proved on the whole much more arid than enlightening — this in addition to its not even having at times any real connection with wit or humor, since we may *laugh* out of mere politeness, or embarrassment, or as an alternative to displaying annoyance. We "properly" laugh, it is obvious, at what we find funny; what may be less obvious, the laughter may spring from something not intrinsically amusing — a familiar group joke, or a community laughingstock, or from someone telling the same story for the twentieth time. In any case, it seems to me that we *laugh* much more at witlessness than at wit, at humorlessness than at humor — if only because nothing can make us feel so superior; whereas first-rate wit or humor inspires more admiration for the author of it than derision for the object.

More specifically, we laugh at situations, predicaments, anti-climaxes; and with these we may encounter something creative or imaginative enough to be splendidly witty and funny both. When, in Wilde's *Importance of Being Earnest*, Jack Worthing, who has contrived to kill off his "brother," suddenly appears on the stage in deep mourning — only for the dead man to be not only alive but right on the premises — the *visual* impact of such extreme and ill-founded bereavement is a great stroke of instantaneous wit. But wit is for the most part a direct product of language; its tactic, says H. W. Fowler, as Sydney Smith said a hundred years earlier, is surprise — as accurate a word as I think one could find for a comment that we cannot see coming and then hits the bull's-eye. Most wit of high quality adds something by illuminating the particular subject matter and subtracts something by criticizing the object of it. But it must do this with words of particular aptness: when Edith Wharton describes a character as one of those ladies "who pursue Culture in bands, as though it were dangerous to meet alone," the satiric wit at once contributes to our knowledge and diminishes our respect. Though the right words are a *sine qua non* of superior wit, in the great masters of it, wit is almost always a matter of attitude as well as adroitness, as much a habitual way of seeing things as of saying them. Such writers have philosophically a comic sense of life, have temperamentally a skeptical, critical nature of their own. Their wit is not just chiefly compounded of salt, it is extremely disdainful of sugar; and those who are superlatively witty — Molière, Congreve, Voltaire, Jane Austen, Peacock, Heine — are so organically so as to be synonyms of wit, as a Keats is a synonym of poetry or a Mozart of music. The whole texture of *Candide* is in a sense as satirically witty as any of its individual hits, such as the reference to sentencing England's Admiral Byng to be shot *"pour encourager les autres."* The whole texture of *Pride and Prejudice* is as committed to witty reflection as is Mr. Bennet's reply to Mr. Collins's boastfully describing the "little delicate compliments" he obsequiously heaps upon Lady Catherine de Burgh: "May I ask whether these pleasing attentions proceed from the impulse of the moment, or are the result of previous study?"

The fact that such masters don't just embellish but impregnate their work with wit indicates how many are its facets, how varied its functions, what a spectrum it constitutes, what a kaleidoscope it creates. It can possess quality through glitter as well as weight, and in the form of other weapons than a rapier: with Byron on Wellington it can be a fieldpiece, with Dr. Johnson a heavy hammer that hits the nail right on the head, with Pope a virtual guillotine. Good wit, we might say, flashes like lightning; very good wit flashes and hits something. In any case, wit moves fast: however aristocratic, it is never solemnly announced by the butler; it bounds like a rabbit out of a hat. The drawing room, or wherever people socially foregather, is the classic scene for unpremeditated yet elegant wit; perhaps the most delightful *social* wit is one of easy, unchecked flow among, as it were, well-matched instrumentalists. Unhappily, there is seldom any record of it; most superior wit that has traveled down the ages has been sharp and brief. It may be Dr. Johnson's famous retort to the shouted abuse of a bargeman on the Thames: "Sir, your wife, under *pretense* of keeping a bawdy house, is a receiver of stolen goods." It may be the chance proximity on a railway platform of a French cardinal and general who hated each other. Inquired the cardinal grandly, "*Mr. Stationmaster,* when does the next train leave for Bordeaux?" Purred the general, "At half past two, madame." It may be John Wilkes's answer to a very smug Catholic's question: "Where was your religion before the Reformation?" "Where," said Wilkes, "was your face before you washed it this morning?"

Among other virtues, in each of these cases there has been sufficient provocation for a withering retort; there is no gratuitous malice, no needless bad manners. All in all, really unfair and bullying wit, even in Dr. Johnson on other occasions, can be — from insufficient "motivation" — of doubtful merit, just as poor plot motivation is in a novel. This is not for a moment to disparage a purely objective maliciousness, as in Lord Chesterfield's cold and brilliant comment on a certain marriage: "Nobody's son has married Everybody's daughter." Opportunity knocked again when Mischa Elman, sitting in a box at Jascha Heifetz's triumphant debut, remarked to Gabrilowitsch, "Isn't it awfully warm in here?" and was answered, "Not for pianists."

When we leave the concert hall or dance floor or drawing room for the library, we find, in literature, a great many species of wit. We might suitably begin with critical wit at the expense of writers, or artists in other fields, themselves. As lethal as it is laconic is Gide's famous reply as to who was the greatest French poet: "Victor Hugo, *hélas.*" And Philip Guedalla achieved a brilliant play on words with his dividing the novels of Henry James into three periods: James the First, James the Second, and the Old Pretender. Of wit's many forms, perhaps satiric wit is the most readily and richly communicable — for here, beyond expert marksmanship, there is often an exhilarating target. Our appreciation may depend in part, as does caricature in drawing, on our familiarity with the victim; though at the highest levels — in a Dryden at his best, or a Pope — the wit is so acute, the strokes are so sure that, to respond, we need not know very much about a Shadwell or a Buckingham or an Addison. In Pope's greatest satiric portraits, as of Lord Hervey, we have nothing less than vituperative wit — venomous, relentless, disproportionate; but so superbly carried out as to be a masterpiece:

> *Let Sporus tremble. — What? that thing of silk,*
> *Sporus, that mere white curd of ass's milk?*
> *Satire or sense, alas, can Sporus feel?*
> *Who breaks a butterfly upon a wheel?*
> *Yet let me flap this bug with gilded wings,*
> *This painted child of dirt, that stinks and stings,*
> *Whose buzz the witty and the fair annoys,*
> *Yet wit ne'er tastes, and beauty ne'er enjoys.*
>
>   . . .
> *Fop at the toilet, flatterer at the board,*
> *Now trips a lady, and now struts a lord.*
>
>   . . .
> *Beauty that shocks you, parts that none will trust,*
> *Wit that can creep, and pride that licks the dust.*

But satiric portrayal of real persons or places is no wittier than satiric invention of fictional ones. It is only necessary to cite a va-

riety of examples — Voltaire's Dr. Pangloss, George Meredith's
Sir Willoughby Patterne, Jane Austen's Mrs. Bennet, Congreve's
Lady Pliant, Etherege's Sir Fopling Flutter, Molière's Monsieur
Jourdain, Petronius's Trimalchio — to recognize now biting ridi-
cule, now glittering mockery, now high-spirited joshing. But, in
addition to a name, satiric wit can have an address: in J. P. Mar-
quand's *Late George Apley*, it will be Boston; in Henry Adams's
Democracy, Washington; in Norman Douglas's *South Wind*,
Capri; in Max Beerbohm's *Zuleika Dobson*, Oxford; in Anatole
France's *Penguin Island*, France; in all these there is quality. Ben
Jonson's satire showed how men's various manias — much the
commonest was greed for money — could dehumanize them. Jonson's can be a kind of misanthropic and moralistic wit — solid but
heavy gold; two centuries later, Thomas Love Peacock, in *Nightmare Abbey* and *Crotchet Castle*, satirized men with more benev-
olent manias, who had witty stylized discussions seated round the
dinner table. A century more, and George Bernard Shaw could be
playfully satiric, as in the trial scene of *The Devil's Disciple*, or far-
cically so in *Androcles and the Lion*, or very eloquently in the hell
scene of *Man and Superman*.

Self-satire joined to social satire can reap very pleasant rewards
— consider Dean Swift writing about his own imagined death; or
E. M. Forster using the centenary of his "death" to josh English
cant and the clichés of the London *Times:*

> There can be no doubt that his contemporaries did not recognize
> the greatness of Forster. Immersed in their own little affairs, they
> either ignored him, or forgot him, or confused him, or, strangest of
> all, discussed him as if he was their equal. We may smile at their
> blindness, but for him it can have been no laughing matter, he
> must have had much to bear, and indeed he could scarcely have
> endured to put forth masterpiece after masterpiece had he not felt
> assured of the verdict of posterity . . . Like Beethoven, like Blake,
> Forster was essentially English, and in commemorating him we can
> yet again celebrate what is best and most permanent in ourselves.

This brings us to parody proper, most of which lacks distinction
either from being too obvious or from fastening on a single tendency or trick — Swinburne's alliteration, Wordsworth's prosy side,

Browning's twisted style (though all three weaknesses have been adroitly parodied). No form of wit is better criticism than parody at its finest; but it *must* truly criticize. This is just what many of Lewis Carroll's parodies fail to do: "How doth the little crocodile," "You are old, Father William," "Twinkle, twinkle, little bat" are amusing and wacky variations on their originals, but not satiric judgments; the proof is that the writers they parody could never have written them. Max Beerbohm's best parodies are decidedly the finest modern parodies of writers that exist: using Christmas as a basis for the bulk of them, Max in the Henry James parody has two tots in a dilemma whether to look at their Christmas stockings; and in the Edmund Gosse has that bustling friend-of-the-great arrange a Christmas lunch between the hearty, all's-right-with-the-world Browning and the sullen, all's-wrong-with-it Ibsen. More important, the prose in each parody is wonderfully right — witness from the James: "The scarred, the poor dear woebegone and so very beguilingly *not* refractory mirror of the moment." At a genial level Robert Benchley rouses laughter with such subjects as program notes for the ballet; for sustained parody that draws blood and laughter both, W. B. Scott's *Chicago Letter* bashes in the whole avant-garde, esoteric, exalté, multilingual, culture-snobbish, name-encrusted, jargon-infested world of the terribly superior quarterly and the loftily pretentious elite.

This is to pulverize ultra-highbrowism into nonsense. Of quality nonsense in itself, *Alice in Wonderland* is both *grande dame* and grandmother. Oscar Wilde's Lady Bracknell, that "monster without being a myth," is another *grande dame*, not least when interviewing Jack Worthing as a possible son-in-law. Stephen Leacock, Donald Ogden Stewart, Robert Benchley, James Thurber, S. J. Perelman have, on this side of the Atlantic, written now and then inspired, frequently enjoyable, and sometimes slow-footed nonsense. On this side also, nonsense has during the last generation become a trade, the method a trick, the *non sequitur* exploited *ad nauseam*. American nonsense has not least been mechanized and vulgarized in the shaggy-dog story where a frog complains of "a man in my throat" and a horse, given extra hay, says "and that ain't money." This is not inferior wit, this is a total and tawdry lack of it.

This brings us to puns and plays-on-words in general. Plainly, they can be good or bad; to take two very agreeable ones, there is John Wilkes's remarking that the Peace of Paris was like the peace of God, which passeth understanding; as there is Charles Poore's remark, in adversely reviewing an art book, "I say this more in Seurat than in Ingres." But most puns and plays-on-words are either obvious or inept, or they somehow clang too loud upon the ear; most of them would scarcely pass muster as wisecracks. Oscar Levant once defined wit as "a wisecrack that has played Carnegie Hall," but that is about like saying that, when put in a Tiffany box, a cultured pearl becomes a real one. Surely it is an indictment of taste to flaunt a label as a guarantee of merit. It is one thing that, just as Homer nods, Laurence Sterne sometimes smirks or Max Beerbohm turns coy. For such men exhibit for the most part genuine distinction, their wit being both filtered by artistry and founded on a greater wish to please themselves than to please other people. The minute the wish is reversed, distinction is clearly in danger and probably doomed; and when the medium is a mass medium, "other people" means millions of other people, who are to be amused at *their* level, whatever the writer's. That is why Broadway comedies, pandering to mass appetites, and TV comedies even more, almost always fail of quality, and never so often as today. For today they are most frequently, and in box-office terms most successfully, gag comedies — the brassy rat-tat-tat of the joking doubling the ragbag nature of the jokes. There are indeed good gags and wisecracks, possessing the sharpness and surprisingness of wit, but they remain gags and wisecracks by virtue of their tone — of something brash, flip, overfamiliar. And they are bound to miss out on real merit, for though low humor and low farce, rooted as they are in character and situation, can be extremely rewarding, low wit cannot. For, *as* wit, it invites harsher criticism than it inflicts; it reflects more damagingly its own crass ambitions than any it would condemn. Russel Crouse, one of Broadway's brightest hacks, summed things up when he remarked that during out-of-town tryouts the "laughs" were all clocked, and jokes that failed to get enough were killed. It seems odd enough that a play groomed for New York should be judged by, say, Philadelphia's reactions; but the real point was the hack's criterion of "Will this get a laugh?" rather than "Is this funny?"

A few words might be said of two other categories of wit — light verse and the epigram. Quality in light verse is often extremely high, though sometimes of a limited kind, as in the too purely verbal fireworks of a W. S. Gilbert, or the impeccable craftsmanship but at times flavorless content of a C. S. Calverley. The best limericks, as flawless as they are improper, stand very high; there is merit also in the terse impropriety of the French "Lot and his Daughters":

Il but,
Il devint tendre;
Et puis il fut
Son gendre.

As for the epigram, it has less claim to truth or wisdom — but more need of trenchancy and wit — than the aphorism. There is a fine succinctness about such an aphorism as La Rochefoucauld's "We refuse praise from a desire to be praised twice," or about Vauvenargues's "Vice stirs up wars, virtue fights," but in neither is there any great brilliance or surprise. There is both, on the other hand, in Chamfort's epigrammatic retort on the claims of the eighteenth-century French nobility to be the intermediary between the King and the people: "Ah yes, just as the hounds are the intermediary between the hunters and the hares."

In several respects, humor differs vitally from wit, though this is not to deny their frequent neighborliness, or sharing the same house or even the same room. There is a touch of both in the Savoyard proverb, "I have so much to do that I am going to bed"; both also inhabit the story of Humbert Wolfe, a pacifist during World War I, being publicly handed a white feather and inquiring with a smile, "Have you a pin?" Without regarding them as absolutes, I think we can define certain differences between wit and humor. Thus, where wit is a form of criticism or mockery, humor includes an element of self-criticism or self-mockery; where wit tends to proclaim imperfection, humor wryly acknowledges it; where wit undresses you, humor goes naked. At its best, humor simultaneously hurts and heals, makes one larger from a willingness to make oneself less. It has essentially much more breadth than wit, from being much more universal in appeal and human in effect. If harder to translate or explain, it often need not be explained or translated at all, revealing itself in a sudden gesture, a happy juxtaposition. We speak constantly of "the humor of the situation," almost never of the wit: just so, virtually everything that is farcical or funny derives from humor gone a bit wild. Besides having more largeness and breadth, humor at its finest has also more depth, or at any rate has something unfathomable or mysterious enough to move us. (The wag is deadpan, but the clown is sad-faced.) Walter Kerr speaks of the moment in *The Circus* when Charlie Chaplin, "having surreptitiously managed to eat the whole of a child's hot-dog, reaches for a napkin and very thoughtfully wipes the child's lips." Humor too has its surprises, but they do not so much illuminate as throw a strange light over the scene.

Chaplin, for what he superlatively — and the clown generally — symbolizes in humanity, helps explain one of humor's greatest endowments and most steadfast affiliations. Humor in this sense is a needed walking stick that can also serve as a weapon for the lame, the lost, the ill-favored, the disreputable — for what we might call the have-nots of the world. These people achieve quality by transforming what could be self-pity or bitterness into something that mocks at the more fortunate while being rueful about themselves. "If this is how Her Majesty treats her prisoners," said Oscar Wilde standing handcuffed in the pouring rain, "she doesn't deserve to have any." An old Negro plaint concludes: "Money thinks I'm dead." "If the rich," runs a Yiddish proverb, "could hire other people to die for them, the poor could make a wonderful living." Perhaps another distinction between wit and humor would in general align wit with the epigram, with society and the drawing room and the terrace; and humor with the proverb, with humanity and the kitchen and the back fence.

Far more familiar and popular, to be sure, is the humor that, from having nonsense in its veins, simply brightens our existence. Of such humor the English are the great masters. We find it again and again in their nonpareils of eccentricity, their *non sequiturs* of thought, in the very existence of an Uncle Toby, the mere entrance of a Micawber; in the lies of Falstaff, the commands of the Red Queen, the pranks of Tony Lumpkin, the precautions of Mr. Woodhouse. Many English novels are so filled with humor that it seems to us the mainspring of their interest, their charm, their vitality; we might, indeed, almost suppose the humorous minor character to be an English invention. There is also an English school of humorous light verse, as good in its way as the school that is witty, as old as the Elizabethans, as famous as Edward Lear, as modern as John Betjeman.

America has had its gifted humorists, most notably Mark Twain, its George Ades and Finley Peter Dunnes, its aforesaid Benchleys and Thurbers, its Erskine Caldwell in *God's Little Acre* and Faulkner in *The Hamlet*, and has had its great stage comics. But in my opinion the mainstream of American humor is short on quality. Thus, compared with an English achievement in the novel alone, which extends from Fielding and Smollett to Jane Austen and Peacock, from Cranford to Barchester, from Mr. Pickwick to Mr. Polly, the American achievement is truly meager. Granting England a big head start, the great difference may be one between a compact, homogeneous caste society (where class distinctions are themselves a source of humor) and a sprawling, heterogeneous, democratic one. From our crude early native humor of the tall tale and the frontier, we switched to a humor predominantly regional or racial, often much too broad and stereotyped: despite a melting-pot culture, each brand of humor stood aloof from the others. Pat and Mike were one thing, Abie and Moe quite another (*Abie's Irish Rose* was belated and sentimental); as were Sambo and Rastus, as were the dry Yankee, the breezy Wild Westerner, the Southern colonel with his drawl. If there was a melting pot of humor it came, very much thinned out and standardized, with the microphone; if there developed a tradition of humor, it lay not in the novel but in the stage joke and the comic strip. In time a few targets changed — the mother-in-law became Mom; but not much else was changed. Even zany humor was largely formula stuff, even homespun humor seemed machine-made, and when something fresh did appear, it was immediately canned to please various palates, with labels reading Book, Play, Movie, Radio, Television, Digest, Sunday Supplement. To a great extent, *humor* in America has lost not only its quality but its very essence; has turned curiously snide, has become self-pityingly or self-lashingly "sick"; our gags celebrate our guile, our banter parades our aggressions. All this is alien to true humor, from offering the insect's bite and not the disinfectant's. At the same time, we tend in any "important" matter, like politics or business, to fear humor, to bracket it with levity and irreverence, to worry that it may backfire. In opposition to such widespread, weak-kneed conformism and philistinism, there has understandably developed in America a harsh, needling, flagellating, ultimately reckless satire. For ours is no age or climate for magnanimous humor or genial wit. In such a climate, we can "hope" perhaps for something of great power and magnitude to appear, for someone like Swift in an oppressed Ireland, Chamfort in a decadent France, or Dickens in a crime-darkened, slum-ridden London.

2

WHATEVER BECAME OF PERSONAL ETHICS?

Madison Avenue also, I imagine, is paved with good intentions. It would be strange if it weren't, what with exhibiting so many other likenesses to hell, whether the temptations that bring men to it, or the torments after arriving. But Madison Avenue's paving stones represent *future* intentions as well as foiled ones: many of its residents mean someday to get out. Thus sang men once of Hollywood too, and of other pernicious settlements; and in truth men did get out, at least a few of them. This particular vow has perhaps been America's most costly illusion, a very graveyard of its culture. Unlike Europe, whose ruins are of stone and brick, ours are of chromium and gray flannel. Unlike Europeans, who can be stingy and sagacious about money, we are generous and suicidal. It is meant to save us hardship and it sentences us to hell. Beyond that, our man-made hells are more insidious than Church-made ones: they are not merely punishments for temptations succumbed to, but are themselves full of temptations to boot. In the man-made hells, the Devil must forever contrive new treats and inducements, higher-paying work, grander-sounding titles. And man-made hells are much more understandable than Church-made ones, not just because they combine high pay with hard labor, but because it is easier to believe in your own weak nature than in a stern, retributive God. *How can I help it?* any child could understand, where *Why should He do this to me?* can seem quite unfathomable. Expiating guilt on God's terms is far more rigorous than learning to live with it on Freud's.

My point, however, is nothing so obvious as that psychoanalysis has become one of our great religions. My point is not about psychoanalysis at all, but only about a new shift by which people hold their guilt at bay. In today's business and professional world that employs the educated, the clever, the gifted — a world of air waves and advertising copy, of publicity and promotion, of newsprint and coated stock, of regional distribution and national circulation — great numbers of those recruited espouse a certain political and social philosophy. They are liberals. They have liberal objectives, vote liberal tickets, support liberal causes. They are genuinely social-minded; are unreservedly for integration, slum clearance, socialized medicine, prison reform; for old-age benefits and reclaimed young delinquents; for due process, for free speech, for the abolition of censorship. In a voting booth they are presumably their own man, in the club car only slightly the corporation's; they take off their blinkers after quitting their desks and their muzzles after leaving the building. A numerous group, they are necessarily of different selves and kinds. Some are violent about Southerners, some about Communists, some about Catholics. Some think practicality the most workable idealism; others fear that power corrupts, whatever its character. Some, worn out by the long grind, grow more militant in their liberalism; others, perked up by the new promotion, grow more perfunctory. But they are all liberals in no very ambiguous sense, on no quickly satirized terms.

Most of them indeed practice what they preach, at the town meeting as well as in the voting booth; in the books they buy, the warm-potato injustices they protest, and only a little less than formerly in the schools where they enroll their children. They firmly believe in the future. *Future*, as it happens, is the key word, the complicating word. For their own future marches side by side, as it were, with mankind's. Or rather, it fails to march side by side, from forever jockeying for position, jostling for precedence. These, after all, are the big futurity stakes, and *their* future can on occasion be at odds with mankind's. How bravely wave the banners of progress! How meanly read the interoffice memos! The contrast between the two is as sharp as that between the exalting dream and the shrilling alarm clock. And the conflict is as fierce as the contrast is pointed.

The schism they have made between the self and society has somewhat the nature of a deal. The basis of the deal is not to hamper the self *in* society, not to make one's social ideals penalize one's personal welfare. Character, that is to say, must not stand in the way of career; belief must not always govern behavior. In a sense, of course, the new schism is as old as the human race; is the eternal clash between our acquisitive instincts and our aspiring ones, between the thrust of ambition and the prick of conscience. But in another sense there is perhaps something truly new about it; as there is further a real variation on something old.

What is perhaps new is what seems so contradictory. People who in the past led lives of educated careerism seldom espoused militantly social-minded aims. They often showed a proper community spirit or denounced political corruption in their own backyards; they favored hospitals and supported orchestras; they did much for growing children and something for wayward girls. But they seldom gave vocal support to social programs that reached beyond personal benevolence. They righted wrongs as against affirming rights; they did not plump for a social progress that might threaten their own. *Political* opportunists may have done so; or crusaders like the New England abolitionists who, as millowners, were exploiters as well. But few business careerists have been open — and purse-open — liberals, rejecting all the arguments of a reasoned conservatism and hailing a future that should redress the wrongs of the past. What today's liberal careerists alone except from all this is the present. The present may require their groveling before the boss, or being a touch treacherous toward a colleague, or taking credit for someone else's bright idea, or transferring the blame for one's own mistake; it may require whooping up the network's clownish censorship or craven cancellations; it may demand a little polite job-lifting or sabotage or slander. But if it does, that springs from bondage to today's dog-eat-dog world and man-bites-man methods, and is in strong contrast to the forward-march into the future, to the crusade against all repression that doesn't obstruct promotion.

What seems new in this is not the fact of such a dichotomy, but its particular nature. Those who earlier aimed straight at success by however devious means always embraced a philosophy, or evolved an ethics, whereby they could glorify what they were doing. They found their sanction in an America that was the land of plenty, or in a democracy that was the gospel of opportunity, or in how hard knocks can strengthen character, or rough handling aid survival. And then, in the fullness of time, they crowned all this with septuagenarian largess. Many of them, indeed, managed to turn their ruthless careerism into "inspiring" careers: in any case, scarcely a one of them but hated Labor, fought humanitarian legislation, and branded social progress Communist.

Most past careerists did this from being a quite different breed from the one I would discuss. The new kind are a sort of debased intellectual class who, by way of their knowledge and skill, have become rather the writing hands of business than outright businessmen. Careers, for them, are not usually a tower to climb to the very top of, but a tunnel to work their way through, with plump economic security at the other end. These people have sought no philosophy to glorify their actions, have seldom rationalized their liberalism to mesh it with their livelihoods. They haven't even, a great many of them, turned hard; they are simply hardened to their roles; not least to New Dealing, as it were, from the bottom of the deck.

This means, as I have said, that in terms of liberal objectives, wherever possible they practice what they preach. And it is often possible — they can help their fellowman whenever he is segregated or jailed or flogged; censored or silenced; slum-dwelling or dispossessed. They only cannot when he is their colleague or competitor. And this seems new to me — a dog-eat-dog careerism that crusades for the underdog. What seems to me, along with it, a real variation on something old is that these people do steadily, quite early in life, what the hard-fisted rich used to do very late. For today's

rat-racers, as they crowd other rats out of the race, suffer twinges of
conscience; and so, when young and by way of their pay checks,
they do what the robber barons once did when old and by way of
their wills. They pay conscience money. But today's money, unlike
yesterday's, is not paid retrospectively in leisurely remorse; with
their knack for being modern, they have evolved Pay-as-you-go
Penance.

Here, as so often today, we must pull up to greet the national
villain in all this, the notorious Bitch-Goddess. Moreover, it's very
easy to excoriate success once we dub it a rat race; easy to condemn
it when we spell out its origins and techniques. But in fairness we
ought not to forget how long and how rousingly, from pulpits and
rostrums, in language eminently exalted and only moderately
vague, Success was made part of bright democratic vistas, of the
fulfillment of self and the furthering of progress. We must not forget for how long, before it became the Bitch-Goddess, it was the
great affirmative gospel of American life. Realistically judged, our
carrying that gospel too far — along with not grasping that as a
"democratic" ideal it was no match for a capitalist imperative —
could not but bring about what prevails today. Also, as higher education became one of democracy's great dividends, it could not but
be reinvested in material enterprise — at length in Organization
enterprise, with the rivalries now painfully intramural, the coveted
job not a mile away but across the hall, the war a civil war, the
rat-racers brother rats.

Along with all this, something resulted that I don't want to exaggerate but that, taking even a most moderate view, seems very
disquieting. There resulted, among far too many intelligent and
educated people, the substitution of social morality for personal
ethics. This seems to me a menacing contemporary phenomenon,
with even a sort of Communist fillip about it — the fillip of the
end justifying the means, of men being entitled to finagle so long
as other men shall be promised their chance. It has also led to having many *really* enlightened people so much stress social morality
as seldom to refer to personal ethics. This to some extent may be

the result of their taking personal ethics for granted; or of their assuming that as social morality advances, personal ethics must also. But I suspect that it measurably results from something else — from a feeling that personal ethics, as a specific exhortation, reeks of both copybook maxims and conservative class thinking. But surely, when liberalism can seem more a sop to conscience than a sign of it, it is time to shift emphasis a little.

Perhaps the best quality of old-fashioned conservatism was its sense of personal honor. The phrase "personal honor" so smacks of code that a dozen years ago one shied away from it, a generation ago even tended to mock it. One would still prefer a phrase like "personal decency"; but the two are not the same, and it is perhaps the very idea of code that now weighs in honor's favor. For the decent man largely *lacks* the prejudices that becloud social vision — where the honorable man behaves well in spite of having them. What was too often amiss with personal honor was its restricting itself to a group or class or nation; was its becoming, at its worst, the Southern-gentleman or old-school-tie kind of thing. But, purged of class limitations, it remains a final touchstone of conduct — first, from its governing regardless of personal bias, from its operating toward enemy no less than friend; and again, from its being born of inner pride and self-respect. To take unfair advantage or use ungenerous means shamed oneself; and on this score — of its creating no guilt or self-contempt — it made for a healthier society, or at least a healthier basis for one. Personal honor, to be sure, often rested on wealth dishonorably gained, and could constitute a kind of luxury ideal. But it operated, and still operates, among all classes, in all sorts of communities: where it all too little operates today is in the intelligent, educated world I am speaking of.

Well, we need not bring back the phrase, with its unwelcome overtones of caste; "personal ethics" will do very nicely. But, observing the steep decline of the thing itself in a "liberal" society, we must have *some* phrase to express it. Think just of surface manifestations today — think of the pokes and sideswipes among all sorts of news personalities; think of the snideness and malice, in public, of all sorts of "superior" people, self-righteous as well as self-seeking. Liberals, almost all of them. Many of them may be nothing more than decidedly touchy and pushy; others nothing worse than compulsively opportunist; doubtless only one in five is really adept at character assassination or at knife-in-the-back. Broadway, for example, abounds in social-minded, cause-conscious people; Broadway resists reaction, opposes censorship; but Broadway provides a proverbially well-lighted stage for the envenomed ego and the venal claw.

Here again we must pull up — to admit that anxiety stalks the scene hardly less than ambition. A frequent defensive plea, among such opportunists themselves, is that the jettisoning of ethics isn't merely callous or cynical, but cruelly deterministic; that in so fierce a struggle the lust to succeed is more than half the need to survive. There is no way to cry "Hold, enough!" Even should you not breathe down the neck of the man ahead of you, the man behind is breathing down yours. Certainly there is truth in all this; not least in the final twist that has made of careerism something where, if you *don't* win a prize, you must pay a forfeit. But it is not the whole truth, nor need it be elevated into a law.

All this, it must surely be clear, has no more to do with attacking liberalism than decrying Sunday Christianity has to do with attacking faith. The morality involved, it seems to me, can be worse than conscience-money morality; can be pure escapist morality, and escapist in two ways. For, however real these people's sympathy with the diverse victims of society, the fact remains that the victims nowhere impinge on these people's world, nowhere threaten it. And there is the second fact that toward all such victims these people can feel a beneficent guilt, a wholly impersonal guilt — for the wrongs done here are done by others, where the wrongs done closer to home all too often are not. Protesting one kind of misbehavior while indulging in a different kind is familiar enough; here, coming from people who do much to shape present-day conduct, it can be all too dangerous as well.

For if, *on their present terms*, these people help create a future victory for social values, it must smack of defeat as well. If people so relatively high-placed more and more shrug off personal ethics, must not other people soon regard doing so as normal? And on that basis what kind of "superior" individuals will inhabit the social-minded world of the future? For that matter, how social-minded can it be — how far can social reform prove a match for personal ruthlessness? Won't we, rather than abolishing the rat race, have simply made it available to everybody? Already there exist TV spokesmen for liberalism whose programs get gossipy and personal and who, while enjoying large incomes from the programs, pay their panelists nothing. Already there are Broadway big shots who have sound enough social ideas, but who can behave like monsters. Already we have newspapers that, under the guise of being humane about what disturbs and distorts people, exploit every humiliating, distorting detail. Even at higher levels, what chance have social goals against careerist finish lines? What price equality when intelligent human beings claw one another for a foot and three-eighths of precedence, or for billing half an inch larger? By all means let us extend, wherever possible, every form of social endeavor. But how ultimately great is the gain to bring up children with no prejudice against race and with every sympathy for the poor, if they are to have no scruples against back-stabbing, and an utter apathy toward fair play?

3

A TASTE OF MONEY

Little in our time has been oftener quoted than Shaw's retort on
Samuel Goldwyn when, in the course of their negotiations,
the businessman stressed art and the artist, money. As a rebuke to
the cant men use to disguise their venality, it was altogether fitting;
but perhaps its deeper interest lay in Shaw's being as distinctly
truthful as Mr. Goldwyn might seem disingenuous. I am also not
sure that Shaw didn't know more about money than Mr. Goldwyn;
or that he didn't care more. In any case, Shaw's steady insistence,
as a great and very famous writer, on his due — his refusal to bate
a sixpence from his royalties, or cut a line out of his plays —
set a monumental example which has doubtless fortified many
writers since. Nor is it odd that it was Shaw who did it, for it was
largely what was odd in Shaw that made him. He wanted money
for no usual reasons. During his most affluent years, he had a rich
wife and no children; did not drink, smoke, gamble, eat meat, have
sex or live grandly. He wanted money for prideful or ironic reasons.
Certainly it could help heal the hurts inflicted by his shabby-gen-
teel background and his early London struggles. As a puritan again,
Shaw — rather like the Quakers — found in moneymaking his
prime worldly satisfaction. As a writer, it somehow gratified him to
be a better businessman than the businessman. As a Socialist, it
might amuse him to be a shrewder capitalist than the capitalist.

In any case, he remained our century's great example of a distinguished writer who made a large fortune — and by being as in-

transigent about his principles as about his payments. And yet, if it rejoiced the puritan in Shaw, it just a little jolts the puritan in us. Shaw, on money, got to be a trifle too insistent: however condign the rebuke to Mr. Goldwyn, it too much reassured all Mr. Goldwyn's scribbling minions. The minions might not live like Shaw — without meat, or cigars, or the rest — and might not write like him, either; but it helped them to know that in one very important respect they and he had something in common.

Untempted by the world's fleshpots, Shaw was also unmoved by its glitter. This was rarer than it may seem. In spite of the valid identification of artists with Bohemia, the two real truths in bohemianism are the artist's loathing of bourgeois morality and his frequent lack of good sense about money. But he is bohemian, not ascetic; dislikes Suburbia far more than society; is anti-Wall Street, not antiwealth. At times indeed he can acquire very luxurious tastes, and be attracted by resplendent and seignorial backgrounds. Snobbery has never been given the serious attention it deserves, if only because few people have viewed it as a serious subject. But in various forms it can go very deep, and it frequently does so with writers. It is too bad that the word *snob* applies today equally to someone overimpressed by his own social position, and to someone overimpressed by other people's; the old distinction of *snob* (the aspiring outsider) and *nob* (the man of position) had real value. More often than we may suspect, the writer is an aspiring outsider. We need only think of the spell that the great world has exerted in all ages on literary men, whether Congreve or Pope, Swift or Sterne, Goethe or Balzac, Henry James or Proust, Scott Fitzgerald or Evelyn Waugh; and again, we need only think why. Being the most imaginative and memory-haunted of men, the writer may, to begin with, be a romantic — in love with a kind of patrician ideal, with a vision of breeding and elegance. His imagination may even make an ass of him; we need only remember, I think in Proust, someone's rapture at being asked to a very grand party and his boredom after he goes to it. And on just those terms imagination, in any perceptive writer, holds open the door while irony enters the room. But the memory-haunted writer may, in a most downright sense, remember slights and snubs that frayed his early life. Or, very simply, the writer could not bear the truth — Meredith, that his father had been in trade; Dickens, that his father had been in prison. Besides, there is even more snobbery about possessing money than about lacking it. By itself money is thought vulgar; it must be chaperoned by something socially acceptable.

And if there is a romantic reason for writers to climb, and a realistic reason as well, there is also a professional one — the interest that many writers have in "manners" and the social scene. Much of this plainly calls for firsthand knowledge. Beyond that, writers can have a desire for money and position thrust upon them — from their being given a taste of luxury that creates an appetite for it.

All these matters vary greatly, of course; and to a large number of writers they do not apply at all. But often one element or another does apply; and even where there is no social aspiration, there can be a cultural or purely economic one. The great point about writers and money today is their unprecedented opportunities for making it. It is all too easy to exaggerate the status of writers *as a whole* — for most of them the economic struggle is still painfully acute, which must be borne in mind with everything that follows. All the same, relatively many writers, often serious and good writers, have the sort of incomes today that a bare generation ago were confined to a handful of great names, or to authors of best sellers and popular stage hits. In today's age of diversified literary rights, of book clubs and paperbacks and digests, of serials and syndicates, of dramatizations and movie sales, of permissions and high-paying journalism, of radio, of TV for one's writings and TV for oneself, of lecturing and recordings, of grants and fellowships, of visiting professorships and residencies — an age in which one book can have nine lives and one fee can have six figures — a great many writers, despite high costs and high taxes, can live in the same world, indeed on the same street, as the rich and the prominent.

With this change in situation has come a decided change in attitude. The serious writer needn't think himself a name for the few, or Grub Street an address for the future. Nor need he see, between money and high standards, any necessary clash. Opportunity may not yet have knocked at his door, but it is assumed to know where he lives. Moreover, the moment Opportunity has knocked, all sorts of helpful other people will be writing and phoning and coming to call. Whoever invented the alphabet was clearly writer-conscious, putting the agent *and* the accountant *and* the analyst, at the very beginning. But even with so large a staff — or thanks to it — the writer can prosper. In his progress upward, he will use no executive elevators, and wherever he goes must still be Upper Bohemia. Upper Bohemia may picket Park Avenue; but it must often — by living on both sides of it — have to cross its own picket lines. And its children's schools, as it progresses, become less progressive; its views, as it advances, grow less advanced.

The point of all this is a quite concrete one: that there exist whole clusters of people in the arts who live *expensively* — at times through inherited wealth or moneyed marriages, but oftenest from what they earn. If we look for direct forebears on a *group* basis, we perhaps most readily find them in the Algonquin group of the 1920s. Here were people with citified interests and sophisticated tastes who made and spent a good deal of money. Even before them, of course, many individual writers had both the means and the desire to live handsomely: yet even much later, scarcely any other literary circle had an aura of expensive living about it. It is noteworthy how many good writers went to places like Yaddo and the MacDowell Colony; or had guest cottages on rich men's estates; or, if flush, rented a place for the summer; or commonly — which fitted their tastes and their purses alike — contrived to live abroad.

Certainly, during this period, writers had their windfalls and fat years, and accordingly their sprees and splurges. But, even where their bank balances could support stylish living, their antibourgeois convictions often protested it. They did not, as so often today, live like rich people, or keep up their end with the rich people they went with. But the salient point is not that till recently writers seldom lived like rich men: it's that they didn't live like businessmen.

They had agents to handle their work, and might seek out a "tax man" each year, from sheer ignorance of the tax laws. But few even very successful writers had agents in the sense they do today; indeed, they couldn't have had them in the sense they do today — as operating a vast, complex switchboard plugging in on all the sources of revenue I have already enumerated. And few writers a generation ago could have needed accountants and lawyers in the sense they do today. Today, just how they receive payment, and just when, bulks as large as how much payment they receive. Today, there is a labyrinth of technicalities to thread, of deductions to master; and perhaps such writers' biggest problems today involve real estate and the stock market, trust funds and self-incorporations. Many writers today are businessmen, not in the sense that they personally look after their own finances, but in the sense that they don't — that they employ experts. And the successful writer's day means, exactly like the businessman's, sessions with a secretary, all sorts of business letters and phone calls, an appointment at ten, a conference at twelve, a business lunch at one, and very likely a cocktail or dinner date with a business side to it. If all these things on any one day are very unlikely, a day without several of them is even more so.

Thus far I am writing of those at the top. But, numerically, there are a good many writers at the top: if not many in proportion to the whole, far more than there have ever been before, and far faster in soaring upward. But — to move decidedly down — even in a world of notoriously inadequate incomes, the academic world, one finds many and diverse new sources of income. I don't mean salaries, which have generally risen at about the rate of living costs. It is rather how many teachers and professors are now editing textbooks and paperbacks; are now published in well-paying magazines, and appearing on radio and TV; are now lecturing extensively, and winning fellowships and grants. Nor does this apply only to big academic names, or to teachers with outside reputations. The door, now, opens and widens for quite young men, men who are creating a new breed of professor — men who lace their scholarship with sass, who can be at once academic and avant-garde, who go on cultural sight-seeing, and even slumming, tours. One particular field for them is the theatre; in the colleges themselves, "the theatre of the absurd," for example, has won many season bookings. Actually humor, satire, irony, wit appear more and more on the academic menu. Urbanity is not often on it, being still too big a problem for the chef; but the sense of change is noticeable, the degree of change enlivening.

The writer's new status — or, at any rate, new scope — constitutes a genuine gain. Many financial opportunities have opened for the better type of writer, often toward desirable ends. A serious article needs to be written on the pros and cons, the pluses and minuses, of superior writers who currently address large popular audiences in magazines, on TV, on the lecture platform. Certainly the mass audience is getting far better than its normal fare; and if not many in the audience are converted or even much stirred, that only stresses the glacier-like slowness of solving the problem. In any case, enough good writers today have such audiences as to constitute a kind of working minority. They are not going to win anyone over from Yerby's level to Yeats's; indeed, their real value may lie less in making cultural recruits than in halting cultural deserters. A great American misfortune is the disintegration of the college graduate in the twenty years after he graduates — his loss of interest in what he had become acquainted with, his lack of interest in anything since. It is just such backsliding readers (who have defaulted to the "wrong" magazines) that, by way of the finer voices in them, might be reclaimed.

In contributing to mass media, the writer himself may often have to simplify, but he need not falsify, and need sometimes not change a comma. To be sure, there may be a more than merely ironic disadvantage involved. The good writer's fringe benefits may be turning into his real financial stake, so that the poet makes money largely off permissions; the playwright counts most on that worst kind of audience, the "benefit" audience; the novelist most prospers on a hack stage version or film version of his novel. And if the tail, beyond wagging the dog, is making rather a lapdog of it to boot, that in itself is no threat to the writer's *creative* career; it can possibly be the one way to ensure it. And certain fringe benefits are, for author and culture alike, true benefits — the serious paper-back readers, the university lectures, the poetry readings and re-cordings at a high level.

The writer's changing financial status necessarily means a change in his psychology. One of the great cultural phenomena of our time is what the sociologist will eventually find a jargon phrase for, but what quite simply can be called the luxury handout. I mean all the forms of expense-account high living that many people earlier enjoyed only vicariously, via magazines and movies. Today even quite unimportant writers frequently share in them, and at a high level. The entertainment of fairly unimportant businessmen, how-ever expensive, has seldom much style to it: it runs to the flashier "name" restaurants; to hit musicals, prize fights, World Series games, bars and nightclubs. But, for the not very no'able writer — who may well be a professor — magazine and publishing-house hospitality often means elegant restaurants, distinguished clubs, dinner with far better known people, besides literary lunch and cocktail parties. The same writer's lecturing involves luxury hotels and rich men's homes. All this becomes part of his professional life, and thus a conditioning factor of his own life. Moreover, along with the luxury handout, there now goes what might be called the swapped milieu. As the less stodgy bourgeois and professional world cultivates an artist-world informality, the artist tends toward more stylish and traditional living. The two groups share a pen-chant for a sort of *couleur-de-rose* peasant culture; the unstuffy rich eschew butlers and dinner jackets for buffet suppers and itinerant bartenders; the artist world fancies good wines and *cordon bleu* cooking, the very same bartenders, and on occasion a caterer.

The fact that the two styles of living have grown largely inter-changeable indicates something new for the writer, whether in terms of income or of inclination. Upper Bohemia, in one form or another, is an old tradition — but mostly with cultivated nonartists, with well-to-do people of "background" who want to keep what seems right with their world and slough off what seems oppressive. They want Bohemia's casualness without its messiness, they want traditionalism's well-bred comfort without its gentility. Something like this has also characterized *writers* of "background": one thinks of Bloomsbury or Gramercy Park. Their Upper Bohemias often acquire an academic air, or a snobbish and eventually stuffy one. Moreover, writers in such milieus can get to be rather dangerously lionized, or, even more dangerously, tamed. In general America's writers have lived a more careless life than this, whether from a lack of means, or of roots, or of desire. Certain writers might retain from their early life certain touchstones; but at least till well on in years they wanted something free and unritualized. Or, if the Left Banks and the Provincetowns and the Majorcas were ritualized in their way, it was an antibourgeois way.

What the old bohemianism signified was not just a frequent lack of money but a fundamental unconcern for it. Some of its insouciance toward money may have been rationalization; or a prevailing radicalism; or a self-dramatizing romanticism. And certainly want of money could cause serious dislocations, could ruin lives and overturn careers. But there was yet a pretty deep-seated feeling that the terms of economic success, even the terms of bourgeois security, came too high. It was one thing for the Goldwyns to try to fatten their bank accounts by talking up "art"; that was an old, old dodge. But the artist himself — and beyond any romanticizing — had a recognition of his special role. He might at times be making a virtue of necessity, he might elevate into martyrdom the personal mess he had made of things. But the sense of vocation was not just high-flown or self-congratulatory; there went with it an awareness of what it entailed — of the people it differed with, the conventions it quarreled with, the sanctities it defied.

To be sure, plenty of serious and gifted artists wanted to make money, wanted to make a lot of it; and a number of them did. Some, like Trollope, were entirely businesslike in their writing habits. Yet the fundamental attitude was different if only because the existing circumstances were. Opportunities were fewer; no book had nine lives. Moreover, bohemian living was not just a protest against bourgeois standards, it was a way of adjusting to economic ups and downs. Writers' lives were often makeshift and nomadic less from having no roots in a community than from having no stake in it. Owning a house meant sweating over a mortgage; possessions had, for a second home, the pawnshop; and banks were for borrowing money, not saving it.

Writing is the legatee, today, of what, whether or not it has reformed our culture, has in some sense revolutionized it. In spite (or because) of all the class-vs.-mass distinctions, and all the battles of the brows, a much widened market exists for capable writers.* Such writers can be had simultaneously, at every brow level — can be read in the same month in *Partisan Review*, *The New Yorker*, and *Look*; can be bought on the same day in a scholarly edition, a paperback abridgement, and a popular Digest; can be heard in the same week at Harvard, at The New School, and on David Susskind. "Pop" culture, indeed, is acquiring much of the character of the old pop concerts. Just as, along with Strauss and Suppé, the concerts offered the more accessible works of Mozart and Beethoven, so today radio and TV provide great audiences with morsels, and sometimes tenderized meat, from the classics — and from today's avant-garde and "controversial" highbrows. Beyond that, on radio and TV there are all sorts of education and classroom programs; of talks by writers and critics; of poets' readings;† and of plays and music. What percentage of the total audience tunes in on such things I don't know; but however small, it is huge compared with any pre-radio or TV audience. What percentage of the programs themselves would pass a cultural Pure Food and Drug Act, I don't know either; but that they very much benefit living artists financially seems certain.

In that very certainty, there is for the have-not writers as well as the haves, for the beginner as well as the veteran, the sense that, with no taint of corruption, the pot of gold lies very close to hand.

---

* Leonard Schechter, in the New York *Post*, described the symposium atmosphere of the first Patterson-Liston fight, with Budd Schulberg, Ben Hecht, A. J. Liebling, Gerald Kersh, Norman Mailer, and James Baldwin all covering it.

† Many poets today, I imagine, make more money from their readings than from their writings.

And already, in certain domains of art, the rewards are blazingly visible. A dozen years after Madison Avenue became a synonym for the big money in advertising and TV, it could as easily, through its art galleries, have become one for the big money in modern painting. In fact it is in painting and the theatre that the arts have most conspicuously become a business — and the artist a business-man in how he functions, a rich man in how he lives. On a very large small scale, there exists today an Upper Bohemia that in its standard of living is wholly top bracket. Its people have the same town and country places as the leisure class; the same kind of servants, of clothes and food and cars; the same architects and interior decorators, the same accommodations in the same ships and hotels. Nor can they be distinguished from Park Avenue on any basis of "bohemian" morality. Drinking, drug taking, and every form of sexual freedom are as decided stigmata today of the rich man's world as of the artist's. No artist can any longer claim to be a bohemian or a rebel — or an artist — merely by invoking Priapus or Dionysius.

The theatre decidedly provides what is most comic and corrupt-ing in the way of "creative" success. Part of what is both is in-herent, from the theatre's own knack for being flashy and its need of being publicized. But part of it derives from Broadway's get-rich-quickness. The classic symbol of this, a generation ago, was Moss Hart, literally stepping out of his clothes to turn his bare back on his past and embark on a "gold-garter" period that, thirty years later, was simply a vast penthouse one. And the symbol has become something of a pattern. There are, for example, theatre people virtually never seen after dark out of evening clothes. One such, a man who first achieved notice celebrating a humbler side of the garment industry, once hailed me at an opening with "How d'you suppose I just *knew* I shouldn't dress tonight?" When, rather staggered, I said solemnly, "After all, it's a Monday night — and raining at that," "No, no, no," he answered. "We just *knew* — the X's aren't dressed either, and I assure you we didn't consult one another!"

What is peculiarly comic is that the splashiness, and the taking it seriously, seem most marked in Broadway comedy writers. Doubtless they have their own way of joking about it all, of being sure to get it said first. All the same, it is not for them a joke. More interestingly, not one of these elegantly fashionable comedy writers has written, with the faintest show of true elegance, a single drawing-room comedy. Yet all this is but the anecdotal side of a great moneyed activity. The sovereignty of money is partly imposed on the playwright by the cost of the investment; is further imposed by the amount of box office needed to keep the show alive; is finally imposed by the tactics, the pressures, the crises attending it all. There ensue all the legitimate differences of opinion and conflicts of interest, all the creative jitters and collaborating wrangling. And then, and far worse, the producer's itching palm may urge compromise; and then his whip hand decree it. The playwright, by now, has paid out so much in time and energy, in sleeplessness and exasperation, in controlling his temper and losing it, that creative satisfaction has vanished and the only reward is hard cash. The money, indeed, seems less a form of earnings than of damages.

In a quite different sense, the art world today seems too commercial and insidiously corrupting. To be sure, the art world has long contaminated people who worked in it in the precise sense that it refined them: it has provided a luxury life on rather a lackey basis. The luxury handout that is relatively new to the writers' world stretches back for centuries in the artists'. In every age the fashionable painter has been patronized and made a pet of by the rich, to inhabit a world of feasting and flattery. What, of course, makes the art world unique is the personal ownership of the artist's work. Composers, novelists, playwrights, poets offer their work to the public. But pictures and sculpture belong to individuals and institutions. And those who *sell* pictures and sculpture are often akin to those who sell tiaras and Rolls-Royces; and the art world, for all its cultivation, can have a voice quite as "full of money" as Scott Fitzgerald's Daisy Buchanan. It is a world that must not just allow for rich men's whims but that, like any courtier, must pander to them; and unobtrusively, like any guide or governess, correct their taste; and, like any interior decorator, minister to their pride of ownership and display.

The elegance of the art world's surroundings has tended to veil the frequent crassness of its motives. But the art world today is becoming more and more like the theatre world; today, too, there is less, almost, of the studio about it than of the stock exchange. And along with their Hollywood bidding and pricing, picture sales display a Hollywood garishness. Not only have the big auctions become plushier occasions than the grandest first nights; the sums involved make better "theatre." There is one sure way now in America to make what is artistic popular — the way of high finance. Thus dollars do make highbrows of us all: the sale value of Gainsborough or Cézanne not only achieves headline prominence, it gains philistine respect. What decidedly helped give culture this new status was the $64,000 Question and all its TV siblings. The public saw culture and knowledge acquiring a big market value; and even after the quizzes were exposed as frauds, the taste they had fostered remained. The public is fascinated when millionaires — or museums — fight over pictures. Surely the museums must know that the gaudy prices they pay will set an unhealthful example. The doubtful wisdom of the Metropolitan paying over $2 million for Rembrandt's *Aristotle Contemplating the Bust of Homer* seemed borne out by the crowds who flocked to see it. I watched them, and their "Ahs" were chiefly for the price and not the picture: they stood in vulgar awe as before a jeweler's window ablaze with huge diamonds. It was itself a spectacle of sorts, contemplating the public contemplating Aristotle contemplating Homer.

Without going into the artistic merits of Abstract Expressionism, surely the prices it has so quickly come to fetch make clear that involved are not just art lovers of Pollock and De Kooning as they might be of Ruysdael and De Hooch, but stockholders in Pollock and De Kooning as they might be of Pan Am and Union Carbide. "Works of art" have great commodity value, are top status symbols. As a result, everyone in the Big-Board art world is associated with the rich. And this touches those on the buying side as well as on the selling. Curators, like college presidents, are kept busy raising money and angling for bequests; and are to be found, oftener than college presidents, feeding at rich men's tables and imbibing the fumes of wealth.

I haven't traveled this road of art-and-finance hellbent on achieving a destination. In itself the road runs through picturesque country, offering much that is new and revealing along the way. But the sense grows on one that it has become a heavily traveled road, and one that does reach a destination. Sensibly starting off, away from the genteel slums and messy Bohemias of writers in the past, it yet winds up in exclusive residential subdivisions and a sort of conspicuous wasteland. The writer's position in all this may not be crucial; but his attitude *toward* his position, it would seem to me, is. Time out of mind, he has been fed high-sounding humbug, has heard that his slender means were not only a blessing, but a source of inspiration to boot. He has heard that what loftily set him apart from other men was his *not* striving for material success. Meanwhile, he whose great mission was to tell the truth had often, for a roof over his head, to curry favor. Well, all that has been exploded. My only wonder is whether, with the routing of the old familiar cant, a sort of reverse cant hasn't come to exist — a writer's cant, this time, in which he becomes his own victim. I have the sense that too often today *any* reservations about the artist's relation to money, any setting of limits to his concern for it, are thought arty, or outmoded, or just a new way to bilk him. I have a sense that it is today considered as much the artist's duty to regard himself as a businessman as it was formerly a businessman's dodge to segregate him as an artist.

This may be too glib an antithesis. But what strikes me as literal truth is that writers, as a whole, have been considerably more altered, and influenced, and infected by the life around them than they have themselves altered or influenced that life. And by writers I mean those with standards and values, those who would ruffle the shortcomings of society, not stroke them; who would protest, not comply. It strikes me that, though such writers don't feed pap to the public, they have begun to swallow the public's pap themselves, and that even as they attack America's materialism, in their own way they are succumbing to it. At any rate, it seems pertinent to determine how much of what they have become is mere surface accommodation to the life around them; how much is understandable adjustment to new forces and pressures; and how much, finally, seems a matter of choice and a subject for anxiety.

Certainly much today in the writer's way of life reflects the helpful side of a highly mechanized society. Whatever his other problems, surely it grows harder — on even a modest income — to suffer all the discomforts of home. Dishwashers prevail; diaper services abound; so do laundromats, and community nursery schools, and sitters, and time-saving appliances, and small summer cottages to be had by the month. All these are distinct benefits, and seldom at odds with a writer's chosen way of life. However varied their backgrounds, most writers, having gone to college, have acquired a similarity of surface behavior. Moreover, many writers today lecture and teach. Life, for most of them, grows what once might have been thought crushingly respectable. The party-going is more decorous; the domestic arrangements are more domestic. Writers' marriages may keep breaking up; but writers remarry today rather than live in sin, and their homes contain somebody's children. The children often go to rather orthodox schools. It all constitutes a much modified Bohemia, less the result, I think, of changed ideas than of changing incomes.

Much of this is a matter of surfaces. But if writers conform more, in the sense that they placard their roles less, that is because their roles today gain general respect, and because their economic positions and professional prestige as often soothe their vanity as assault it. Where fundamentals are concerned, most writers worth their salt still live and think on their own terms. Writers haven't had their mouths stopped; and society, perhaps more than ever, is having its nose punched. What seems to me a danger has less to do with middle-classness than with materialism. Still untouched by the old shibboleths, writers are not nearly so immune to the new status symbols. Indeed, the danger may well lie in the actual by-passing of the kind of middle-class standard of living toward which all professional people move — bypassing it for the high-income scale of living which many writers already maintain.

They may still be relatively few, but they bulk large enough to provide an incentive. Moreover, they don't live expensively, in the gambler-style way that artists once did from hitting the jackpot; they do so with every assumption of permanence. Hence certain new factors have entered in. To begin with, when one lives expensively one starts going with others who do, and something embarrassed or self-conscious arises toward writers less affluent. As for the others who live expensively, they can be of many kinds — blue-blooded country neighbors, or lion-hunters in town, or executives met on luxury liners. Mixing with them can be both instructive and enjoyable, but it can also foster dangerous identifications. The real danger is that the writer nowadays *can* often truly identify; and can, as seldom in the past, keep financially in step. Nowadays too, as seldom in the past, he may not be much out of step politically. There are few "dangerous radicals" in today's world of letters, while in its social world there are more and more liberals of a sort. A writer's morality may continue sound; but, rather than combat the world, it must often have to skirmish with his own way of life.

An ironical factor in his new approach to living is quite literally the business of the wife and kiddies. It need not even mean a very conservative or conventional wife; she may just be feminine and elegant. At any rate, it is usually she who enforces a more affluent standard once it is reached. Seldom is any of this blueprinted: it just works out that way. But to live so high the respectable writer must often work too hard — the more so, from refusing to prostitute himself. Or, simply from being frequently approached, he will take on too many assignments. And half-smudged creative work born of being too much in demand can prove as harmful as hackwork born of being too little. And what is dangerous, is that each material temptation involves no artistic misconduct, no conscious backsliding. But, after ten years, just where will it leave him?

Not too badly off, perhaps. At the end of ten years, he will still not be stuffy, or Babbitty, or reactionary. He will still eat and drink, and get up and go to bed, exactly as he pleases. He will hate bores, and not be one. He will be unintimidated by fashions in architecture or art or letters; make his own discoveries, reach his own conclusions; speak up for what he believes in and vote for the better man.

The trouble is that all these virtues which still apply to him will apply equally to thousands of enlightened, self-governing businessmen.

4

FASHIONS IN VULGARITY

Nothing, in a sense, would be easier to chronicle than a history of bad taste. The past is strewn with horrible examples; we need only look at the drearier or declining sections of cities, or in junk or antique shops, or — since on occasion vulgarity begins at home — in our own family attics. There are McKinley-period trophies in architecture, German-beermug-era trophies in décor. Everywhere there are reminders of a false refinement; or novels that ladies quite as much as ladies' maids once wept over. Every age yields fictional accounts of moneyed upstarts — Trimalchio in ancient Rome, M. Jourdain in seventeenth-century France, the Veneerings in nineteenth-century England. Was "bad taste" ever more rife than among Victorian England's indigestible wedding cakes in stone? Yet, was "vulgarity" ever so ridiculous as with the great Lord Chesterfield, who deemed it vulgar to laugh aloud; or with the French classical drama, that forbade mention of the word *mouchoir*, since on its exalted stage not noses were blown, but trumpets.

Yet, though nothing were more easily compiled than a chronicle of bad taste, nothing, after a time, calls out more for revision. Let fifty years go by, and it is not the items in the catalogue that shriek bad taste; it is the cataloguer. Not what he excoriated will seem vulgar, but what he extolled. In the early 1920s a critic of décor, championing the most functional furniture, might have whacked away at the curlicued accessories of the Victorians. Today all too many people wish their keepsakes had been kept, sigh in vain for their grandparents' square pianos and rosewood sofas; and shudder at the metal frames and tubular stems that passed for furniture. Clearly, since taste began, one generation's fashion has become the next generation's fright.

In the degree, then, that it posits touchstones and untouchables, proclaims What's Done and proscribes What Will Never Do, every catalogue of bad taste is a comedy of overassurance. Virtually the same era that banished the handkerchief from the drama, and laughter from the drawing room, cheerfully made butts of cuckolds and sport of madmen. The Augustans, while thinking it effeminate for men to carry umbrellas, deemed it manly for them to carry muffs. The Victorians, while forbidding mention of most illnesses and all sex, doted on rancid practical jokes. Yet, for all such warnings of booby traps, there is perhaps some point in our trying to discover vulgarity's more permanent traits. From the past, we get at least a clue in its verbal alliances, in the company it kept. There was once constant reference to "vulgar display," to "vulgar curiosity," to "vulgar presumption." Vulgar display, probably the arch offender, calls up visions of too much finery and jewelry, of bric-a-brac and be-silvered-and-china'd dining-room tables — or simply of too much dinner. All this particularly brings the last century to mind, for with it emerged large, prosperous middle-class families that, by requiring large houses, encouraged lavish living. Moreover, an age that admired plump, high-busted women put no tax on heavy meals. Then, too, so prudish an age banned so many other forms of indulgence as perhaps to make lavishness less an initial desire than a kind of last resort. A respectable matron dared not smoke a cigarette; on the other hand she could virtuously eat three slices of cake.

Actually, even the more tasteful Victorians never stigmatized display in itself; they merely stigmatized this thing or that on display. Passing up, for the moment, any distinction between vulgarity and bad taste, we still might note that vulgarity isn't avoided merely through good taste in individual selection; there must also be a sense of proportion about the whole. Nor need we confine

ourselves to the marble and plush atrocities of upstarts: the desire
to exhibit on a vast scale has much ancient and aristocratic warrant. Most lordly establishments impart a too strutting sense of
ownership, of greedy heaping-up and senseless size. Measured
against a perfect taste, the patrician's giving material form to his
pride of rank can be just as vulgar as the parvenu's proclaiming
his lack of any.

There was that other once-common phrase, "vulgar presumption." It has largely fallen into disuse, not because people have
stopped being presumptuous but because the phrase became a
caste reproof — something applied to whomever one deemed one's
social inferior. The culprit might often be vulgar enough, whether
from a bumptious attempt to get on or a blatant attempt to dazzle; but he was hardly presumptuous: it was rather his detractors
who presumed. But of course the class bias that stamps so many
things vulgar goes very deep — indeed to the roots of the word itself, to *vulgus* or the common people. Something, in other words,
was vulgar that had a lower-class stamp — or at least the stamp of
a lower class than one's own.

This class bias is not uninstructive; but though we have still to
define vulgarity, plainly in its subtler connotations today it has not
just overflowed "lower class" banks; it has been rechanneled in a
different direction. We might even contend that it is only the
common people — along with some decidedly uncommon ones —
who are not vulgar. What were once designated the lower orders
may be coarse or crude, may indeed be common or cheap or disgusting. But the things they do that are most beyond the pale —
belch or spit, eat with their knives or sleep in their underwear —
do not quite fit our current sense of "vulgar." It is crude to eat
with your knife; what is vulgar is to drink tea with your little finger
extended. It is disgusting to pick your teeth; what is vulgar is to
use a gold toothpick. It is illiterate to say "ain't I"; what is vulgar
is to say "aren't I." The common people, as a group, are not vulgar
if only because they don't know enough or care enough to be.

It is among those who would once have been termed their
betters that we encounter vulgarity full blast. We encounter it,

that is, when signs of education have entered in; when there is a certain awareness of social or cultural or aesthetic right and wrong; when there is a craving to attract notice or seem to belong. We are never, said La Rochefoucauld, so ridiculous through the qualities we have as through those we pretend to; and we are never, he might have added, so cheap. For, together with such pretensions, there almost always goes the attempt to mask them — the coy tactic, the devious maneuver. Vulgarity, I would think, involves motivation. People are vulgar when, for self-interested reasons, they resort to unworthy methods — whenever they do something to falsify or floodlight their prestige or importance, their claims to position or talent or knowledge. They are equally vulgar when, from the same kind of motives, they fail to do something. One of the columnists told of a Broadway figure who displayed a new gold cigarette case. "I'm sick of gold," he remarked — "what I'd have really liked was a platinum cigarette case: but my friends would have thought it was silver."

At an innocuous level, vulgarity is mere vanity — people's wanting to look their best, or better than their best. Oliver Cromwell might exhort the portraitist to paint him warts and all; most of us desire to have the warts removed, and dimples added. Few of us speak as readily of the ancestor who was hanged as of the ancestor who was knighted. But if we weren't a little vulgar in matters of this sort we might be something much worse, we might be unbearably priggish. It is not till people, in manifesting superiority, begin to seem sniffy and cheap — or no better than what they disparage — that vulgarity turns offensive. The well placed have for generations made a vulgar ploy of vulgarity: Jones, they will remark, had "the bad taste" to refer to something they didn't want mentioned; or Smith had "the insolence" to remind them of something they preferred to forget. This sort of high-handedness always has vulgar blood; high-handedness, indeed, must pass an aesthetic test of being more stylish or witty than it is arrogant and rude. Equally, there are right and wrong snubs. The wrong ones can be as ill-bred as anything they wish to pulverize. For a nice snub, consider the very nobly born Frenchman to whom someone not half so wellborn was bragging of his vast family mansion with its great high-domed dining room. "With us," the Frenchman finally murmured, "it's just the other way. Our dining room is so low that all we can eat is fried sole."

Obviously, there are ways in which human and artistic vulgarity differ. Vulgarity in life is not just an aesthetic offense; it has a falseness or impurity about it, an *inner* cheapness. Vulgar people often display perfect form; can talk well, live smartly, even get discreetly ahead in the world. But as they grow superficially more presentable, they grow, if anything, inwardly more insensitive. There is even a kind of vulgarity so self-assured as to take pride in flaunting itself: a very famous theatre personage sent out, as a Christmas card, a picture of himself posing for a beer ad. Vulgarity in art, on the other hand, usually involves form as well as substance, and questions of aesthetic effect. But it, too, largely derives from a false or flashy motive, from a greater wish to be impressive than sound. Often in men of much talent we find a streak of it — of excess or exhibitionism, specious beauty or spurious virtue. Swinburne can be too lilting or lush; Wilde and Disraeli use too much pomade; Tennessee Williams can be lavishly sensational, William Saroyan ostentatiously humane.

On the other hand, we must distinguish between styles in art and the vulgarization of a style. Thus, gingerbread architecture with its childlike Hansel-and-Gretel playfulness may be far less vulgar than "classical" mansions that look like U.S. subtreasuries. One may not respond to the baroque of Tiepolo's frescoes or Prandtauer's architecture; but except where misapplied, baroque is not vulgar in the least. Indeed, the real test of taste perhaps only arises at the level of the ornamented or theatrical. Anyone, by playing safe, by wearing only gray and navy blue, by sticking to the best Georgian spoons, by reading Virgil or Racine, can be unassailably tasteful. The test of taste comes in one's particular use of bright paint and loud colors, or harps and trumpets, or marble and jewels. Almost anyone can grasp the vulgarity of Liszt and the lack of it in Mozart; it is more difficult to grasp the vulgar lapses in Wagner and the lack of them in Berlioz. And certainly one great form of vulgarity is the fear of vulgarity; it flaws the work of even a Henry James.

Vulgarity does not stand still: there are fashions in it, it shows progress, it gains on one front and loses on another. The world of today differs strikingly from that of two centuries ago — machinery and mass production, literacy and mass communication, democracy and relatively classless living have proved banes and blessings alike. Material display — the overmuch, the overlarge, the overstuffed, the overshiny — has in great part been streamlined into submission. Our material tastes have not only learned from the excesses of the past, they are shaped by the exigencies of the present. What with a general lack of space today, and lack of servants; with doctors and diets, with the rise of sport and decline of prudery, most people eat, dress, live, travel, entertain more simply. To gorge or splurge is curiously unchic. Most people indeed live like most other people, in a world of deep-freezes, dishwashers, station wagons, casseroles, and baby-sitters. A pantry maid is almost as remote as a coach-and-four; and a man may see the same dress on his secretary as on his wife. And with so much social and cultural leveling off, vulgar display has steeply declined.

The new vulgarity is different. The old vulgarity followed that classic rule for the playwright — always show rather than tell. The vulgar used to show how grand they were by the size of their houses, the massiveness of their plate, the snootiness of their butlers; by how they overdressed, overtipped, overrode those about them. They never said they were rich; they never had to.

Today the old stage formula has been discarded for the blunter vulgarity of *announcing* one's importance. Self-display has passed over into self-advertisement; and it is not so much the business world that conducts itself so as the world of journalism, of Hollywood and Broadway, of TV and "the communication arts." In that world people, beyond frequently engaging paid publicists, distribute their own testimonials, write their own plugs, sing their own praises, stress their own good deeds. And when not patting their own backs, they are slapping — or stabbing — other people's. When they cannot command the limelight, they invade it. This is an age of name-dropping — and of last-name-dropping even more — when on meeting a famous man of sixty, a man of twenty-four straightway calls him Bill. And as the first name flourishes in speech, so does the first person in writing. Serious writers turn out waggish pieces as a way of plugging their books. Columnists brag, when the most piffling news story breaks, how they had predicted it months before. Into the body of their newspaper stints people inject commercials about their TV appearances. Even all sense of occasion has vanished. At a small private New Year's Eve party, while the guests were watching, on TV, the crowds gathered in Times Square, one television man sang out loudly to another, "They wanted *me* to handle this — but we couldn't get together on the dough." The remark, to be sure, isn't much more vulgar than the sort of gathering that makes it possible. In the professional world today, entertainment tends to be the merest form of self-advancement, of blandly feeding the mouth that bites you, of managing to be seen, of striking up useful connections on sofas, of cooking up deals over drinks. Even those hostesses who are above the battle and imagine they are exhibiting lions are actually racing rats.

All this, however appalling, is today perhaps inevitable. What with ratings and samplings, press-agentry and polls, people who are supposed to mold and influence others must more and more promote themselves, make shopwindows of their offices, show windows of their homes. Truman Capote, in his book about the visit of the *Porgy and Bess* troupe to the Soviet Union, told how, while most of those on board the train going into Russia relaxed and joked, a columnist was kidded for sitting in a compartment alone, pounding relentlessly away at his typewriter. "People don't get into my income-tax bracket," he explained, "by looking at scenery."

Furthermore, the whole fashion in entertaining, or interviewing, or "educating" mass audiences today tends to throw privacy to the winds, to make publicity not just an unreprehensible, but a greatly respected, side of modern life. To use zoological terms once more — it keeps getting harder to use strictly human ones — there now goes on a kind of human horse show, in which blue-ribboned personalities are trotted up and down, are photographed, queried, televised; or are just put on view as distinguished hosts or pedigreed hostesses endorsing Scotch or bed sheets or soap. For the amateurs in all this, the appeal to vanity may be enough: for the professionals, it is part of a fierce struggle to survive. Big-name feuding is no longer mere internecine strife; it is a spectator sport. Which of two feuders will come out ahead is on a par with which of two football teams.

The worst part of all this is that it has *become* such a spectator sport. It was said, long ago, that evil communications corrupt good manners: it might be said more pertinently today that mass communication corrupts good manners, that we are all being gradually worn down, that without even being aware of it, we are acquiescing in what would have appalled us twenty-five years ago. And how not, with the very air we breathe commercialized, with the very lives we live treated as so much copy? Quite literally, it is the gossip columnist's business to write about what is none of his business. The quiz programs with their venal lure and test-of-virtue stakes have vanished; but another kind of quiz program survives, where interviewers ask people — before millions of listeners — questions that their closest friends might hesitate to ask them when alone.

It is perfectly true that it takes two to make up such interviews — and millions, listening in, to make a go of them. Clearly, were there no people willing to be questioned, and no large audiences intent upon the answers, such programs could not exist. But, psychologically and sociologically, the thing is not so simple. With the person interviewed, vanity; love of the limelight; the fear that it will go elsewhere, are strong inducements; and in an age when publicity has become respectable and when psychiatry has licensed people to Tell All, fewer and fewer are those who when invited will say No. But what has happened to the performer is really less important than what has happened to the public. Of course, the average person is full of curiosity and enjoys gossip. But to argue that — because he's something of a peeping tom — it's his inquisitiveness that produces such interviews, is pure peeping-tommyrot. We bring up our children, we order our lives, we regulate our society on the contrary principle that our shoddier instincts should not be deliberately pandered to. Those most genuinely concerned for freedom of speech are no less concerned for the right of privacy; nor are they misled when sensationalism appears purporting to be the servant of truth, or when psychiatry is commercially invoked to chaperone smut. The motive of the scandal magazines is all too clear. It is where the motive is masked, when privacy is invaded on the pretext of a sociological search warrant, that a more menacing vulgarization appears; and as the product of such corrupting alliances, what sort of children will inhabit the world of tomorrow? For in time values not only get tarnished: they even get turned around. A few years ago George S. Kaufman, by complaining that *Stille Nacht* was being turned into a kind of cheap Christmas commercial, roused a storm of furious protest against himself: in the face of such things, who shall dare to argue that people can distinguish God from Mammon?

We live in a world where TV is now sovereign, is so enthroned that 50 million Americans sit bareheaded before it for hours on end, enduring blare for the sake of glare, and forever plagued by those powers behind the throne — the sponsors with their intrusions. *Of course* there are good television programs; but that is sociologically beyond the point. The point is that for tens of millions of people TV has become habit-forming, brain-softening, taste-degrading; has altered for the worse the whole cultural climate of American life. Privacy was in sufficient danger before TV appeared; and TV has given it its death blow. And as all liking for privacy vanishes, all dislike of publicity must vanish too. Men that one would have supposed had distinction are nowadays Men of Distinction by way of the ads. Indeed, the better known a man is for his taste or good character, the more he is sought out, the more

he is importuned, to sully or betray them. When those who shape
our manners shout at parties about not getting together over the
dough, or send out their beer blurbs as Christmas cards, who shall
maintain that the vulgarity that once featured a clock planted in a
Venus de Milo's belly has disappeared? Some of us might even
put back the clock if we could.

II

THE AMERICAN WAY

5

AMERICA AND ART

The compelling fact about art in America is that it is not organic. It has almost no share in shaping our life; it offers, rather, compensation for the shapelessness. And just because we prescribe a certain amount of art for ourselves as a kind of corrective — being "deficient" in art as we might be in calcium or iron — we regard it less as ordinary nourishment than as a tonic, something we gulp rather than sip, regard with esteem and yet suspicion, and either require to be made up with a pleasant taste or exult in because it tastes unpleasant. The American feeling, or lack of feeling, for art has been immemorially easy to satirize, whether at the one extreme of Babbittry or at the other of Bohemia. All the same, for whatever reasons, such feeling has long been part of the American character — which is to say that the American bent, the American genius, has honestly moved in other directions. Like the Romans and the Germans, we are not an artistic people. This may be partly the result of our so long being able to reach out, rather than having to turn inward; of our possessing a vast continent to traverse, subdue, explore, develop, grow rich on, so that there was no husbanding or skilled handling of resources, no modifying what we started with or were saddled with into something gracious and expressive. A race, like an individual, develops a style in part through what it has uniquely, in part through what it has too little of. French prose owes its dry, neat lucidity to the same things that produced a general lack of magic in French poetry; French

women owe their chic, I would think, to their general lack of girlish
beauty. Americans have suffered from overabundance — from not
needing to substitute art for nature, form for substance, method for
materials. At the very point where a patina might begin to appear,
or mellowness to suffuse, we have abandoned what we made for
something newer, brisker, shinier; and with each such act we have
become a little less "artistic" in our approach. But of course there
is more to it than that. An artistic people — the French, the
Chinese, the ancient Greeks — is one whose necessities are made
the comelier by its dreams, but whose dreaming is equally con-
trolled by its necessities: the two are integrated, are never so
harshly at odds that the dreaming must serve as a lurid compensation. With an artistic people a kind of good sense regulates both
its acquisitive side and its aspiring one; and from deprecating excess
on a large scale, it eventually does so in small ways as well. Hence
the design of existence stands forth more powerfully than the décor;
and because design, unlike décor, affects a whole society, the national traits and instincts and responses get beyond cost or size or
class, and equally characterize the rich and the poor, the cultivated
and the unlettered. There is always a sense of bone structure about
an artistic people — think of the Spaniards — a touch of severity,
of economy. There is, I suppose, something rather classic than
romantic — a sense of the ancestor as well as the individual.

An artistic people need not (and very likely will not) be profoundly poetic or mystical, as the English and the Germans are. It
is plainly because the English and the Germans lead such double
lives, because one extreme must almost atone for the other, because dreaming grows out of repressions or helps to stamp out
reality, that two nations so given to vulgar instincts and material
aims should be capable of such splendid intensities — intensities
which, for all that, do constitute excesses. And we too, as a people,
are driven to compensate; are so excessively aspiring for being so
excessively acquisitive; come back to God through guilt or satiety;
go on binges with Beauty because it is no part of our daily life —
and we somehow think the extent of the undertaking will make up
for the quality. Our magnates are always giving away millions not

too shiningly acquired; our aging plutocrats leave a spendthrift order for art like the flashy sports who buy their women ten dozen
American Beauty roses. Nothing amuses or appalls us more than a
gangster's funeral with its carloads of flowers and wreaths; and
nothing teaches us less. The gangster's funeral is actually the model
for Broadway's supermusicals, for the murals on civic architecture,
for Florida's luxury resorts; and the gangster's funeral is itself a late
development, the descendant of the Newport "cottage" — the only
difference being that at Newport conspicuous waste was confined
to living, where in Chicago it specialized in death.

But it is not just the excesses born of wealth that have failed to
make us an artistic people. After all, corsairs and conquistadors are
the ancestors of *most* cultures; and French châteaux and Italian
palazzi of even the best periods stress sheer display quite as much
as they stress beauty. We may just come near enough to being an
artistic people to explain why we *are* not and perhaps *cannot be*
one. We are an inventive and adaptive people; and thus our whole
effort, our whole genius, is to modify rather than mold, to make
more efficient rather than more expressive. We are dedicated to
improvement — to improving our minds and our mousetraps, our
inventions and our diets. We are so dedicated to improvement
that we neither ask nor care whether a thing needs to be improved,
is able to be improved, or, qualifying as an improvement, will
necessarily seem a benefit. We never seem to wonder whether we
may not be complicating things by simplifying them, or making
them useless by so constantly making them over. But the ability to
invent, the desire to improve, may partly spring from our having
got so much later a start than other civilizations — from our being
at a log-cabin and homespun stage when Europe had long achieved
silks and marble, and then lagging for so long behind them. We
first were made competitive from a sense of our marked inferiority
to others; we then became, from our sense of our natural wealth
and resources, competitive among ourselves; and we are now, of
course, inventive *because* we are competitive: last year's model
must be disparaged so that this year's model can be sold. But no
matter how genuine was the original impulse, or how sheerly com-

mercial it is today, inventiveness has become ingrained in our practice, and our source of constant pride; and even among the best of us — unless we are extremely vigilant — it is now an influence on our taste. Abroad, avant-gardism expressed the crying need among old cultures for new forms and feelings; here, we often seem to be breaking with tradition before establishing it; here, experiment has a gadget air, a will-to-invent about it, as often as a sense of rebellion or release.

This gadget aspect crops up everywhere, in the most unexpected places. Thus our highbrow criticism is constantly inventing and amending a vocabulary — one that somehow will seem a special, up-to-the-minute possession for critics, exactly as the latest models in cars or television sets will seem a special, up-to-the-minute possession of prosperous businessmen. The actual character, too, of our present-day literary jargon — so much of it psychiatric and sociological — is that of a profoundly inartistic, indeed, an aesthetically quite barbarous, yet irrepressibly inventive people. Take just one simple example. In the entire language I doubt whether there exists an uglier word, or one less needed for the use it has been put to, than the word *sensitivity*. One special and particular meaning could be allowed it — the sensitivity, let us say, of a photographic plate to light. But even among critics with a historical sense and a cultivated ear, it has almost completely ousted the two words that for centuries so happily shouldered, and so neatly divided, the burden: *sensibility* and *sensitiveness*. But the whole highbrow vocabulary, the whole need for new spring-and-fall models in literary language — *subsume* one year, *mystique* the next, *exfoliate* the year after — exhibits our national need to adapt and amend and apply at any cost, with no great concern for the urgency, and perhaps even less for the rightness, of the words themselves. And even more indicative than their original "coinage" is the indecent speed with which they become almost unbearable clichés; even more, also, than their coinage itself is the fact that they are so uniformly pretentious, so very rarely picturesque. If only critics would read Dr. Johnson for his wisdom and not for his unhappier choices in words. We are inartistic, indeed, in our very approach to art.

We have never as a people regarded art as something to live with, to freely delight in, to call by its first name. Perhaps this derives from something beyond an inventive streak that keeps us restless, or an awe that makes us uncomfortable: perhaps had we had more opportunity to live with art, we might have acquired a more relaxed attitude toward it. It has never been on our doorstep; we have had to go in search of it, go doubly in search — as much to discover what it is as where it is. The journeys have had a little of the air of pilgrimages; the works of art, a great deal of the sanctity of shrines. The whole burden of our criticism, our constant cultural plaint, is how scant, and impure, and imperfect, and isolated, art in America has been — which, inevitably, has conditioned our approach to it. We insist on strong, emphatic, unmistakable reactions; we either swoon or snub, analyze at tedious length or dismiss with a mere wave of the hand. We go at art, in other words, not like casual, cultivated shoppers, but like a race of antique-shop dealers for whom everything is either magnificently authentic or the merest fake; and the result — though of course there are other reasons, too — is that we cannot take art in our stride. So belated and uneasy an approach has made us about art what Prohibition made my whole generation about wine: either frank, unblushing ignoramuses or comically solemn snobs. Different levels of Americans reveal very different attitudes toward art; but what is perhaps most significant is that they all reveal one marked kind of attitude or another. They either tend to hold back lest they commit howlers; or to go into raptures lest they be taken for clods; or to pooh-pooh the whole business lest they seem long-haired and sissified; or to purse their lips and utter pronunciamentos lest they seem just vulgarly susceptible or humanly responsive.

If classifying them as fence straddlers or as poseurs or as philistines or as prigs is to simplify and even travesty the matter, it may yet help account for the fact that we are not a people for whom, at any level, art is just a natural and congenial aspect of existence. The very "uselessness" of it — the fact that art, like virtue, is its own reward; again, the very magic of it — the fact that it cannot be reduced to a formula or equation; the utter arrogance of it — the fact that money cannot buy it nor American salesmanship or elbow grease achieve it: these are, at the very outset, reasons for mystification and distrust. *Its* kind of arrogance, of refusal to be won on extrinsic terms — as of a high-mettled, beautiful girl whom no suitor can win on the strength of his bank account, his family background, or his sober, industrious habits — seems improper, even unethical, to a people who can respect putting a high price on something, who can approve and even enjoy a hard tussle till things are won, but who can no more understand than they can approve that something is beyond negotiations, is just not to be bought. Art to their minds is not a high-mettled girl, but an extremely unreasonable woman. Art's kind of magic again — art's refusal to be achieved through laboratory methods, through getting up charts or symposiums or sales conferences, through looking at smears under the microscope — its magic seems behind the times, almost downright retarded, to a people with a genius for the synthetic. Art's kind of uselessness, finally — its non-vitamin-giving health, its non-pep-you-up modes of pleasure, its nonmaterialistic enrichment — quite genuinely confuses a people who have been educated to have something to show for their efforts, if only a title or a medal or a diploma. Art, for most Americans, is a very queer fish — it can't be reasoned with, it can't be bribed, it can't be doped out or duplicated; above all, it can't be cashed in on.

Someone, Max Beerbohm perhaps, once defined a bohemian as a person who uses things for what they're not intended — a window drapery, let us say, for a ball dress, or a goldfish bowl for a soup tureen. And this just a little defines the American sense of the artistic. We must endow everything with a new twist, an added value, an extra function. We literally cannot let well enough alone; hence we very often make it worse — and never more, perhaps, than when we also make it better. The new element, the new effect, the new use to which an art form is put, very often has to do with achieving something more tractable or palatable or painless or time- or labor-saving; with offering, at the very least, old wine in new bottles, and much more to our satisfaction, old wine in plastic containers or ice-cream cones. Thus we have Somerset Maugham reedit and abridge the classics; we get a present-day version of Buckingham's *The Rehearsal,* a Negro *Juno and the Paycock,* a *Cherry Orchard* laid in Mississippi; we have Mr. Orson Welles telescoping five of Shakespeare's plays into one; we have something written for the piano performed on the violin, something intended for men taken over by women. We're not, to be sure, the only nation that does such things, but I think we're the only nation that feels a compulsive urge to do them. Where the Germans have a particular genius for ersatz, for substitutions, we have one for new twists and gimmicks, new mixtures and combinations. We simply *have* to tamper: if we don't cut the words, we must add to the music; if we don't change the story, we must shift the locale. Nowhere else, surely, can there be such a compulsion to make plays out of books, musicals out of plays, *Aïda's* into *My Darlin' Aïda's;* to insert scenes, delete characters, include commentators; to turn gas stations into cathedrals, or churches into dance halls. Out of Plato and Berkeley we get Transcendentalism; out of Transcendentalism we concoct Christian Science; and then, almost immediately, Jewish Science out of Christian. Many nations have discovered the Devil in dancing, but we are perhaps the first to find God through calisthenics.

And no doubt we create, from all this, the illusion that we are notably experimental in the arts, ever seeking new forms, contriving new functions, establishing new perspectives. But, even ignoring the material or commercial side of it all, our contrivance of so many artful blends and twists and variants is really our avoidance of art itself, exactly as our craving for sensations argues a distaste or fear of experiences. Our whole artistic effort, if it does not parallel, at least involves our genius for concocting the mixed drink and for putting the packaging ahead of the product. The result — from which almost all of us suffer more than we realize — is a kind of vulgarization, and one that can take place at high levels no less than at low ones. Our stressing significance in art rather than intensity, our present search for symbolic figures and concealed meanings and multiple levels: isn't this part of our compulsion to introduce something new, add something extra, offer something unprecedented? Does it not bear witness, also, to our intellectual ingenuity rather than our aesthetic responsiveness? Hasn't the new multilevel *Pierre* or *Confidence Man* a kinship with the new split-level house, or the concealed meanings with the concealed plumbing, or the indirect approach with the indirect lighting, or the taste for knotty problems with the taste for knotty pine? I do not think I am being anti-intellectual when I say that in America the intellect itself is being overused and misused in the world of art, where — after all — the most thoughtful elucidation avails nothing without the right, pure, instinctive response; for in art the reverse of Wordsworth's saying is also true and immensely important: in art, there are tears that do often lie too deep for thoughts.

Given our inventiveness, such endless and manifold vulgarization is inevitable. No race can make an idea go farther than we can. We get the last ounce of derivable income from it; we carry it, indeed, to distances that virtually obscure the original starting point. From the classic sandwich made with bread we evolve the triple-decker made with ice cream; from the first motel, that could hardly have competed with a bathhouse, we are now contriving structures that will outdo — if not soon outmode — the Ritz. And quite beyond our double-barreled desire to make things profitable as well as attractive, all this technical skill and inventive cleverness must in the end conspire as much against our creative instincts as against our artistic ones. A nation that can so marvelously concoct must less and less feel any need to create. We are developing a genius for rewrite at the expense of one for writing, for stage directors who shall do the work of dramatists, for orchestrators who shall do the work of composers. Everything today must carefully and exactly conform to public taste, yet offer a new wrinkle into the bargain — we insist on what might be called a kind of Murphy bed of Procrustes.

The effect of this vulgarization is almost sure to be pervasive and permanent. There is something disarming, often indeed unnoticeable, about vulgarization itself. Sheer vulgarity quickly stands self-condemned, hence tends quickly to correct itself. Or where it persists — as representing something congenial to a particular social milieu or human type — it is so blatant as to isolate itself and proclaim its own quarantine. So long as what is "wrong" can be quickly spotted, and thereafter vividly contrasted with what is "right," whether or not it continues to exist, it can no longer triumph. The most insidious aspect of vulgarity, I would think, concerns not those to whom its appeal is obvious and immediate, but those, rather, whom it gradually and imperceptibly manages to win over, those who in the beginning are partly superior to it and who only by habituation sink to its level. A vulgarity that can thus contaminate won't often, it seems clear, be of a primitive or glaring sort; it will be, rather, a worm in the apple, a sort of Greek bearing gifts. In the world of art, such vulgarity may boast that it does far more good than it does harm, that it makes many people respond to what they might otherwise pass by. I'm not speaking of the out-and-out popularization, but rather of such things as the movie version of *Henry V* or Stokowski's arrangements of Bach — of things offered under the auspices of culture and aimed at reasonably cultured people. This form of vulgarization will by no means altogether misrepresent or even too greatly discolor. And though a severe taste may resist or reject it at once, a fairly sensitive taste — what I suppose is most conveniently called a middlebrow taste that, if left alone, might come to appreciate Bach or Shakespeare "neat" — will not resist or reject the adulteration, will soon, in fact, come to prefer and eventually to require it.

Vulgarization isn't always a matter of making things pleasanter to the taste, or easier to swallow; it can also consist — which can constitute the highbrow maneuver — in making them more difficult and abstruse, rather resembling the homely girl who goes out of her way to accentuate her homeliness. It is as possible to defeat the primary end of art, the sense of beauty, by minimizing it as by rouging it up. Shortcuts represent one kind of vulgarization, labyrinths represent another. The highbrow procedure, if we were to raid the vocabulary that accompanies it, might be called countervulgarization. It constitutes, in any case, no cure or corrective for the middlebrow ailment, but rather a different kind of disease; and though its very lack of cheap allure will cause it to render art far less of a disservice than the rouge-and-syrup process, it is yet equally a barrier to our becoming an artistic people. What with art being something, on the one side, that slides smoothly down our gullets and, on the other, something to be chewed long after any flavor is left, we can seldom any longer, I think, get the fine, sharp, vivid, simple first experience of art that must be the preliminary to any more complex one. Something is always doused over it or drained out of it, hiding the flavor or heightening it, removing gristle or adding lumps; or the thought or look of the thing, before we even bite into it, conditions us. A man can no longer even read, let us say, the "Ode to a Nightingale" without the slightly guilty or, at any rate, self-conscious feeling that it is "romantic poetry."

As a result of the vulgarizing effort to make things palatable, and of a countervulgarization that renders things parched, there is being beggared out of existence a high yet workable cultural ideal, a climate in which a *sense* of art can flourish. And it seems to me that the lack of a proper climate for art is a much more serious shortcoming in America than the actual number of works of art themselves. Culture — in the old-fashioned, well-rounded sense of something civilized and civilizing alike — has not simply failed as a reality in America, but is fast fading as an ideal. Such a culture stands in relation to formal education as good wine to the grape: it is a fermentation, a mellowing, a very special and at the same time wholly characterizing element; and it permeates society in terms of its sensibilities no less than its art. One can, of course, all too easily exalt such a culture as a way of disparaging much that is essential and even healthful in modern life; and one can sigh for it on a sentimental basis, in standpat terms. All the same, any way of life that lacks its best qualities can scarcely be looked upon as cultivated at all; at any rate, no amount of education or knowledge or skill can begin to mean the same thing. And actually the climate I desiderate is no more than a salubrious, breeze-swept temperate zone; it is not forbidding, nor oppressively patrician, nor strenuously democratic. A cool, dry judgment is mingled there with gusto and generous appreciation; the people there are no more mired in the past than running wild in the present; its tone is altogether urbane without being even faintly genteel; it boasts neither untouchables nor sacred cows; it displays a constant corrective irony and perhaps not overmuch virtue; and everyone there is just sufficiently wrongheaded and prejudiced and inconsistent to be attractively human.

Being a curiously inartistic and ingenious people; being, also, too serious-minded to look on pleasure bare, and so commercialized as to put a price tag on Beauty, we approach art by many routes, but never by the most direct. Most frequently vulgarization sets in, the point of the story is sacrificed to the plot, Shakespeare is streamlined or Chekhov fattened up. Among the overserious there is often a process of dehydration, with only such fluid retained as has medicinal properties; or the work of art is converted from thoroughbred to packhorse and forced to stagger under a heavy sociological and psychiatric load.

Although what frankly seem to me the most delightful and rewarding qualities of art are precisely these that are slighted in many highbrow ranks today, I must admit that it is not done altogether without reason. The slighting constitutes a form of dissociation, even of protest. The sight of panders everywhere must inevitably call forth the prig; the sight of art being everywhere rouged and perfumed, groomed and tricked out for harlotry, must inspire a violent contrary wish — a wish to have art, like an orthodox Jewish bride, shorn of her locks and made as unalluring as possible. Middlebrow adulteration, its slight softening of every texture, its faint sweetening of every taste, have clearly had a hand in creating the current highbrow distrust of charms and graces. This isn't to say there need be an abundance of such qualities or that, in an age like ours, there can be. In this unquiet age, an age not even of scars but of outright wounds, clearly very little that is charming or delightful will seem central or germane. Yet though there is truth in such a statement, there is also cant. It is perhaps not necessary to dance on the edge of volcanoes; but need one ignore, or even disapprove of, the sunset because the sky may soon grow dark with bomber planes? Again, is shaving off the hair an answer to over-rouging the cheeks, or a desert the corrective to a swamp? Even so, one might agree that one kind of excess tends, not unprofitably, to breed another — did not highbrow criticism, in the very act of professing to probe the tensions of contemporary life, seem so pedagogically remote from them. Art is not something marketable but neither is it something mummified; and indeed, if it is not chiefly and most palpably a form of transcendence and release, pray then what is? If the impress of style, the vivid air of distinction, the artist's ability to be uniquely expressive and intense — if these do not invite, do not indeed impose, some immediate, electrical response, can the result — however rich in cerebral or moral mineral matter — really have much to do with art itself?

I was not surprised, reading an Inquiring Reporter column on "What Is Charm?" to find a sculptor identifying charm with the prettier examples of eighteenth-century painting. It was to be assumed that charm's status would be relatively low, its character rigorously limited; that it would be equated with Sir Joshua Reynolds's children or, by extension, with Sir James M. Barrie's grown-ups; that it would at most signify Lancret and Fragonard, minuets and romantic ballets, Hans Andersen or Charles Lamb. No doubt the word itself has acquired vapid and even repellent connotations; and plainly writers who spray charm about without discretion are like women who mistreat an atomizer. Moreover, charm can be a strong ally of gentility and a quite conscienceless weapon of fraud: we usually do right, I think, to ask to see its credentials. But that is very far from trying to have it deported; and to suggest that, because many writers misuse charm, there is no virtue to fragrance is to come closer, I would think, to the gospel of unyielding naturalism than to any goal of truth. Ignoring such obvious charmers as Poulenc or Dufy or Walter de la Mare, if contemporary artists so unlike as Picasso, E. E. Cummings and Marianne Moore haven't, among other things, a very decided charm, what have they? Art, today, sometimes seems in danger of acquiring all the vices of science without any of the virtues. What with being anthropology's field worker and psychiatry's receptionist, art is quite prevented from cultivating its own garden.

Charm is by now too ambiguous, too merely decorative a word
to be made the symbol of my own dissatisfaction. But it is clear
that all the old, traditional, taken-for-granted "surface" qualities of
art — distinction, fragrance, elegance, gaiety, style: those things
for which we prize a Mendelssohn or a Vermeer, a Tennyson or a
Congreve — such qualities, it is clear, are being slighted or ig-
nored. No doubt *The Tempest* can be profitably viewed as something more than a masque; but to interpret it as something quite
other, to regard it as principally a study in expiation, seems to me
to make Shakespeare very much of an age — and an age, moreover,
not his own. Possibly we are falling into the shallowness of despis-
ing the "shallow." He was the mightiest of puritans no less than of
philistines who first insisted that beauty is only skin deep. Depth,
and its stepdaughter Complexity, and its handmaiden Symbolism,
are so much revered today, so much courted and curtsied to, as almost to obscure the fact of exactly what we mean by them, or
whether — on the terms set — they aren't properly associated with
philosophy rather than art. Perhaps the greatest of all our critics
remarked that "poetry gives most pleasure when only generally and
not perfectly understood," and he offered it as a principle to honor,
not as a puzzle to resent. But so pressing now has become the
critical obligation to explain or reinterpret that it is almost manda-
tory to pitch on something either obscure enough to need explain-
ing or misunderstood enough by all previous critics to need to be
straightened out. And since no one can burrow deep where the author happens to be shallow, we must make canyons out of mole-
holes; we must everywhere find size and significance, those idols so
much less of art than of America; and more and more our criticism
suggests the tread of elephants approaching a temple.

Given our feeble artistic sense, the whole present tendency isn't
too hard to grasp. Anything journalistic must be outlawed —
which could be a virtue; but outlawed in terms of the pedagogical,
which is almost always a vice. Everywhere people reappraise some
simple classic for the small ingenious theory that isn't worth the
paper that is written on it. All too frequently the creative is turned
into the intellectual, soaring is replaced by delving; while art, which
has always constituted the highest and noblest form of release, is

more and more tinged with something so gnawing and anxious as to seem more like remorse. But surely one very great characteristic of any inherently artistic people is a sense of play — play of mind, most of all, not mere prankishness — and a natural sense of irony. The reigning current mood has quite ousted all sense of play and exhibits no working sense of irony. To be sure, irony is a much approved and discussed and dissected quality in today's approach to literature, and wherever possible, and perhaps sometimes where not, critics isolate and decipher it; but it doesn't seem very contagious.

Mr. Richard Chase, in his recent book on Emily Dickinson, deplores what he calls the rococo element in her poetry — the minor, dainty, toylike, bibelot aspect. And in anyone who at her best is so deeply imaginative and intense an artist as Emily Dickinson, the persistence of this merely whimsical and fanciful streak causes real injury, becomes a real misfortune. We could similarly wish that the English Metaphysicals had indulged in much fewer conceits, or that Sterne, or even Shakespeare himself — but I needn't dig for other examples. Yet where the superior artist is harmed by not rising above what we may call, with Mr. Chase, the rococo, a nation is very often harmed by not reaching up to it. The artist can dispense with the small forms of beauty, but the public cannot. The artist can function largely in a world of his own making — too much culture is perhaps even "weakening" for genius, and beautiful material objects may in a sense be the enemy of beauty. But nonartists, noncreative people, the world at large, need the atmosphere, the ornaments, the décor of culture. A predominantly bibelot-like culture could only, of course, be frivolous, dilettantish, effeminate. But a purely functional, no-nonsense, always-abreast-of-the-times culture, where in one's bookcase Toynbee leans only on Schweitzer and Schweitzer leans only on Freud — does this bespeak anything temperamental or personal, or is it only a part of the times? It's not a question of Old Guard and avant-garde, or whether a Canaletto print does more for a home than a Mexican primitive, or oldish things made of mahogany more than brand-new things made of metal, but whether there are not amenities and graces of the spirit; whether there are not cultures, as well as cups, that cheer. I don't contend that Jung or Margaret Mead or Frank Lloyd Wright aren't more central to our time than Osvald Siren or Sir Charles Singer; or that in order to be cultured, or well adjusted, or happy, one need be able to distinguish R. L. from G. B. Hobson, A. W. from A. F. Pollard, Oliver from André Simon, Vincent from Gertrude, or Gertrude from T. E., or T. E. from W. W., or W. W. from W. J., or W. J. from D. H. Lawrence. But for every ten educated people who have read Margaret Mead, is there one who knows which Hobson was the great authority on bindings and which on Chinese art?

Much of our own antirococoism stems, I think, from something puritan in us. We are only given to a kind of love of the graces, a feeling for the charming in culture, when the wind is blowing from Europe; and it hasn't blown steadily from there since the 1920s. The twenties, of course, have latterly been as much romanticized as they were formerly run down. The mood of the twenties was made up of many things — not least, of that sense of promise in life, and of profusion in literature, that made us emotionally both spend-thrift and carefree. But upstart and disordered and excessive though the twenties were, they were in impulse genuinely anti-bourgeois, antipuritan, antipedagogical: they reacted to the creative, they relished the creative, they aspired passionately to create. We lacked, then, the measure and control, the ability to select, delete, hew to the line, that constitute an artistic people; but we had, at any rate, the capacity to absorb and participate, to feel release and indulge in appreciation. We lacked the discipline, but we had the positive qualities that needed disciplining. The mood of the twenties had to pass, Depression or not; while, granted the Depression, the mood of the thirties had to be what it was. But the enduring significance of the thirties is less the purpose and propaganda that writers put into their work than the high spirits they took out of it. For the propaganda has been long discredited, but the joyousness has never been restored.

The present age is in the strong grip of cultural authoritarianism and of the most dogmatic kind. For great natural cultural lawgivers

of Dr. Johnson's type there is much to be said, though even here
"there is much to be said on both sides." And of course today there
are not only all those who would legislate and lead, there are all
the many more who hunger to be led, who crave to cry "Master."
Lionel Trilling has rather chided E. M. Forster — in an age so generally contrariwise — for his "refusal to be great." One knows what
Mr. Trilling means, one knows what is valid in what he means —
whether with Forster specifically or with intellectuals and artists in
general. A "refusal to be great" can mask a certain evasion of
moral responsibility, of final decisions and allegiances. It can reflect
too a certain self-consciousness, on the refuser's part, that is mere
vanity; it can constitute a special, perhaps quite extreme, form of
egoism. And Forster himself seems at times not merely casual but
playful and frivolous. All the same, whatever personal shortcomings or debatable human traits may lodge with this attitude, it yet
seems the backbone of a very notable, a very much honored, tradition — of that indeed very great tradition of skeptical humanism.
It is a tradition that having said *Thus I think* next always asks
What do I know? a tradition that forces the very bringer of light to
assay the light he brings as sharply as the darkness he dispels. In the
history of thought and culture the dark nights have perhaps in
some ways cost mankind less grief than the false dawns, the prison
houses in which hope persists less grief than the Promised Lands
where hope expires. Skeptical humanism is no enemy of positive
values or even of resolute action; but men bred to that tradition
will continue to feel that their values must be exhibited, warts and
all, and must in the end be made to speak for themselves. About
any other method, including the acceptance of greatness, there is
always at least a touch of *force majeure* and perhaps even a drop or
two of patent medicine. Today anyone's refusal to be great seems
the more formulated for being so out of line with prevailing
thought. The Great Men, the Strong Men, of literature today are
men of fierce passions and strong convictions, men playing the role
of prophet, teacher, moralist, martyr, saint, sinner, seer — the Mel-
villes, Nietzsches, Kierkegaards, the Gides, Dostoevskys, D. H.
Lawrences. Some of these men are as individual, one or two are

now and then as skeptical, as Forster; but the real point is to what degree have they encouraged independence, individualism, skepticism, the relaxed will, in others?

If only because the tide has been running strong against the old humanist attitude, the Forsters with their relaxed wills and their refusals to be great must take on a special value. The tradition of Socrates, of Montaigne and Erasmus, of Hume and of the Enlightenment, all the more because it never flourishes *below* the cultured classes, is immensely vital to them, is what we might almost call their claim to culture. It seems to me an absolutely essential tradition for societies and nations in need of something equable as well as affirmative, in need of lasting daylight as well as glowing dawns. It is a tradition that has never really established itself in America — a corollary, I think, to our being an inartistic people; it is a tradition, at any rate, at variance with a people who love the *idea* of greatness, who love panaceas, and formulas, and solutions, and absolutions, and reassuring answers. To a nation that worships God and Mammon both there must be something profoundly uncongenial in an attitude that blindly worships nothing. From the failure of the humanist tradition to participate fully or to act decisively, civilization may perhaps crumble or perish at the hands of barbarians. But unless the humanist tradition itself in some form survives, there can really be no civilization at all.

6

IN PURSUIT OF THE ALMIGHTY DOLLAR

In our history and literature, the ordinary businessman tends to be either a prosaic figure or a subject for satire and is, on the whole, reasonably well behaved. The big businessman is frequently something quite different, an outstanding figure of drama who turns marketplaces into bloody battlefields. Thus, the making of the great fortunes, and the makers of them, have had their own kind of merciless plunder and iniquitous charm, and their own prominent role in the making of America; and when the chronicling of their lives goes beyond merely trying to divert or dazzle us, it can be very rewarding. The late Ben B. Seligman's *The Potentates* in great measure has this value. Though the climate he works in and its leading characters and more lurid conquests are often familiar, his portrayal of business from colonial to computer times is the work of an economist who can articulate issues, of a historian who can delineate changes, and of a Labor functionary who wields a formidable measuring stick — or call it birch rod — in administering judgments.

The historian offers four significant changes in the nature of his potentates, characterizing them chronologically as The Individualists, The Masters, The Makers, and The Procurators — useful distinctions in terms of *autres temps* but with an overpowering element of *plus ça change* in the pursuit of profits. Indeed, the more accurate theme of *The Potentates* is a lust after exorbitant profits, after outrageous fortunes. In the period of the Individualists — roughly from the early fur traders to the heyday of the greatest fur trader of them all, John Jacob Astor — this exists, to be sure, on a relatively miniature scale, just as it functions, for much of the way, under a mercantilist system. For Britain permitted the colonies to trade only with the mother country and paid the colonists in merchandise rather than money. This produced, however, an illicit pattern for eluding the prescribed one, whether as outright smuggling or as three-cornered trading — for example, in colonial rum, West African slaves, and West Indian sugar. If the colonial farmer seemed small potatoes, his was yet the root profession, and from living off the land he might acquire a great deal more of it. If the trapper seemed like penny buckshot, a fur trader like William Pynchon could be exporting, by the 1650s, 14,000 pounds of beaver skins.

In the cities, as time passed, merchants grew wealthy and influential; by the mid-eighteenth century Thomas Hancock of Boston had become "wholesaler, retailer, importer, banker and landlord," his store a kind of premature department store, his interests extending to manufactures and mines. Hancock's fortune passed to his nephew, the famous John, who was in actual fact somewhat infamous, being writ large for smuggling, bribing, and the use of thugs. As business expanded, its need for manpower brought across the Atlantic indentured servants, then 50,000 British convicts, and finally African slaves, these last the making of New England's first millionaires.

Shipping, real estate, and mercantile activity dominated the North's pre-Revolutionary economy; a depression in the 1760s, born of British restrictions, set the scene for the Tea Party and Paul Revere, and for a war during which business far from suffered, and trading with the enemy was by no means a sin. The rebels could be profiteers as well; supplies were withheld from the army to force prices up, and our first big moneyman, Robert Morris, as Superintendent of Finance for the Continental Congress, frequently let his friends and himself in on a good thing in the matter of contracts. Despite a term in debtors' prison, Morris was by

1787 the richest man in America; it has often been said that he financed the Revolution; it has also been said that the Revolution financed him. Either way it was largely done with paper money: so great did inflation become that in Philadelphia stockings cost four hundred dollars a pair. After the war, the new sovereign states quarreled so often over commerce as to need, and to create, a Constitution which became "a document intended to advance the common economic interests of men of business."

During the half-century that followed, business briskly expanded. Poor land in New England sent men to the building of ships and to sailing the seas; to the China trade and the whaling trade; to privateering and piracy; to carrying many kinds of cargo, even ice for hot countries. Manufacturing took hold in New England; elsewhere, John Jacob Astor came to dominate the fur trade by cheating when he bought and overcharging when he sold. By 1816 there were almost 250 state banks, possessing far more currency than specie. Boston's Andrew Dexter got hold of a bank and its banknote plates, ran off bills for himself which he had his cashier sign after work and which he then sold. Getting hold of a second bank, he andrewdextrously fed each with the other, and from a $45 investment issued $800,000 in notes.

Business also expanded geographically. The Louisiana Purchase had opened great spaces for farming and prospecting; beyond the Appalachians other great spaces were opened, with speculators trying to buy huge tracts of land, such as a million acres, from Congress. By merely sitting at home Astor bought up all the land on Manhattan Island he could lay his hands on, to become by 1847 the richest man in America. But it was not a stay-at-home era; new transportation — first canals and then railroads — made for travel, emigration, increased business. From a single Staten Island ferryboat Cornelius Vanderbilt had come to own thirty-four steamships and ferries and seventeen ocean liners before his elderly switch to railroads — they to become the greatest and most viciously fought over of nineteenth-century industries. But by then the rough, barefisted Individualists had given way to the ruthless, barefaced Masters.

By the 1840s the railroads had pushed beyond the Appalachians, were carrying the mail, were getting vast federal, state, and local subsidies — every town involved dreamed of becoming a terminus — and great land grants as well. By 1853 the first of the big railroad men, Erastus Corning, had created the New York Central, soon to become the largest corporation in America, and quite large in paper holdings and watered stock. By the time Vanderbilt divested Corning and Dean Richmond of the Central, the great railroad drama — or serial story — had begun. Mr. Seligman has not drawn on Peter Lyon's blasting of the principal railbirds in *To Hell in a Day Coach*, but certainly he nowhere challenges Lyon's depiction of nineteenth-century railroad history as an epic of rapacity and swindling, with an all-star scoundrel cast that make bit parts of the Jesse Jameses. The century's two most acrimonious clashes came, first in the 1860s over the Erie, in which Vanderbilt got licked by Jay Gould; and then, at the end of the century, in the Northern Pacific–Great Northern war when James J. Hill, J. P. Morgan, *et al.*, fought E. H. Harriman, Jacob H. Schiff, James Stillman, *et al.* — a threatened slaughter that virtually wound up in a standstill. To polish off the Titan among industries, the railroad continued to lead in importance through the first quarter or more of the twentieth century; since then, despite its passenger-be-damned tactics and its tin-cup histrionics, it would seem to have a pretty fair record of profit-making poverty.

For half a century cotton proved of decided importance to business as the South's great staple and even greater export. Tremendously dependent on slave labor, the South, in its need for it, had thoughts of annexing Cuba. Slavery itself, says Mr. Seligman, was not a big issue; indeed, until well into the Civil War it proved economically a workable system, with investment returns running as high as 12 percent. (Slaves also counted politically, with five blacks the equal of three whites in apportioning House seats.) The War, while financially wrecking the South, greatly enriched Northern manufacturers and businessmen. Their war profits led to reckless spending and parvenu ostentation, this the gaudy vestibule to the Gilded Age. War profits hastened the coming of age of the new Masters, whose major geography was East and West rather than North and South. There were all sorts of industrial expansion; of technological innovation, such as the sewing machine; and of new techniques, such as selling the sewing machine on the installment plan. The tactics and antics of the railroad men would be imitated, the sleight of hand with securities proliferated, the new breed in potentates would gladly learn from the old — how, for example, Commodore Vanderbilt boasted of outwitting a friend in business; or, after a squabble over a new house, threw his wife into an insane asylum.

The Masters, though they would establish the huge impersonality of corporation rule, could claim a striking image, an appalling carnage, a robber-baron polity. They robbed the Indians, they cheated the white man, they chucked out the squatters, they squeezed out the farmers, they greased palms, they twisted arms, they knifed one another. With them, a mere eye for an eye would have seemed imbecilic philanthropy. But where "Southerners stole thousands, Northerners took millions." Not everything, to be sure, smacked of railroad yards or Wall Street; there was a big new traffic in, among other things, meat packing, trolley cars, tobacco, the department store, the five-and-ten-cent store, the mail-order business. Furthermore, two of Mr. Seligman's Big Three among the Masters were to rule over "new" industries: "Steel belonged to Carnegie, oil to Rockefeller," along with Wall Street to J. P. Morgan.

The history of all three is far from unknown, in outline if not in detail: a Rockefeller detail new to me is that John D., Sr.'s father "prided himself on training his sons to be sharp by cheating them whenever he could." His son John, who early in his career was to reject oil as "too wild a business," was to attain through it the "most complete monopoly ever built in America." Monopoly, it seems, was from far back Rockefeller's goal and was granted him, he believed, by divine decree. By the time Standard Oil's enrollment had reached forty companies, Rockefeller, in the manner of a college president, allotted his partners various professorial chairs — in pipelines, contracts, marketing, manufacturing, and finance; his own pet course on the secret rebate, or kickbacks on freight charges, proved an immense success. On and on, and bigger and bigger, went Standard, an international empire declared an illegal monopoly by the Supreme Court in 1892; on and on it blandly continued, undemonopolized, to be excoriated by Henry Demarest Lloyd, exposed by Ida Tarbell, and fined $29 million by Judge Kenesaw Mountain Landis (this overturned on appeal), until in 1909 it was ordered dissolved by the Supreme Court. But the family fortune went marching on. Its history is commensurate with its holdings, both of them too vast for easy summarizing.

Andrew Carnegie, who read books and went to concerts, hobnobbed with Herbert Spencer, and played host to Matthew Arnold, was different: he wore gloves over his brass knucks, displayed crocodile tears along with crocodile jaws, and spouted moral maxims while spreading nasty rumors about his rivals. Nor, we are told, was he a practical iron man or even a true steel one; his forte was salesmanship. His love of the workingman led him to direct the notorious Homestead Strike from abroad, while pretending to know nothing about it. He bought people at the "book price," but when he tried to do this to his wide-awake partner, Henry Clay Frick, Frick stalked out and brought suit, denouncing Carnegie as a fraud and a cheat; what chiefly emerged was the company's enormous profits. Indeed, so enormous by now was Carnegie's fortune that he was as ready to sell out as were his rivals to buy him; in a transaction negotiated by J. P. Morgan, Carnegie stepped aside for almost $500 million in gold bonds.

Morgan wore no gloves and wielded a mallet. His story also is not easily summarized but can be epitomized as sheer dictatorship; he dealt, it has been said, in ultimatums. He would also float stocks and water them, create crises and settle them; his operations became worldwide: at one time he or his partners held seventy-two directorships in "forty-seven of the larger corporations," and the year before he died he "owned or dominated" twenty-eight railroads. He was a mighty Master and scarcely equaled was his masterpiece: the formation of U.S. Steel. Hatefully magnificent, he needed no statue, being cast in marble.

With the corporation fully created by the turn of the century, its enjoyment of limited liability proved an unlimited asset. It had become "the legal device by which a nation's resources could be plundered. . . . [It] hastened the growth of a paper economy, one that dealt in intangibles and promises to pay as a major form of wealth." All this found a gospel in versions of laissez-faire and in Social Darwinism, an economic survival of the fittest. It had lawyers invoking that previously radical document, the Declaration of Independence, and judges discovering that the "pursuit of happiness" meant the right to enjoy property as one saw fit.

By now the Makers were supplementing the Masters; they were inventors, adapters, and the like, who did not forget to invent a suitable symbol, the cash register. With Edison and others as pacesetters, there was a kind of technological gold rush: some inventions wore huge price tags, others were up for grabs, and by hook or by crook, by perjure or merger, all sorts of potential sources of profit changed ownership. One of these, the automobile, changed American life, and to some extent, its economy. In it, says Mr. Seligman, steel found its biggest customer; and certainly oil and rubber must have been made happy also. Though the automobile was European born, by 1903 America led in production of it. What was needed for *mass* production was an assembly-line technique; what was needed from it was a good low-priced car. Henry Ford soon turned out a very successful one for $850; in 1908 he once more turned out, for $850, his sturdy indestructible Model T, which put Ford far in the lead of his competitors — by 1912 there were seven thousand Ford dealers. To achieve such success Ford merely converted the worker into part of the machinery, with a job that seemed to take place in a jail. Ford's famous five-dollar "profit-sharing" day — a benefaction that won him the name of a radical — was actually denied to a large percentage of workers, and simply drove even harder, on the assembly line, those who were granted it. His career as a leading Maker, and, with his anti-Semitism and antilabor tactics, a troublemaker, ended in a senility from which his grandson Henry II rescued the business. The other big pioneer automobile man, W. C. Durant, would early merge Buick, Cadillac, Oldsmobile, Pontiac-to-be, and much else as

General Motors. Having created an empire, he got into financial trouble with it and, though he held on, first Walter P. Chrysler, then Chevrolet, and finally Du Pont managed or took control of it.

Mr. Seligman includes the Du Ponts and the Mellons among the Makers, and certainly the Du Ponts are. What with their tremendous expansion from a gunpowder start — dynamite, chemicals, paints, plastics, Nylon (which their chief chemist discovered), twelve hundred items in all by 1958 — theirs is a great laboratory fortune, estimated at $7 billion. But the Mellons — at any rate their Maker, Andrew — were really Masters. They too boast a great many items, if industries can be called items — steel, oil, aluminum, coal, coke, carborundum, trolley cars, shipbuilding, plate glass, banks; but there is nothing resembling a laboratory. Indeed, Andrew Mellon did a good deal of business with the old Masters — Frick, Carnegie, Rockefeller; he also conspicuously promoted the interests of business while three times Secretary of the Treasury; and he had gone many times to court before going to the Court of St. James's. When Mellon's big Aluminum Corporation was enjoined from monopolistic practices in 1912, "the proscription was blithely ignored." When monopolistic charges were renewed in the 1920s, and the Attorney General, Harlan Fiske Stone, was ready to prosecute, he was hurriedly elevated to the Supreme Court, and the company totally exonerated by a Justice Department examiner who was not a lawyer, not an economist, not even an accountant, but merely a former clerk. In his elegantly icy and greedy way Andrew W. Mellon seems perhaps the least "sympathetic" potentate of them all.

With our last group, the Procurators, we are bumping up against today's realities. Mr. Seligman is treating of "representatives" who, within a corporation structure, have taken over one company after another; is treating of corporations that have taken over one industry after another; and again of corporations that have moved into one country after another. "The Procurators" carries us from the Boom and the Crash (the Guaranty Trust judged the market collapse "a favorable development") through the Depression (Mencken thought FDR the weakest man the Democrats could have nominated) into the explosive prosperity following World War II. In size and dollar signs alike, almost everything doubled in less than twenty years. Millions, by the sixties, had become mere pocket money; business talked in billions — as the assets of more than thirty utilities, the deposits in close to fifty banks, the sales of over a hundred industrial firms. The economy was corporation-rampant and corporation-run, while still to come was the mammoth era of mergers — almost three thousand in the year 1967. In his final chapter on the Procurators, Mr. Seligman sums up the period economically as the Age of Space, which is to say of commercial air travel from its early mail-carrying through passenger-carrying to military-industrial and astronaut days.

A quite long book, *The Potentates* covers a great deal of ground in all parts of America and all periods of its history; treats of a great many businesses and a vast gallery — a virtual rogues' gallery — of businessmen. There is a good deal, also, of the role that government and the law have played in our business history. All this is done at the sound level of *haute vulgarisation*, of channeling knowledge into applied rather than abstract economics, of brightening analysis with anecdote, and of largely elucidating the "principles" of big business through the practices of big businessmen.

Doubtless economists and historians will question some of Mr. Seligman's interpretations and judgments, which have behind them something of Veblen, Gustavus Myers, Charles Beard, and others; but the book is free of the suppressions of the "authorized" biographies and the shoddiness of the overpopularized ones. There are minor matters to cavil at. The last third of the book suffers from a literal *embarras de richesses*, its clutter of fortunes making for a certain effect of sprawl, and some of its biographical sketches seeming pretty perfunctory. The book can also be rather jumpy in its chronology — thus AT&T precedes Alexander Graham Bell, and Henry Ford has lived and died before Thomas Edison comes on the scene. The only omission I would complain about is TV. True, the book deals earlier, though briefly, with radio; but TV is surely the most pervasive element in today's cultural life, and in the most commercial form. It is all the worse big business because it should never have become big business, but should, after the British fashion, have been chiefly a public service. As it stands, it is big business operating in a lackey relationship with bigger business. It has about it nothing of the great potentates' bullying or swagger; with its vulgarizing, its compromising, its bowdlerizing, it recalls, in cultural terms, Disraeli's crack about O'Connell, that he "committed every crime that does not require courage."

7

1876: IS THAT ALL THERE WAS?

With several Eastern cities already very conscious today of America's coming bicentenary, and indeed very competitive about the less purely patriotic aspects of celebrating it, there may be topical as well as historical interest in William Peirce Randel's *Centennial: American Life in 1876.* For one thing, the greatest popular event of 1876 was the Centennial Exposition in Philadelphia, something which serves in Mr. Randel's book as a kind of mini-mirror of the times, and so could prove, if only quaintly, instructive for perhaps the greatest popular event of 1976. And the fact that 1876 commemorates for us not just our country's hundredth birthday but its halfway mark could give *Centennial* a niche in any appraisal of our national expansion, and how far that also means progress, or of our national achievement, and how far that also means greatness.

Centennial itself, however, is not a book that sets 1876 against 1976; it is a reconstruction, with much reading behind it, of the life of the country in a given, if special, year; of fashions in thought and feeling; of what went on in high places, which could also be dark ones; of regional differences, and sociological and industrial developments. Robbed by his very title of any chronological or single approach to so many-sided a subject, Mr. Randel has gone in for a circular one, a sort of U.S.-on-Exhibition tour of such displays as Politics, Business, Religion, Education, Public Opinion, and the Arts. And indeed, he encountered in 1876 a very great deal that he could write about, though a great deal less that clamored for celebration.

For that matter, the actual celebrating in 1876 calls for only limited celebration today. From the outset, there were problems of financing the Exhibition in Philadelphia's Fairmount Park, and only at the last minute did Congress grant it a credit of $1.5 million. Though, financially speaking, it had a rather short run — May 10 to November 10 — it remained, owing to Protestant pressure, closed on Sunday; and publicizing, as it did, a highly diversified nation, it drew very dissimilar regional reactions. The Northern East proved by all odds the most responsive; many Southern states weren't even officially represented, many Western regions had virtually nothing to represent them. Yet paucity, on the whole, was less detrimental than abundance, for aesthetically much of the Exhibition was a hodgepodge of mediocrity and a riot of plush-and-gilt thinking. There was an architectural "motley of styles" — Lewis Mumford, retrospectively, found it "hard to think of anything lower"; and surveying the gallimaufry of display items, William Dean Howells could nowhere find a unifying principle or meaning. The art often jogged along with the architecture; if, of art that mattered, Winslow Homer's *Crack the Whip* was admitted, Eakins's great, just completed *Clinic of Dr. Gross* was barred and consigned to the medical section because "Dr. Gross's hands showed blood." Prominently displayed was an "excruciating" Italian-plaster George Washington astride an eagle, the eagle life-sized, George over six feet from the waist up; and extremely popular was a wax Cleopatra with an arm that moved. Europe, except for England, was not too helpful, or trustful: the Rembrandts that Holland sent were all copies. Big names could well mean bad news: Richard Wagner's specially commissioned opening-day grand march was "perhaps the worst music" he ever composed. As for the distinguished nature of the awards, three different piano firms received medals for "the world's best piano." More significantly, the Exhibition left behind no milestone like the London Crystal Palace, the Eiffel Tower, or the Chicago Transportation Building.

The Exhibition had its bad breaks, such as a blazing hot summer, with the buildings like ovens; attendance in August averaged 33,000 a day, in October 89,000. A politically harassed President Grant opened the Exhibition, in one account, to "more groans and hisses than huzzas," failed to show up on the Great Day, July 4, and in November wound up the Exhibition in twelve perfunctory words. But it had proved a fairly successful spectacle, having caught the public eye with everything from Yale locks to Pullman berths, with objects as brand-new as linoleum and as revolutionizing as the telephone. ("My God," cried the Emperor of Brazil, "it talks!")

The Exhibition shared the headlines with less festive news, for on several counts 1876 achieved a high point in low practices. Grant might with reason have ducked the Exhibition on the Fourth of July, for the notorious disasters which had plagued his presidency from Black Friday in 1869 on continued explosively during his last year or so in the White House. First Grant's Secretary of the Treasury, Benjamin Bristow, cracked down on the Whiskey Ring to expose excise-tax evasions that transferred millions of U.S. Treasury dollars to thieving trouser pockets, evasions that reached as high up as the Chief Clerk of the Treasury and Grant's own confidential secretary, General Orville Babcock. Thanks to a presidential deposition in Babcock's favor, he alone out of 350 defendants was acquitted.

Next on the 1876 docket was the exposure of Grant's Secretary of War, William W. Belknap, as a large-scale grafter, and so flagrant a one that his old Princeton roommate, asking as chairman of a House committee that Belknap be impeached, spoke of "a record of official corruption and crime such as there is no parallel for in our history." Belknap's haul came to a million dollars, $90,000 of it from contracts for headstones on Union graves. All over the country fears now circulated that Grant's whole Cabinet was corrupt, which proved groundless, barring the Secretary of the Navy; he, also a Princeton man, had maneuvered Navy contracts into a $320,000 personal bank account.

But perhaps nothing so ill became Grant's incumbency as his

leaving it, to the scandalous reverberations of the disputed 1876 Hayes-Tilden presidential election — too familiar a story, and too long drawn out a one to recapitulate, but one that certified Grant's fellow Republican Hayes as President only on the very eve of Inauguration Day, and that inspired one of the Republican party's most high-minded communiqués. With victory depending on the disputed electoral vote in four states, the Republican National Chairman wired to the governor of one of them: "Florida must be made Republican. Troops and money will be furnished." In Louisiana, after much Republican tampering, Tilden still led by seven thousand votes, so the tampering continued while, with nonpartisan zeal, the chairman of the Returns Board tried to sell the election, first to the Republicans and then to the Democrats, first for a million dollars and then for a mere $200,000. Small wonder that Grant, an honest man surrounded by dishonest ones, should have made of his last message to Congress an abject apology.

If politically life in America wobbled from sordid farce to lurid melodrama, culturally it existed at very different regional levels, which Mr. Randel designates as the Civilized East, the Frontier, and the Wilderness. He laments, as may we, that 1876 produced no book by a keen, preferably foreign observer of our culture — if not an invaluable Tocqueville, at least a trenchantly carping Dickens or Mrs. Trollope. And indeed, native or foreign, the commentators in 1876 seldom rise very far above picturesque trivia. Thus Jacques Offenbach, in America to conduct thirty centennial-year concerts, reports that when he ordered an elegant dinner at the swank Fifth Avenue Hotel, to his consternation everything was brought to the table at the same time. Another French visitor, Jules Leclerq, was equally impressed by the beautiful American women and the use of baggage checks; and was a touch startled to be served, in a Kansas City hotel, "*ragoût de* prairie dog." And Joseph Hatton of London stated that of 4000 Chinese women in San Francisco, 3900 were prostitutes.

Fortunately Mr. Randel himself does a good deal better for us with his stockpile of hard facts, cold statistics, clashing ambitions, controversial issues, and seasonable remarks out of the mouths of knaves. If his method fails to integrate his various findings, many of them are evident enough, if not indeed well known. Certainly American business often walked ethically arm in arm with American politics. The 1870s was a synonym for swindle and corruption, an era of Boss Tweeds and Wall Street panics and robber barons, with the naked claw concealed not beneath a velvet glove but beneath a catcher's mitt. In the seventies, lobbying in Washington itself became an industry, while big business saw its largely-commodities past — iron, steel, textiles, clothing — shifting to a largely-utilities future: the telegraph and telephone, chemicals, electrical devices, petroleum. As for lobbying, Collis P. Huntington divided congressmen into three categories: clean ones, who didn't need to be paid; commercial ones, who could be bought; and Communists, who couldn't. As for petroleum, in 1876 John D. Rockefeller was about to move in on the New York area, in the process of creating "the one great monopoly in our business history."

But if the United States in 1876 exhibited all the stains of a ruthless capitalism, it provided all the contrasts of a staggered culture. Mr. Randel's Civilized East could be intensely money-minded after the stab-and-grab fashion of New York or the pinch-and-squeeze fashion of New England; yet if Massachusetts in 1876 had 734 savings banks, it also had remarkably many colleges, four of them for women. Ohio had an impressive number of colleges, too, and a prosperity born of commanding all three great routes of Western travel: the Great Lakes, the first national road west, and the Ohio River. Locomotion was part of the cultural staggering: the farther west you went, the more important river traffic became, and the more prominent wagon freight (Wells Fargo, the Adams and American Express companies). In the wilderness, the era of Indian raids was ending, but that of holdups was at its height; there were almost none, however, on river steamboats, where gamblers, hand in glove with holdup gangs, did the fleecing.

The wilderness in 1876 was still envisaged as a kind of great economic empire of the future; Seward, who had negotiated the purchase of Alaska in 1867, eyed Western Canada, too, and dreamed of acquiring Mexico as a state and making Mexico City our national capital. Meanwhile, gold seekers and buffalo hunters were encroaching on Indian reservations; in 1875 the government even tried to buy the Black Hills from the Sioux; and the following June saw the Centennial Year's most dramatic and tragic event: the battle of Little Bighorn and Custer's Last Stand against Sitting Bull. There the Indians were avenging a shameful army policy, pretty well set forth in General Sheridan's notorious "The only good Indian is a dead Indian," to which a congressman had retorted that it cost a million dollars to kill an Indian but only two thousand dollars to keep him alive. At the same time in the Wild West, the stuff of a hundred future movies — the James brothers, Billy the Kid, Wyatt Earp, Calamity Jane — was painful actualities. Against all this, helping to tame the West, was a small brandnew device called barbed wire; in 1874 ten thousand pounds of it were sold, in 1876 nearly three million.

Beyond the wilderness, at the other end of the country, lay a spottily civilized West: a Portland, Oregon, almost as proper and prim as New England; a high-stepping San Francisco with the racketiest night life — the Barbary Coast — in the country, and the greatest luxury hotel — the Palace — in the world; while, casting its shadow before, the University of California at Berkeley was suffering from so much political interference that its president quit in disgust.

In the West, 1876 saw Wild Bill Hickok killed during a poker game and Colorado admitted to the Union. In more domesticated regions, 1876 saw the first practical carpet sweeper emerge, Lydia Pinkham's Vegetable Compound put on the market, Central Park completed, Edison patenting the mimeograph and Alexander Bell the telephone. (Western Union could have bought the rights to it for $100,000.) It was an era when all sorts of new things bobbed up — eggbeaters, ice-cream freezers, soda fountains — and when it was difficult not to gain weight. Who has not seen the vast table d'hôte hotel and railroad menus offering terrapin, quail, steak, and a dozen other things for a dollar? It was overwhelmingly an age of middle-class too-muchness, in furnishings as well as food, in underclothing as well as ornaments, in euphemisms as well as offspring (a wife who was "expecting" might provide both). It was a moment, too, when the mighty railroad conveyed countless country boys, not all of them Alger heroes, to the bright-lighted city, where vice was rampant, children were trained pickpockets, and very young slum girls sold matches as a blind to soliciting.

The display that Mr. Randel thinks made the best showing in 1876 was Education. For one thing, along with solid citizens, many distinctly unsaintly millionaires saw in higher education an inviting form of philanthropy, whether as a thanks-offering to God or as a pill for relieving guilt. More significantly, an enlarged conception of education, including agricultural and scientific programs, was fast gaining ground: the University of Minnesota proclaimed it would teach everything "from hog cholera to Plato." At Harvard Dr. Eliot had started putting through reforms, whether creating the first economics department in the United States or abolishing the custom that a professor's income was determined by how many students he could attract. And Harvard in 1876 had perhaps the most distinguished faculty in all our academic history: James Russell Lowell in modern languages, Francis James Child (of the Ballads) in English, Oliver Wendell Holmes in anatomy, Asa Gray in botany, Wolcott Gibbs in applied science, Henry Adams in history, William James in physiology, and Benjamin Peirce in astronomy. The Harvard *Lampoon* also dates from 1876, as do Johns Hopkins University, and in a kindred field, the American Library Association, the *Library Journal*, and the book that introduced the Dewey decimal system. The same year the American Intercollegiate Football Association was founded (it decided to have football played in the fall rather than the spring); and so sports-minded was the American public becoming that 1876 saw the founding of the National League, the first U.S. lawn tennis tournament, and the U.S. debut of polo.

What might seem a grand final display booth in Mr. Randel's national tour — the arts — merely tends to bear out the Philadelphia Exhibition offerings. Eakins and Ryder, to be sure, were men of stature in painting, and H. H. Richardson in architecture; but the Age of Ostentation was at its height, which meant far too much too-muchness, far too many curlicues, and even the well-bred doting on gingerbread. In architecture Moorish might frolic with Gothic, or any other two or three styles join hands. There were reactions to this: the English-born architect Charles Eastlake, for example, was by 1876 successfully preaching simplicity and "sincerity," but often replacing gingerbread with boiled potatoes. The theatre was a pretty frowsily bespangled business, with no concern for realism and too much for the star system. All the same, it flourished tremendously, whether in city playhouses, in small-town "opera houses," or out west on a "small, raised platform in the corner of a barroom." Out west also the Gold Rush Twins — Central City, Colorado, and Virginia City, Nevada — offered, with excellent singers, actual opera in sumptuous new opera houses.

In the literary world of 1876 the prevailing effect is a good deal like that in the other arts, with sentimentality or vulgarity minding the back door and gentility guarding the front. Through opposites, these sometimes met, for both the hussy and the homebody, the tearful and the timid, could make aesthetics their victim. It was harmless books that in bulk caused harm, it was literary journals that stalled literature, it was "tasteful" critics that lowered the blinds instead of letting in light. Yet 1876 saw the publication of *Tom Sawyer*, of Melville's *Clarel*, of Henry James's *Roderick Hudson*, with James's *The American* being serialized in the *Atlantic*.

Mr. Randel has assembled 460 pages of largely pertinent and interesting material, but in the service of a single year and often so loosely dropped into the text as to seem more like source material. From his not providing an ampler perspective, one tends oneself, after a while, to bring the centennial year into comparison with the bicentennial, to think of likenesses and differences, of what's relevant and what's remote. Technologically, with not very long to go, one doesn't dare to predict what last-minute wonders the 1976 Exhibition will display, or how many planets as well as nations will be represented. Aesthetically, too, even so short a time is a leap in the dark and may feature such strange fads or startling uses of paint as one cannot conceive. Indeed, the 1876 and 1976 Exhibitions will probably stand farther apart than the 1876 and 1976

Americas, for in several of today's dominant if chiefly dubious traits, 1876 is "the baby figure of the giant mass." Certainly Grant's Administration, with its noisome scandals and scoundrelism, helped set the tone for our plutocratic future and our over-materialistic culture, and the politics it introduced was not just corrupt but corrupting. And it clearly plays a part in the unblushing ethics, today, of the Eleventh Commandment, Thou shalt not be found out, and in the checkbook aesthetics of the Cartier diamond. To be sure, in their externals and their proportions, these inheritances are so altered that, after a hundred years, perhaps only one of them remains in the same place and goes by the same name. But perhaps that one is enough: for with Wall Street, all the others are in some way connected.

8

WHO SHOT THE IRON HORSE?

The railroad, assuredly one of the supreme achievements of the nineteenth century, has become, in America at least, one of the most blasted burdens of the twentieth. At best today it resembles a fabled ruin, a vast fallen empire. More commonly it suggests a stodgy and even dirtier-looking subway; a sprawling anachronism that conveys not ruin but mess, not age but senility, not something speeding across continents but stalled between stations. To the air-minded, it is a beastly by-product of fog; to car-driving millions, it is a curio about to share the fate of the corset, the icebox, the Welsbach lamp, the napkin ring, and the livery stable.

Yet in 1966 shareholders of railroad stock were paid $502 million in cash dividends, "more than in any other year in the industry's history." So we are informed very early in Peter Lyon's *To Hell in a Day Coach,* a work which bears the subtitle "An Exasperated Look at American Railroads." Mr. Lyon is one of those people, themselves verging on anachronism, who enjoy traveling on trains, yet can enjoy very few of the trains they travel on. But Mr. Lyon offers no plaintive lament, no elegy written in a country waiting room; his scrutiny is as dry-eyed as it seems lynx-eyed; his splutterings run not to swearwords but statistics; his treatment, from the bad old days of plunder to the recent cries of pain, is bluntly financial. His book is brisk and a little breezy in manner, but his bibliography seems solid, and his citations are specific, nor does he offer — or need to offer — sensationalism in place of truth.

Our nineteenth-century railroad history is an obstreperous drama of rapacity and romance, with an all-star cast of scoundrels, compared with whom mere train robbers, the James brothers or the Daltons, play bit parts. It is an epic of swindling, of neo-Viking pillaging, of neanderthalish power grabs, whose methods turned legislatures into lackeys, whose transactions turned watered stock into wine. It is a flag-draped dossier of chicanery at the hilly end of Pennsylvania Avenue and of timidity at the other. The Iron Horse as an industry, like the horse itself, was forever belching smoke and banging into whatever got in its way. However gifted its rivals in our most florid age of robber barons, railroading was the Abou Ben Adhem of industrial villainy.

This is true not least because, from the very outset, our premier villain was looked upon as a public servant, as a national benefactor; hence was deserving of public funds, hence was entitled to grants of land, hence was the plump heiress of Eminent Domain. Public grants became the darling of private greed; hence the heiress was wooed wherever possible, or was jilted wherever expedient. Before even ten thousand miles of U.S. track had been laid down, railroad policy, says Mr. Lyon, had already crystallized as ignoring, dismissing, and sweeping under the roadbed the public interest. Already during the 1840s there were anguished public outcries about "discriminatory freight rates, poor passenger service, filthy accommodations," and the like. There were squawks and cries that the state should own the railroads, something not easily consummated since the railroads owned the statehouse. Thus, Erasmus Corning, the earliest of the great public servants and a power in Albany, sensibly became a state senator himself, while his colleague from Buffalo, Dean Richmond, became Democratic state chairman. Making trained seals of other politicos, the two men linked arms and railroads, and lo, the New York Central was born.

With that the grease-palmed prologue ends, and the curtain goes up on the brass-knuckled first act. With that, we are in the presence of famous names and on the eve of infamous events, with scoundrelism rampant and scandals rife. Just a few years more and the four great Eastern trunk lines — the New York Central, the Pennsylvania, the Erie, and the B & O — will combine, in the way of rates and the like, against the public, while colliding among themselves. The first generation of railroad magnificoes — Commodore Vanderbilt, Daniel Drew, Jay Gould, Jim Fisk, Russell Sage — will trample on everything, even one another. Thus the Commodore, having captured the Central, laid siege to the Erie, precipitating that "public spectacle of greed" which "stands alone in our history" — the Erie War, wherein Vanderbilt was licked by his juniors, Gould and Fisk, one of whose very first acts was to put on their board of directors William Marcy Tweed. Licking his wounds, the aquatic Commodore watered the Central's stock, while Gould and Fisk permitted the Erie's stockholders "ten million dollars of debt." In the course of events, Drew used fishy securities and fled to New Jersey with $6 million in cash "wrung" from the Commodore, who conspired to have him kidnaped back to New York. During all this, New York's legislature was openly bribed, and its Supreme Court corrupted.

The East's Big Four in railroads being now in good hands, the West responded with its Big Four in men. Nonrailroaders, but otherwise unimpeachably qualified, Mark Hopkins, Charles Crocker, Leland Stanford, and Collis P. Huntington became transportation-minded, and in due course, at Promontory Point, Utah, the Golden Spike was driven in. Around one of the most restful words in the language, *pacific* — whether Union, Central, Southern, Northern, or Western, plus the Great Northern for kicks — were to develop, with the arrival of Harriman and Hill, with the intrusion of Morgan and Wall Street, some exceedingly superior crises and some of the most valiant blows for freebooting ever struck.

Doing for a turn-of-the-century generation what the Erie War had done after the Civil War, the titanic Northern Pacific–Great Northern hostility set Hill, Pierpont Morgan, and George F. Baker, with the Vanderbilts and U.S. Steel "looming in the background," against Harriman, Jacob H. Schiff of Kuhn, Loeb, and

James Stillman of the National City Bank, with, looming in the background, William Rockefeller and H. H. Rogers of Standard Oil. After many coups and much carnage, but no decisive conquest, Morgan devised an "entente" that led TR, as President, to take action against it, and the Supreme Court to decree its dissolution. Harriman, whom Mr. Lyon calls "the most brilliant railroad executive in American history," came off best, getting back securities costing him $80 million that he could sell for twice as much.

Mr. Lyon distributes other awards and honorary degrees. Of the early great, Russell Sage was the "most pernicious . . . miserly, devious, an habitual liar, a perjurer and a betrayer of his associates"; a convicted usurer, a corrupter of governors and legislatures at a cost of two million and a profit of well over twenty. Collis P. Huntington Mr. Lyons salutes as the biggest of the Four: "ruthless, grim, cold, crafty," whom someone neatly described as "scrupulously dishonest," though I personally prefer a remark, which Mr. Lyon fails to quote, attributed to Huntington himself: "Whatever is not nailed down is mine. Whatever I can pry loose is not nailed down." We all know how the Central's W. H. Vanderbilt spoke of the public; the elder Morgan, for whom all Roads led to Wall Street, said less profanely, "I owe the public nothing." A president-maker of railroads, Morgan one day phoned a certain Charles S. Mellen. Their conversation, as recalled at a public hearing by Mellen:

> MORGAN: Is that you, Mr. Mellen?
> MELLEN: Yes.
> MORGAN: Anybody hear what you say?
> MELLEN: No.
> MORGAN: Will you take over the Northern Pacific?
> MELLEN: Yes.
> MORGAN: Will you leave it all to me?
> MELLEN: Yes.
> MORGAN: Goodbye.

Morgan also, in 1903, made Mellen president of the New Haven, and Mr. Lyon makes Morgan progenitor of all the New Haven's woes.

As the century turned, the wheel of fortune held steady; by 1905 no other industry equaled the railroads in revenue or power: their capital was estimated at ten times that of the country's banks and trust companies. Sixty years later a single "rival" corporation, General Motors, could boast greater revenues than the entire railroad industry. It is easy to account for much of the decline with the single word technology — cars, buses, planes, and trucks have competed and increasingly conquered. Add motels to cars, and you have 100 percent door-to-door living. Subtract planes from business, and you don't merely put back the clock, you all but restore the hourglass. Yet, granting such competition, what of tactics and countermoves? Are there no longer any great railroad strategists?

Well, it seems that for a long while the railroads sneered at such upstarts as trucks, which, under 400,000 in 1921, numbered more than 3 million by 1933. Even earlier, railroads showed no great affection for their big breadwinner, freight. So far as they were concerned with our country's welfare, World War I could have been World War lost: in 1917, the United States was short 158,-000 freight cars, while nearly 200,000 of them "stood idle on the tracks of the Eastern roads." The government finally took over the railroads, from January 1, 1918, to March 1, 1920, pouring money into repairs and improvements, while the railroads, in due course, filed claims for damages. The New York Central, for example, claimed $11 million, and finally paid the government $23. The Pennsylvania sought nothing for itself, knowing that the United States had spent $218 million on it; after much hollering, it was let off with paying $90 million.

The Pennsylvania has been the G.O.M. of railroads, often a key to their mergers, gobbles, and grabs, and its 1960s marriage to the New York Central suggests that of a sort of iron duke to a highborn dowager with a limp, and less for love than to cut down on the housekeeping. Of course the Chinese-boxes form of ownership that is now fashionable in all industries has been axiomatic for generations with the biggest railroads. Thus, they once for five months disputed who should own the Lackawanna before the Lackawanna's president even heard what was going on. In the

1920s, with railroad profits exceeding a billion a year, empire-snatching went right along with bull-market gymnastics. After 1929, everything in railways tottered and tumbled, till by 1932 profits had sagged to $325 million; five years more, and over $3 billion worth of railroad bonds were in default of interest. World War II put the industry back on its feet, but the railroads mistook their present for their future, while the trucks were all the time taking the future over. As railroad freight business went down, railroad rates went up, and business went down further, from 67 percent of the freight traffic in 1945 to 46 percent in 1958; and by 1959 the railroads were hauling, for one example, less than 8 percent of new cars. Since then, owing partly to outsiders' bright ideas, have come much brighter days. Piggybacks and auto racks, hopper cars and unit trains have, to antiphonal screams from truckers and bargemen, brought freight back to its ancestral home. By 1966 railroads were hauling nearly 50 percent of new cars, hopper cars had become great granaries on wheels, and the old faithful, freight, was riding to glory.

There remains Mr. Lyon's day coach, en route elsewhere. Mr. Lyon is exasperated indeed about current passenger service; he cites many horrendous examples of how brutal, how abominable, how indefensible it is — or, worse, how nonexistent. To be sure, the first economic truth that my generation mastered — it was an open secret in the fourth grade — was that freight trains made money and that passenger trains lost it. Hence for railroad bigwigs the passenger has not just been any old worm, but a costly tapeworm. Mr. Lyon thinks this attitude started more than a century ago when passenger fares had been legally restricted to two cents a mile, in retaliation for which the industry today would presumably restrict passenger service to two trains a month.

I fully agree with all Mr. Lyon's accusations and indictments of the past, but, thanks to a friend whose splendidly independent thinking has impressed me since boyhood, I must wonder whether Mr. Lyon's thoughts on the present may not, from his great love of trains, be emotionally blinkered. As my friend, who wishes his name withheld, puts it, could what Mr. Lyon considers a cold-blooded railroad ploy to wipe out *human* freight be in reality something quite different and highly commendable — namely, a fine, manly condemnation of certain discreditable traits in America's business life? In other words, might not the railroads' current approach to passenger service constitute a *deliberate re-jection* of America's dog-eat-dog competitiveness, of its craze for new technological gadgets, of its gaudy drum-beating promotion, of its glossy unmeaningful packaging, of its indecent pandering to that wallet-fingering hero who is Always Right, the Customer? Frankly, asks my friend, isn't the railroads' relaxed policy a blessed relief in the face of Avis tailgating Hertz, or of this airline offering caviar for breakfast, or that one free manicures and hairdos? In what Mr. Lyon sees as calculated passenger hardships, may not others find a sort of industrial idyll, a shift on the part of business from the commercial to the cultural? Let me jot down a few points.

1. In striking contrast to their once greedy policy of clamoring for government money for passenger service, railroads today have been spectacularly refusing it. They have actually beseeched the government to be let off carrying the mail — with the impressive result that, as against 10,000 mail-carrying-for-money passenger trains in 1935, there were in 1967 only 876.

2. At a time when the shocking business of demolishing historic landmarks all over America is being everywhere protested as a cultural crime, the New Haven Railroad — to give just one example — is carefully preserving 129 grade crossings and 179 bridges which cannot but delight the connoisseur of relics, being all of them from fifty to seventy-five years old.

3. All the same, the New Haven isn't taking an irresponsibly aesthetic view of such bracing sights; isn't for a moment setting beauty above bumps and bruises, or art above bandaged heads. In line with its policy of not risking human lives, it some time back conscientiously reduced its passenger service; beyond that, it would much prefer that the public visit these historic spots by taxicab or car pool.

4. In yet another way, the railroads are putting culture above cash: for people who strongly favor rail travel, the railroads have worked out ingenious connections between one train and another, so as to offer passengers, en route, not only king-sized rest periods in commodious terminals, but the chance to tour many of our most picturesque cities, often for six or eight hours — time enough to visit the leading parks and squares, the zoo, the art museum, the city hall, the new model reformatory, besides looking in on an old school friend or a cousin with money.

5. In paying homage to the past, and eschewing the parvenu brand-new, the railroads are in effect creating portable museums — what my friend terms Williamsburgs-on-wheels; are proffering prime examples of the proud craftsmanship and impeccable coach-work of more leisured days. In time, it is hoped, there will be identifying plaques and inscriptions accompanying this fine period equipment: *Warren G. Harding Dozed Here; This Leather First Cracked Under the Weight of William Howard Taft.*

Can such arguments be idly dismissed? Mr. Lyon, to be sure, riding his own theory, manages by juggling facts and figures to contribute a more sinister interpretation. A tireless burrower, he finds evidence that the Post Office Department *canceled* contracts with the railroads because, for example, they required thirty-eight to fifty-six hours to deliver mail at $438 to $516 a van, as against truck deliveries in twenty-six hours at $420 a bigger van. He also argues that the railroads deliberately tried to get rid of the mail as a way of getting rid of the trains. He asserts, again, that in "two states" and "several sizable cities" there is "no railway passenger service whatever." He claims that Robert R. Young, a popularity seeker who reorganized the B & O and the New York Central, ran paid advertisements reading: "A Hog Can Cross the Country Without Changing Trains — But You Can't." Well, well. Just *imagine* a hog changing trains — why, the sight of it would be the action picture, the news story, of the week.

Mr. Lyon further charges the railroads with deliberately failing to list certain trains; with instructing ticket-office agents to deny that certain others exist; he even charges the Santa Fe with "advising people to fly." He claims that certain information clerks are "evidently instructed to take the phone off the hook and forget to put it back, resulting in an all-day busy signal, until at 5 P.M. a recording suggests trying again at 9 A.M. the next day." Mr. Lyon cites Governor Hughes of New Jersey, who kept getting a busy signal for forty-five minutes before a Pennsylvania R.R. information clerk answered the phone. Is that so odd? I've gotten a busy signal for fifty-five minutes just phoning my wife — and as for having the phone off the hook, I have it off the hook right now so as not to be disturbed while writing this, and I'll wager Mr. Lyon had his off the hook while writing *To Hell in a Day Coach.* How else can anybody, including overburdened information clerks, ever get their work done?

I certainly don't want to seem pigheaded in all this: Mr. Lyon does have a good deal of what I suppose might be called ammunition. Even concerning the general thesis that passenger trains have always provided an operating deficit, Mr. Lyon insists that this is a "phantom deficit," a "statistical mirage," and that "millions of dollars of maintenance and other overhead costs" are levied against passenger charges "which would still have to be paid if every passenger train disappeared tomorrow." It has been well said that there are two sides to every story, and on purely sentimental grounds, I must confess I'm on Mr. Lyon's side. For I look farther back than he can, to an age of train travel when, if railroads were America's most ruthless industry, for a growing boy they were its most romantic. The charcoal-broiled steaks — a rarity then — in the diner; the fried chicken, as the C & O stopped at stations in Virginia, sold from baskets through the train-car windows; the chance to ride in the locomotive cab, with permission to blow the whistle; the child's nose pressed against the lower-berth window as the train raced through flickeringly lighted villages at midnight . . . Well, suppose Mr. Lyon is right. What can we do to bring his coldhearted, cash-minded railroad executives to their knees? I can't imagine that the classic device would help much — nothing would make these men happier than a boycott.

9

OF BABBITTS & BOHEMIANS

The twenties in America, Elizabeth Stevenson remarks in a book
about them, *Babbitts & Bohemians*, have turned into mythology
without becoming history. Certainly they have so stamped themselves on the imagination, so dramatized themselves in recollec-
tion, as often to seem romantic where merely irresponsible, and nostalgic where most unkempt. The production has been drowned in
the stage lighting, the story shredded into slogans — "The Roaring Twenties," "The Jazz Age," "The Era of Beautiful Nonsense."
Along with other eras — the 1890s, the English Restoration — the
twenties connote giddy holiday periods in history, when the Zeit-
geist took to wenching, or culture lurched and hiccuped, or art
swam in the nude. At the same time, what was shocking might also
have style, or what was stodgy get belted by satire; while the vol-
cano that was serving as a dance hall might suddenly overflow
with lava. The twenties perhaps evoke the flask and the flesh on
warm summer nights, in contrast to the bare ruined thirties that
came after them: indeed, the two eras suggest a pair of Hogarthian
moralities — Wantonness, shall we say, and Want.

All in all, the twenties are more easily contrasted than characterized, for though they planted many of the seeds of America's
future, the immediate future bore no good fruit; and though, during the decade, the arts were pressing ahead, life was going tipsily
around in circles. Yet about it all, as Miss Stevenson says, there was
a "sense of opportunity," and an official cheerfulness; but clearly
the world had been made anything but safe for democracy, and in

America democracy was most notable for the evils it is particularly prone to. Yet it is things like the Babbitts and the bohemians with their picturesque trappings that we remember best from the twenties. Such concrete recollections provide animated cartoons of any-which-way traffic, of jaywalking and barfly weaving, of Stutz Bear-cats and fake hearses, of monkey trials and Elks parades that give us a bewildering map of which not even hindsight can make a quite accurate chart. But looking back, even those who lived through the period can see what gave it a permissive confusion, what still exerts a surface fascination; and can grasp how the cultural message it has left conforms to a physical law — to the fact that cream and scum equally rise to the top.

One of the best things about *Babbitts & Bohemians* is that it spotlights much of the 1920s that we do not readily remember. One of the key words of the period, which I don't think turns up in the book, was *debunk*; and without diminishing the era's brighter virtues Miss Stevenson has herself debunked a good deal of its mythology, which applies even to its villains. The scandals of the Harding Administration, the evils of the Capone administration, the Red Scare raids that the curtain went up on, and the stock-market crash with which it came down — these we know all too well. Miss Stevenson, however, treating Rum-running, Republicanism, and Reaction in their more legalized forms, has chronicled a more elusive iniquitousness, the scum that, at least immediately, did not rise to the top. She has also documented that sense of national aloofness which would fester into America Firstness. She has scrutinized an age of wild living and spending to record how little the population as a whole had to live on and spend; and so has reminded us that in certain vital ways the set contrast between the twenties and the thirties can be not only too emphatic, but even wrong. Thus, the decade of official destitution was much the greater one of general assistance; the New Deal, the reader concludes, gave to Labor far more than the Depression took away. For in their social thinking, the intellectuals and bohemians of the twenties could be as misguidedly apathetic as in the thirties they were misguidedly fervent.

This is of course only part of the story; and it is only part of

Miss Stevenson's. The rest of it she has done a generally good job with, confronting an era overloaded with décor and running riot in detail, but careless and amorphous in design. Chronological rather than thematic, her book keeps to how history unfolds rather than, for the hindsighted historian, it afterwards takes shape. But she has brought to it an open-minded, essentially enlightened capacity to judge, and despite a prose style not everywhere firm, a frequent gift of phrase. If the book has limitations, it is largely because its very dimensions set limits. In treating at ordinary book length and a reasonably popular level the politics and economics, the morals and manners, the culture and art, the society and humanity, the disorder and crime of the decade, Miss Stevenson has again and again had to compress, curtail, omit, throwing many subjects, notably some of the arts, a mere bone. But all in all she has allotted her space soundly and put it to good use.

Babbitts & Bohemians begins judiciously in the previous decade, in an atmosphere of Wobblies and Progressives countered by warmongers and political bosses. Woodrow Wilson was President, but Pa Ferguson and Theodore Bilbo were governors, and Frank Hague, James Michael Curley, and William Hale Thompson, mayors. Congress was not idle, whether creating Mother's Day in 1913 or later, during the War, passing the egregious Espionage Act. The War itself saw us too proud to fight and then too pressured to refrain. After the War came a rain of strikes, from policemen (enter Calvin Coolidge) to miners, and most notoriously the steel strike: U.S. Steel's "undivided surplus of profits" had risen from $135 million in 1914 to $493 million in 1919, while half the steelworkers worked a twelve-hour day at a third below the government's figure for subsistence wages. Public enterprise kept pace with private, with Wilson's Attorney General, A. Mitchell Palmer, persecuting "alien radicals" by way of "patriotic-club" informers, and making arrests with warrants in which "the names were to be filled in after the arrests," or with no warrants at all. Fortunately, Louis F. Post, as Acting Secretary of Labor, conscientiously read all the indictments, throwing out most of them and freeing the imprisoned men. This was 1920, when a temperance movement had waked up to be addressed as Prohibition, when a halt was called on immigration, and the great *cause célèbre* of the ensuing decade began with the arrest of Sacco and Vanzetti.

Despite such bequests, the expiring decade had seemed more nationally alive to progress, to public-spiritedness, to protest, than its heir would be. The least of the Harding Administration's sins was its outright boycott of progress; so unforgettable was its corruptness that the Boston Tea Party still has a black-sheep-brother phrase in Teapot Dome. As for Calvin Coolidge, "he allowed respectability," says Miss Stevenson, "to seem to triumph" and was in fact "part of a system of legal corruption perhaps worse than the kind Daugherty had taken part in." (I had forgotten Cal on enforcing European debt payments: "They hired the money, didn't they?") With the third Republican President of the twenties, Herbert Hoover, we had a highly touted administrator whom Walter Lippmann characterized at the time as a weakling "in the presence of politics and politicians." Nor should we forget the decade's chill, elegant Thin Man, Andrew Mellon, Secretary of the Treasury in all three administrations, whose "principles were two: that wealth should be encouraged to pursue its own ends and that government in keeping to promote these ends, should retire into as small a compass as possible." Hence the maximum surtax on incomes dropped from 65 percent in 1921 to 20 percent in 1925, and gift and inheritance taxes were in time repealed.

In view of all this, the national economy of the period, with its brash bull-market headlines and its faint, smudged small print, is not very surprising. In mid-decade, the average minister's salary was $1622, the average federal employee's, $1515, and nowhere during the decade did the agricultural worker reattain the $800 a year he had made in 1920. Even culturally — where in many ways the period is most dynamic and impressive — the Babbitts, to judge by an inspection I have made of the best sellers of the 1920s, scarcely gave the bohemians a look-in. The one novelist who consistently made the list was the author of *Babbitt*, with the book itself a two-year best seller, and with — for one year each — *Main Street*,

Arrowsmith, Elmer Gantry, and *Dodsworth.* The only other novels of *any* consequence to join the top ten over a ten-year period were *The Age of Innocence, Gentlemen Prefer Blondes, The Bridge of San Luis Rey,* and *All Quiet on the Western Front.* Against this, Zane Grey, Harold Bell Wright, Gene Stratton Porter, and Ethel M. Dell were monotonously triumphant early in the decade; nor, though less well entrenched, were their successors much more resplendent.

If the period was, for all this, one to promote a legitimate mythology, and for those who lived through it, to glow in memory, so that its excesses seem a fair price for its achievements, on what grounds can this be accounted for?

Well, I, in writing of the twenties, am writing of my own twenties and doubtless with a bias that, beyond being touched with nostalgia, has stubborn roots of period sensibility. Not just my recollections but my responses and even many of my values are derived from it. This isn't to become uncritical or even uncensorious; but certain things, perhaps, that I would not acquit I am willing to pardon. In any case, I agree with Miss Stevenson that a sense of opportunity pervaded the period; that one of its governing attitudes was "the openness of the future"; that, as she says, "there was room enough, there was time enough." One could, accordingly, saunter; could saunter, in fact, out of step. It was an age that encouraged the individual temperament, the individualist aspiration; it would have nothing of authoritarianism; and if the bulk of those who fled the suburbs were not mindful enough of the slums, were far more concerned with art than with politics, this was from espousing a soup-stained "bohemianism" that might itself resemble the slums. Miss Stevenson's title, at any rate in the literary sense, is well chosen, for it was because Babbittry in the twenties was so dominant and spotlighted that bohemianism could build up a heckling chorus, and itself catch the limelight and kick up its heels. The two groups were a made-to-order antithesis, a kind of running plot and subplot; were a twain that did nothing but meet — if only head-on; a twosome that the Menckens could in equal parts have fun with; and a pair of opposites that denounced the country club as a philistine desert, and the Village dive as a phonies' swamp. Yet the country club and the Village dive were curiously made one by hooch and hangovers and rolling in the hay; even in very stuffy bourgeois circles, Prohibition sent inhibition reeling. And when, in a rambunctious bull market, money-making became as unhallowed and promiscuous for businessmen as lovemaking for bohemians, a whole society lost its balance, and plot and subplot swayed in unison. But where the main plot exploded in fiscal disaster, the subplot got religion, became painfully aware of the slums, the sweatshops, the strikebreakers, the state of the world. Blushing with guilt, the bohemian collectivized his ego and all too often ruined his art.

If this is to dramatize the period, it is not least because it tended to dramatize itself; almost no one, at any rate, was wholly realistic about it. There was so beckoning a sense of what lay ahead; the future, to the twenties, was much like knowing you were in your rich uncle's will. The very frivolity of the period bespoke a kind of security, and the very opposition of Babbitts and bohemians argued unambiguous values rather than mongrel ones. In the end, indeed, the antithesis is a kind of value judgment: all in all, the ignominy of the twenties rests with the Babbitts, or with their mentors; with chicanery and corruption in high places, with meager earnings and bloated profits; and a certain luster hovers around the "bohemians," at least in what they wrote and painted and composed; even in their small haughty defiances and the Little Magazines and the Left Bank. Today the sharpness of the antithesis seems most salubrious just because there was so little dubious middle ground. It was not simply that Business still snarled at Culture where today it labors to seduce it; but Culture had no thoughts as yet of becoming Business. Young men did not then go in for higher degrees as commercial assets, acquiring an M.A. which presumably stands for Madison Avenue. There was no television, there was nothing very cerebral about radio or sophisticated about advertising. Group journalism was cutting its milk teeth, and Hollywood was for hacks (talent only flocked there with the talkies). Hence people in the arts, whatever the lure of money, were not primarily — in jargon then unborn — money-oriented.

In the matter of handling human problems, there can be no sound comparing of the twenties with what is attempted today. Culturally, however, there are problems today that the twenties partly or wholly lacked. Indeed, that very sense of the future which buoyed up the twenties and gave their Bohemia a seacoast has, though in rather surprising forms, proved valid — so palpably in the arts as to completely remodel their bohemianism. That the writer or painter has become far more of a businessman, with a far more lucrative business, is not in itself disturbing. But beyond their vastly improved standard of living, writers and painters now often follow a businessman's or a rich man's *way of life*. They are status-minded and publicity-minded and often publicity-mad; presumable tastemakers, they live on borrowed taste, even to their interior decorating.

That, again, people of talent in the arts should be featured to-day on mass media may be all to the good; but they are the smallest part of a big-money mass-media world that has created a fad-ridden culture in which talent and trash, audacity and expediency, *frisson* and cliché, mini-truths and mammoth fictions embrace one another. Miss Stevenson speaks of the "syncopation of taste" in the twenties, but it seems very slow freight compared with today, when the last word in culture is televised to 50 million people in only faintly tinted, slightly tainted form. In the twenties, such things as Joyce's linguistic experiments, E. E. Cummings's typographical frolics, and a George Antheil's *Ballet Méchanique*, with its refrigerators, might have their shock or novelty or exhibitionist value, but wholly on noncommercial, art-world terms. Camp and Westerns and happenings and pop art and op art and art nouveau today are largely cultural merchandise with most of them, instead of being avant-garde, half tongue-in-cheek forms of revival.

Probably the nearest thing in the twenties to today's high-income world of the arts was the Algonquin group — Dorothy Parker, Robert Benchley, Robert Sherwood, George S. Kaufman,

Alexander Woollcott, F.P.A., Heywood Broun, and others. Displaying, many of them, a sophisticated touch and satiric wit, mirroring New York's superior frivolities, they lived — thanks to Broadway, Hollywood, *The New Yorker* — expensively, and often became the pets and playmates of the kind of rich people who were bored with rich people. The two groups coalesced, on an enlarged basis, into the first generation of café society. One of the less talented Algonquinites was Alexander Woollcott, a writer and anecdotist with just two personal sources of supply, the tear duct and the bile duct. By the thirties a great radio success as the Town Crier, he made best sellers of the books he doted on — good or bad — as no mass-media commentator had done before. Yet the Algonquin group pleasantly exemplify something that the twenties were rich in and that today is not — playfulness. They made jokes, they spun yarns, they played games, they grew rich off repartee, they were not afraid to be silly, and insult was more their métier than their neurosis. They, much like the era's wacky comics — Fanny Brice, Ed Wynn, Joe Cook, the Marx Brothers — were enliveners and entertainers of the public, and of one another.

Prohibition, which one cannot but return to, throws considerable light on what muddled the twenties, since it made lawbreakers of almost everybody, and often misbehavers as well. Without it, there must have been less cynicism, less shoot-the-works spending, less short-order sex — and far less drinking or drunkenness. The saloon, with its beer pocketbook and swing-door legality, had been for men only; the speakeasy smiled on women and on picking up women, acquired social overtones and presented exorbitant tabs. Moreover, the twenties did not really end until 1934 and Repeal, which sounded taps on a long reign of rowdy gaiety and on our principal form of racketeering. Surely a very salient point is not how much less crime there would have been without Prohibition, but how much less organized crime. Miss Stevenson soundly stresses the importance of Chicago to the twenties, not least for its jazz but particularly for its unruliness, and the rise of Al Capone, which "would end the spontaneity of gang life."

Sound about Chicago, *Babbitts & Bohemians* seems inadequate about New York, whose spotty side saw the rise of Dutch Schultz, Legs Diamond, and that "Morgan of the Underworld," Arnold Rothstein. Miss Stevenson does not even mention the Algonquin group, offers the flapper without John Held, Jr., Jimmy Walker without Grover Whalen, Gilbert Seldes without the 7 Lively Arts, the Village without its favorite haunts. Yet Manhattan during the twenties was the university of all the bright young college dropouts, featuring life at firsthand in its curriculum along with free-lancing and free love. For the young today, with their contempt for set forms and their concern for causes, life is in a sense a mixture of the twenties and the thirties; yet what it crucially lacks of those two eras of contradictory hopes is a hopefulness of its own.

I have said that *Babbitts & Bohemians* is short on some of the arts and their milieus. But in a chapter called "The Year Nothing Happened" it does epitomize the creative fruitfulness of the twenties. The year 1925 produced, in literature alone, *An American Tragedy, The Great Gatsby, In Our Time, Arrowsmith,* and *Gentlemen Prefer Blondes;* Marianne Moore's *Observations,* Cummings's *XLI Poems,* Jeffers's *Roan Stallion,* Pound's *Cantos I-XVI,* and William Carlos Williams's *In the American Grain.* It is a very pleasant sort of paradox that during a decade when twentieth-century American life could often seem most ephemeral and adolescent, its literature proved so lasting and mature.

10

THE THIRTIES: FRAYED COLLARS AND LARGE VISIONS

In any attempt at truth, perhaps nothing can be more subjective, impressionist, Pirandellian, than one's memories of a bygone era. The associations are so many, so garlanded with nostalgia, so cankered with ego; the corroborations so few. The mind "lets go a thousand things"; even worse, it hangs on, raggedly, crookedly, to a thousand others; and when what we happen to confront is the confluence of many minds, or many volumes of memoirs, even fairly recent history can become astigmatic and blurred.

About the 1930s in America — not just the spotlighted thirties of Wall Street and the White House, or of the apple sellers and the breadline, but the thirties of the intellectual, artistic, professional world — there is a certain common remembrance of things past, in part because the *things* were so vivid, in part because life itself so strove to be communal. The thirties are relatively "clear" because they moved, with gathering momentum, in one direction. Certain events — Hitler, Anschluss, the Nazi-Soviet pact — were like fire alarms; certain others — Ethiopia, Catalonia, concentration camps — like tolling bells; others still — the Reichstag fire or the Russian trials — like baleful flares in the night. Yet of how many of even such crises have those who were grown-up in the thirties a precise awareness? Unless we were orderly and accurate diarists at the time, we are by now the heirs of all too many other diaries, the dupes of all too many tricks and transpositions of memory. What

most people recall is less the historic station stops n the way to
Munich or Moscow or Armageddon than what it was like, or how
they acted, or whom they consorted with, on the train. Furthermore, there were so many people getting breathlessly on or, later,
brusquely off; there was so much rerouting and being shunted onto
sidings; and all the reading matter and the bulky luggage and the
officious, loquacious conductors; and the abrupt changes of scenery,
of climate, of weather — not least the storms that would "clear the
air." It was, in a sense, the worst of times and the best of times;
everything, that is to say, seemed to be falling apart, but was to be
much better put together again.

The train and the passengers, the conductors and the station
stops, so often recalled to us, are evoked again in two very recent
accounts: Alfred Kazin's *Starting Out in the Thirties* and Granville Hicks's autobiography, *Part of the Truth*. The two men, if
decidedly unlike in makeup and approach, are yet linked for representing the two kinds of thoughtful people whom the thirties had a
most particular relevance and power to engage. Here were two
classic, protesting American types — the New York intellectual Jew
with a working-class background, the Walker in the City, as Mr.
Kazin called his earlier volume of memoirs; and the small-town
New Englander, the Thoreauvian and puritan Protestant, the
walker in the country. For any such Jew, political and social protest was a matter of conditioning; for any such Gentile, it became
a matter of conscience. What for the Jew, given his disabilities and
his historic "homelessness," constituted an ingrained point of view
and a sense of home, a kind of adjustment to maladjustment, constituted for the New Englander a tocsined point of departure and
a cause for outrage. Where the Jew tends to grow hoarse and dis-
putatious over tenets and texts, the New Englander more often acts
out a stern and simple *Ich kann nicht anders*. Together, the Jew's
enlightened sense of persecution and the New Englander's awak-
ened sense of obligation have been now the watchdogs of American injustice, and now the bloodhounds. During the 1930s they
could many times seem both.

Though *Part of the Truth* spans Mr. Hicks's life from birth until

very recently, its most noteworthy, if not most typical, pages concern the thirties — move from his emerging Communist sympathies, through his years of open Party membership, to his break
with the Party after the Hitler-Stalin pact. Certainly within the
modest confines of Mr. Hicks's title, his account of these years is
admirably forthright, with nothing vital begged or hidden, and
with nothing gratuitously highlighted. Indeed, because of its spare,
resolute factuality, the book takes on a certain Yankee flatness of
tone. One surmises that much of it was transcribed from a faithful
and unadorned diary, so that dealing (even during the thirties)
with considerable variety of matter, Mr. Hicks's account runs to
facts oftener than faces, to the outward event as much as the inward experience. But just because Mr. Hicks did not view the
thirties as simply a form of drama, his book may have the greater
value as a document.

Mr. Kazin's title, *Starting Out in the Thirties*, keys his book perfectly, since it treats of a person in terms of a period. Coming from
a Socialist Brooklyn home, the nineteen-year-old Alfred Kazin
stepped out, in 1934, upon a stage that was in some ways an extension of his upbringing. It was much more brightly, not to say
luridly, lighted, however, and came to feature a well-known cast of
characters — James Farrell, John Chamberlain, Robert Cantwell,
V. F. Calverton, Otis Ferguson, Malcolm Cowley, Clifford Odets.
Hence autobiography that is also a period piece is also a portrait
gallery, the three elements happily blended, the canvas as a whole
correspondingly enriched. A City College undergraduate when the
book opens, Kazin, before the decade ends, is himself a practicing
critic. By then he had got to know a great many writers; he had
moved in and out of the period's living rooms and basements, its
cafeterias and bars, its magazine offices and meeting places. Politically he had been where Socialists, Stalinists, Trotskyites, Loveston-
ites, United Fronters variously assembled, enacting all manner of
rites among the faithful, of rows among the hostile, of romance, on
occasion, among both. Strongly anti-Communist in his radicalism
then, what Mr. Kazin offers now is no sober steel engraving, or sav-
age Party-line-drawing, but a picture bright with incident and

flushed with youth. His thirties run brilliantly to personal experiences, to inquiry rather than commitment. He is often the dissenting dissenter, recording the blurred notes from all the blaring trumpets: where in Hicks during the thirties the literary man was submerged in the political, in Kazin he was unsubmergible.

The two accounts commemorate a great deal. But the thirties, in the end, were wider than Hicks's straight-and-narrow plank, longer than Kazin's celebration of their later half. And conceivably it was their earlier half that, if it now seems more wavering in outline, was more vibrant in actuality. The earlier half was still formative, tentative, transitional, when dispute was not yet frozen into dogma, and the soapbox speech and the speakeasy footrail were often conjoined. In the earliest thirties there were still loud echoes of the Crash rather than deep rumbles of the oncoming storm; people lost their jobs for economic rather than political reasons; the center of things came to be Washington, the cynosure FDR, the catchword the New Deal, the immediate issues domestic and near at hand. There were already, to be sure, a good many politically seasoned intellectuals; but most people who in the early thirties raised their voices and lost their tempers arguing about Marx did so much as they had argued about Schönberg or Joyce, and in much the same atmosphere. Mr. Kazin comes in just as Prohibition is going out.

And with its going, there went something that should not be forgotten: a somewhat messy holdover, or markdown, from the ebullient life of the twenties, a life now turned shabby-ungenteel, with the last carousings in bathtub gin, the last "pressings" of dago red, the last entrance to drinking parlors via seeing-eye doors. For those who were young, who were writers, artists, journalists, free-lances, highbrows of a kind, the Depression was simply a lower-keyed Bohemia. It was a period in the literary world when a front-page review in the *New York Times* paid you twenty-five dollars, and when the Big Money was no more than the title of a forthcoming book. The talk was of strikes, Scottsboro, Harlan County, Huey Long. Moreover, the early thirties marked the emergence of a propagandist literature and drama, and during its first years there could be something stimulating at times even about what was strident. Furthermore, if the movement was soon to excoriate far better writers than it extolled, at the start it disposed of a good many fading petals, it finished off mannerists like Cabell and Hergesheimer, it turned a never very sturdy ivory tower into a leaning one. Isms, generally, were replacing art forms, the Fascist had ousted the Philistine, Marx was outstripping Freud.

By 1934, however, "the age of Hitler," in Kazin's words, "was in full swing." The era of ideological window-shopping was about over. By then unemployment and injustice at home had merged with the spread of totalitarianism abroad. Suddenly, on various terms, a great number of people were caught up in what today must suggest a madly grim infatuation — at any rate, there it was, with Greenwich Village drifters anchored to a cause, with guilt-ridden Hollywood writers doing frantic, exhibitionistic penance. And now came the Communist party's notable ploy: the United Front. There were Hitler, Mussolini, and then Franco to be united against; as for Stalin and Russia, it would almost seem now that with such an assemblage of villains, one of them could be elevated into an ally; with such a panorama of horror, one segment of it might serve to inspire hope. Even those who were wholly deaf to Communism's siren songs could be blind at times, in their antifascist zeal, to its maneuvers. And in truth, the Communists scarcely let other people be antifascist without them. Under one high-sounding letterhead or another, they were forever contriving petitions, scaring up benefits, inviting you to parties; they made raids on *Who's Who*, they riffled through the *Social Register*. There really was, to be sure, a common enemy; until, one fine day, there was instead a Nazi-Soviet pact.

Still, one's recollections can turn as monolithic as history asserts the decade itself to have been; just here, Mr. Kazin's diversified adventures help restore perspective. Doubtless the decade's crises did shape a good deal of its culture; but a good deal else, even among artists and writers, derived from more residual attitudes or individual aspirations. People may have been hard up, but they weren't terribly concerned with *making* money. Even when working on a prosperous magazine, you saw it as a job and not as a career, and might work six months a year to enjoy six months' free time — which could mean living in a very low-cost Europe. There were still, and very conspicuously, ball games and poker games, movies and jazz, liquor and girls, shoptalk and gossip; there were still timeless, as well as tendentious, gratifications in the arts. For the destitute, and for older people skirting destitution, it was an altogether terrible time. But for those who were young and less acutely harassed, it could be a rather cooperative period of low-priced meals and cut-rate living and unapologetic makeshifts, and of (via due bills) hotel rooms and ocean crossings at tremendous discounts. Status as we knew it then was all but suspended; and status as we conceive it today did not exist. Nor for us did the rat race either: there was simply a scramble for small-salaried jobs. One Christmas brought me, at a highly respectable job, a holly-wreathed gift envelope containing a five-dollar bill. It was an age when one could go to Yaddo or the MacDowell Colony, or be lent someone's apartment in summer or a barn on someone's estate, or when Nathanael West, as the manager of a New York hotel, played a kind of all-year-round Santa Claus. The point is that a great many people preferred the independence and leisure that went with ups and downs to the pressures that went with success. Or perhaps they were simply less tempted: it was not only a world where good jobs were scarce; it was a world where TV appearances, lecture empires, highbrow articles in big-pay magazines were nonexistent.

Though they otherwise pose a very sharp, and indeed didactic, contrast, the 1920s and the 1930s were in two respects united — through something positive, primary-colored, reducible-to-a-phrase in their general makeup; and through something positive, of a different sort, in their confidence in the future. For when the unthinking optimism and sense of a Land of Plenty were extinguished by the Crash, there could still emerge from a depleted America and a despot's Europe a dream of tomorrow, a vision of the Promised Land. There has been neither outlook since; the two eras seem equally historical, their two moods equally unrealistic. No doubt, in terms of standard of living, ours is something of a Land of

Plenty today; and in terms of racial, social, economic gains, ours is a land where the promise has been partly fulfilled. Furthermore, today's concern over social injustice and civil rights brings back something of the thirties. But there is also something very unlike. There may be more determined action today, but there is much less reassurance about tomorrow. For today, with every door we open, we encounter a closed one behind it; with every problem we solve, a greater one seems to jut up. It is the future, now, that tends to make us anxious; and not just the future in terms of the bomb. "Progress," life itself are what seem to be getting out of hand. For even were true democracy achieved, there would be a terrifying population problem still to cope with; were the rat race slowed down, there would be an automation problem still to resolve. Even if the moon, in due course, offers a change of venue for the weekend, there will still be the rest of the week.

III

A MANIA FOR MAGNIFICENCE

11

THE SETTING OF THE SUN KING

The reign, the court life, the personal and inviolable majesty of
Louis XIV have attracted biographers in every age, and been
steadily in demand among readers. This is not hard to account for:
in addition to being the lengthiest of reigns, Louis's was the most
resplendent; was the most scandalous as well as ceremonious of
courts; and Louis himself was the grandest mannered as well as the
most terrifying of monarchs. No other king, again, has had three
ladies around the house who to this day are household names; nor
presided over so many splendid establishments, from the Louvre,
which he avoided, to the Versailles, which he adored; and none
either, that I know of, had so many famous writers- and artists-in-
residence, whether as composers or historiographers or dramatists
or diarists or chaplains or gardeners or tutors.

And now Nancy Mitford, whose writing has nicely mingled real
French people — Voltaire, Madame de Pompadour — with fictional
English ones, has paused to celebrate Louis, and turned back to his
fabulous and rather monstrous world in *The Sun King*. Her book
is not a from-the-cradle-to-the-grave biography, since it really begins with the King, in his early twenties, assuming absolute power
at Mazarin's death; nor does it open a very wide window on history,
since it deals hardly at all with Louis's place in the Europe of his
time, and very little more with his actual governing of France. The
book is firmly centered in that most renowned of Louis's creations,
Versailles; it begins, indeed, with his impulse to "create" it, and

Versailles becomes not simply the scene of most of *The Sun King*, but very often its principal subject matter. It is court life that Miss Mitford perambulates, social history that she proffers — which is to say, palace duplicity in the very obvious sense of the word, palace domesticity in the not everywhere wholesome sense, palace promiscuity in the form of locked doors and lurking figures, not to mention matters of genealogy, precedence, protocol, to which it is hard to say whether Louis XIV or Miss Mitford attaches the greater importance. All this involves, of course, one of the most extraordinary casts of characters available in a single setting and period; and all this, on its own terms, is abundant sustenance enough and *sauce piquante* enough for a great feast of high life, swimming in anecdote about small disasters on great occasions, and flowing with gossip about the worst side of the Best People.

At a court of such magnitude it is a memory test to keep track of who's who, let alone of their grandmothers; and of vast help as well as genuine delight are the book's fine illustrations, many of them in superb color. These support Miss Mitford's own eye for scene and gifts of language, alternating close-ups with panoramas, grandees with gardens, period atmosphere with personal detail. With so long a reign to traverse and so large a company to keep in touch with, the fixedness of Versailles — which includes the many years it was building — proves a narrative blessing. To be sure, Louis, in addition to his military tours, was off on occasion to Marly or Meudon or Fontainebleau, though almost never to Paris, which he shunned; but these were excursions, progresses, whims of his, and it is Versailles that comes to mean home. Its being home links *The Sun King* with another recent and rewarding book, *At the Court of Versailles* (edited by Gilette Ziegler), the text annotating passages from the letters and memoirs of various observers of our fifty-year-long scene.

There is only one commanding actor of this scene: the King, despite monotonous quirks and magnificent competition, dwarfs everyone else. And in the end, there can be only one historian of it, much drawn upon here: the Duc de Saint-Simon, who, though prejudiced, long-winded, and a latecomer, is as essential to Louis and Versailles as is Boswell to Johnson (and who is also as peculiar a genius). But there is *not* just one Versailles. I count at least three: one a very grand spectacle; another, full of weird figures and sideshows; a third, all backstage grime and stealth.

We all know the glittering storybook Versailles: the stately ceremonial, the polished comedy of manners, the coroneted *chronique scandaleuse*. This is the Versailles of Miss Mitford's best pages and of almost all the book's illustrations. In it the King promenades and gives ear to courtiers; the King dines, alone but observed by multitudes; the King hunts: it is a diversion he loves. There are tournaments, garden parties, supper parties, masked balls, musicales. *At the Court of Versailles* records a grand week-long entertainment. By day, knights ride at full gallop, lance in hand, to unhook and carry off rings hanging from a stake; in the brilliantly lighted dusk, Lully advances at the head of a vast troupe marching in time with his new music; simultaneously, moving down a different avenue emerge The Four Seasons — Spring on a great Spanish horse, Summer on an elephant, Autumn on a camel, Winter on a bear. Later that week comes the famous *première* (and, for some time, *dernière*) of *Tartuffe*. So life proceeds, with an elaborate protocol governing every great, and almost every routine, occasion. People were shown civilities based on rank — those greeted or au-revoired at the Door, those offered an Armchair, those worthy of being seen off in their Coach. There were customs, too, that began with ladies arriving in their coach and in due course passing through a door; whether an armchair came next is less certain. Such incidents are the commonplaces of Versailles and of a hundred historical novels; the attendant or subsequent scandals gave Versailles its small talk and made of it a whispering gallery. In all such presentations of *The King and I*, the star of Act I was Mademoiselle de la Vallière; of Act II, Madame de Montespan; of Act III, Madame de Maintenon. Much protocol, much *geste* obtained even here: so long as his Queen lived, the King always slept in her bed.

Contributing to the splendors of Versailles, but receiving little attention in *The Sun King*, were the artists Louis XIV patronized and domiciled, and their achievements in art. Just how much

Louis cared for art, as distinguished from magnificent effects, is doubtful (though he genuinely liked music and plays). But he knew the worth of talent, and his Versailles boasts a blazing constellation of names. Molière and Racine helped write its plays, Bossuet preached its sermons, La Bruyère and Fénelon tutored its sons, Lully composed its music, Mansart was its architect, Le Nôtre its gardener. Nor was Saint-Simon its only distinguished chronicler: Madame de Sévigné and Madame de la Fayette were others. The paintings displayed at Versailles, by Giorgione, Mantegna, Raphael, Veronese, Poussin, and Rubens, now hang in the Louvre. And all this great spectacle was conducted on an unprecedentedly great scale: there "lived" at the palace some fifteen thousand people — standing, squatting, kneeling, bowing, bending forward, walking backward, but very seldom seated, in the presence of the King.

There is a second Versailles, where Old Masters give way to caricature, eulogy turns to jest, breeding to inbreeding, and noble personages appear as "characters." There is considerable petty malice here and considerable reason for it; and here, with his flair for gossip and eye for the grotesque, Saint-Simon is invaluable, though others contribute also. A puritan duke personally smashes all the "indecent" statues he inherits from a cardinal. A great lady, asked whether she recites the Lord's Prayer, says yes, all but the forgiving trespasses. As the King's brother expires, his widow shrieks at the top of her lungs, "No convent for me! Don't you talk to me about convents! I won't go to a convent!" Wives, for a joke, have other ladies impersonate them in bed; in deadly earnest, a madly ambitious courtier lies all night under the bed of Madame de Montespan and the King to find out what they think of him.

But such anecdotes cannot fully convey what an opulent madhouse or human menagerie Versailles could be. It is less at anecdote than at portraiture that Saint-Simon excels, whether from among the living personages, or from among the living freaks and monsters, who enter and exit, reenter and reexit over thousands of pages. There is just space to sample Saint-Simon's obituary of the exalted Prince de Condé. No man, we are told, had more ability, or when he chose, was more discerning, noble, graceful. But none could be odder. He had four dinners waiting for him every day in four different houses. Once, entering the Maréchale de Noailles's bedroom as her bed was being made, he cried out, "Oh, the nice pretty bed, the nice pretty bed!" leapt upon it, rolled over and over in it, and climbed down apologizing that it was so clean and inviting, what else could he do? At one period, he thought he was a dog, and during the King's going-to-bed ceremonies, threw his head in the air and opened his mouth wide, imitating one. Late in life, he refused to eat, announcing that he was dead and that the dead do not eat. Fearing that if he didn't eat he *would* die, his doctors agreed that he was dead but insisted that the dead did sometimes eat, and produced a few such. The trick worked, but M. le Prince would eat only with these dead men and his doctor.

Yet, more perhaps than Louis's Versailles was ceremonial grandeur or idiot farce, it was something of a nightmare or a horror story. Under the jewels and furs and velvets might be found bodies hideous with sores; after the great dinners and suppers came ghastly paroxysms of pain; in the midst of life there was everywhere the specter of death. None of this is symbolic; it was actual, true. Even wearing a mask under a mask wasn't symbolic; it was a season's doubtless very useful vogue. There were genuine drawbacks to being highborn and rich. If, with 498 people attending the King's dinner table, or 1500 jets of water playing at Versailles, there was a good deal of Hollywood about it all, there was perhaps even more of hell. What it nowadays means to be sick, at Versailles was deemed good health. Everyone, from a gluttonous King down, regularly took gargantuan purges; whom one dined with might be spreading smallpox, whom one danced with might be wasted with cancer. In an age of fiendishly misguided medical theory, the rich, able to afford slews of doctors and doomed to die of their prescriptions, could be worse off than the poor. Almost every ailment meant constant bloodletting; almost any mishap could end in blood poisoning.

The King, moreover, who insisted that the court attend him at Versailles, and was a past master at taking attendance, also insisted that women he liked attend him on his travels; and they, whether big with child or burning with fever, had to sit with him in his coach, could never nap, never refuse food, never relieve themselves, never droop — "to feel sick," wrote Saint-Simon, "was an unforgivable sin." Hence even the one person Louis adored, his grandson's wife, the Duchesse de Bourgogne, could be jogged into a miscarriage. She, moreover, along with three successive heirs to the throne — her father-in-law, her husband, and her son — died within eleven months of smallpox, measles, doctoring; and her younger son, but for his governess hiding him from the doctors, might never have lived to be Louis XV.

But hell at Versailles was not just a gruesome infirmary. Mischief, slander, conspiracy abounded. Poisoning was virtually the rage, from *poudres à héritage*, "medicine" to dispose of unwanted rich relations, to hospitality, from which magnificoes might die in agony, and for which great ladies were burned at the stake. But the very air was poisoned, with espionage, treachery, debauchery. Versailles boasted a whole titled homosexual society, with, right in the palace, princes "scurrying through the night." When Madame de Maintenon remonstrated with the King, he answered, "Am I to begin then with my own brother?" Even paying the King homage was a hazard. Louis, when young, attended an entertainment in his honor which proved so presumptuously grand that Louis's bread-and-butter letter was a *lettre de cachet*, locking up his host "perpetually" in a fortress. And Louis, when old, resentful of military disasters, remorseful for various misdeeds, and all too aware that the night cometh, could be more than ever, more harshly, more unaccountably, autocratic.

Louis the *man* is perhaps not too difficult to grasp, being, if monumentally large, relatively one-dimensional. He was every inch, and in his every thought, a king, making of divine right a superb, often rather diabolical, role, and making *hubris* in other men seem like downright humility. He had a gimlet eye, a medieval mind, a Bourbon's memory; his rebukes could annihilate, his condescensions sometimes enchant. With matters spiritual he was not always at one. He thought that Christ's language should have been more upper-class; and after a great military defeat, he said, "God seems to have forgotten all I have done for Him." War gave Louis a blazing noon — at forty he was lord of all Europe. It gave him equally a bloody sunset — a France exhausted and distressed. Women gave him lifelong pleasure and were his greatest weakness, whether from their being able to tempt or to manage him. His subjects' welfare gave him small concern: he refused to hear about millions of wretches who froze, or starved, or died like flies carrying out his vast building schemes. Late in life he made three extremely costly mistakes. He revoked the Edict of Nantes, which drove half a million (many of them notable) Protestants into exile; he helped set his grandson on the throne of Spain, which, threatening the balance of power, beclouded any hopes of peace; and at the exiled James II.'s death, he recognized his son as James III of England, which let slip the dogs of war.

In viewing *le roi soleil*, Miss Mitford at times wears sunglasses, at other times rose-colored ones. She notes most of his failings, but glides — or, more accurately, hurries — over them, since it is the Grand Monarque, the master of Versailles, the company he keeps, the ladies he smiles on, the nobles he snubs, the festivities he graces, that attract and inspirit her. All this side of things Miss Mitford handles with decided vivacity, and much of the royal couch, *chaise percée*, and arsenic-in-the-soup side, too. Her book is wonderfully readable. But though the grandeurs it celebrates do not dim her wit, they let her sense of humor doze, and flatten out her sense of style. The royal misfortunes induce servant-girl-literature clichés. "One hopes," writes Miss Mitford, "that the King found comfort [in his new chapel] in the trials that lay ahead"; or "The events of February 1712 are almost too heartrending to relate." On the other hand, the misfortunes of the King's subjects draw from Miss Mitford such dinner-party adjectives as "horrid" and "dreadful," which are perhaps the only licensed upper-class words for referring to unspeakable torture or mass starvation. And, to Miss Mitford, Louis's story offers no fresher moral, if it offers that, than *vanitas vanitatum*, and no more stringent morality than when and with whom to be polite. She pronounces for Louis XIV as "perhaps the most truly polite king who ever lived." But contradictory evidence on his part aside, on this subject Miss Mitford is perhaps not altogether trustworthy, in view of that memorable Edict of Nancy some years ago, that the only possible response to any non-U phrase, such as a friendly "It was so nice meeting you," is total silence. Whether or not supremely polite, Louis could show kingly control as when, to keep from thrashing a courtier he was furious with, he flung his cane out of the window.

On the seamy side there is more material in *At the Court of Versailles* than in *The Sun King*, along with additional sidelights and details. But much derives from our great chronicler who for twenty-odd years shadowed the Sun King, and as it is with Saint-Simon that any writer on Louis and Versailles begins, so I think must any fully life-size account of them end. Not in Saint-Simon either do we get political history, but we do get the vast methodology of a whole society and way of life; here, indeed, one after another of La Rochefoucauld's worldly maxims turn to flesh and blood, breathe and whisper and walk about. No wonder Proust pored endlessly over Saint-Simon. And Saint-Simon is more than a tireless chronicler; he has a great novelist's power of portrayal, and his blind spots, however many, fall far short of his perceptions. His name is ineffaceably stamped on the crowded scene he portrays; and his *Memoirs*, though of staggering length, will richly repay a little dipping into, say a couple of hundred pages in one place, and a couple of hundred more in another.

12

A MANIA FOR MAGNIFICENCE

After literature, it is perhaps architecture that has most stirred the English nature, most roused it to be at once artistic and practical, creative and imitative, proclamatory and immured. No nation has shown a greater feeling for both the public appearance and the private life, for towers and ceremonies and for high hedges and solitude. Aware that an Englishman's home is his castle, the English, since the Renaissance, have built homes that were just about everything else; and a few castles as well. Their countryside is dotted with all sorts of historic dwellings, many of them inspired by what B. Sprague Allen called "the Building Mania of the Eighteenth Century." Let us be its bystanders, outside and inside the houses, along with the gardens and landscapes.

England's landowners were still, during most of the century, England's rulers; for land, as it was the earliest, was still the mightiest form of wealth. During the 1700s men had their East Indies holdings and their West Indian plantations; and merchant and banking and shipbuilding wealth notably increased. But the great landowners were not only very rich, they were lords of the neighborhood and even the county; and one way in which they had come to lord over it was by the impressiveness, the commandingness of their habitations. Their seats (as the period spoke of them) might sometimes be old enough to have been better designed for fortresses than for family life; or might be ancient and accumulative enough to look like small towns. But ever since the Renaissance, and the coming of Inigo Jones soon after, there had developed a considerable show of architectural self-assertion which, halted during the Civil Wars, was renewed at the Restoration, much helped in one way by the Great Fire, in another by a great genius — one who, designing St. Paul's and fifty-four London churches, Greenwich Hospital and the rebuilt Hampton Court, Oxford's Tom Tower and Cambridge's Trinity Library, effected a superb architectural Wrenaissance. Actually Inigo Jones, despite all the country houses attributed to him, seems to have personally built almost none; while Wren has not even had many attributed to him, and may well have done none at all. But in the wake of Wren, in the rebuilding of a gutted London, in the growing demand for colleges, hospitals, town halls, there emerged a tremendous itch to build for oneself.

By the early eighteenth century there was also a vigorous impetus. Peace and prosperity under Sir Robert Walpole loosened purse strings, while now the elegant taste of the Augustans, the new City wealth that craved landed leisure, and the old country-house inconveniences that cried out for domestic improvements created the Building Mania, the era of residential brick and stone. There was one further incentive: the influence of the Burlingtonians. Under Lord Burlington's impassioned leadership, a revived style became an all-but-reverenced fashion; the child of Palladio and Inigo Jones appeared in its most culturally visible, socially desirable, and personally available form.

Derived from English visits to Italy, the fashion for a Palladian classicism submerged a tendency in England not without distant Italian connections: that stirring of the baroque in such architects as Vanbrugh and Hawksmoor, that native sap in a foreign tree which — except as Wren and, later, James Gibbs took what they wanted of it — is almost all that England can show of an architecture which for something like a century was foremost on the Continent, with notable monuments in Italy, and supreme ones in South Germany and Austria. Not fortuitously, baroque flowers best in Catholic soil, in churches, castles, palaces and their interiors all brilliant color and sensuous curves, where life (and death) invoke ritual, pageantry, drama. Never given to understatement, baroque was never very English. Certainly nothing is understated with a Castle Howard or a Blenheim Palace. Nor is the proud, somberly dramatic Northumbrian aloofness of Vanbrugh's Seaton Delaval very English (actually, the "mad Delavals" themselves once hired Drury Lane for a night; and the male line died of drink and debauchery, and never in bed). Of Hawksmoor it suffices to instance, among much else, his superb Mausoleum at Castle Howard, baroque enough in its domed roundness, yet classically pillared and sufficiently austere to outdo the classicists at their own game. Yet they, not the Hawksmoors, now triumphed.

With the classicists at their worst, with their rigid adherence to rules, a mausoleum chill could pervade the pedantic rightness of their living quarters. They have, however, been too often judged by their worst. The reign of the Burlingtonians was actually quite understandable: it flourished off the Grand Tour, it suited upper-class taste and ambitions, it formalized English propriety without falsifying English good sense; and in spite of itself it could achieve very dramatic effects. Moreover, what could become perhaps its greatest aesthetic fault could also be its strongest practical virtue: it was based on strict rules, so that the most ignorant parvenu and the most dull-witted architect could not go wrong.

But if Lord Burlington, who had discovered Palladio in Italy, was the impresario, the star performer was William Kent, a man who as much succeeded as a decorator and landscape gardener as he failed as a painter. Kent could be, indeed, master of all styles as well as all trades; "he could be Roman," said John Fleming, "he could be baroque, he could be gothic, he could be fantastic." In helping Burlington with his unimpressive Palladian villa at Chiswick, Kent was least himself; he was most distinguished with the Horse Guards in Whitehall (left uncompleted at his death) which, as Sacheverell Sitwell says, might well be a country house in a great park — although on such reasoning many a country house might almost be mistaken for the Horse Guards. On the other hand, Kent's Great Hall at Holkham is an apotheosis of marble expanse, Roman magnificence, awesome wealth. Much smaller, but splendidly so is Kent's Worcester Lodge at Badminton — one of those grand minor works which give the century's architecture a particular patrician charm.

The next-best-known Burlingtonian, and all in all the best — the Scotsman Colin Campbell — designed a Mereworth which, modeled even more on Palladio's Villa Capra than is Chiswick, comes off a good deal more impressively. Campbell also designed, with proper Palladian "thoughts," Sir Robert Walpole's Houghton. In 600-feet-long Wentworth Woodhouse, a minor Burlingtonian, Henry Flitcroft, produced the largest house, if house it can be called, in England. It communicates the danger of such piles: their rather commonplace overassertiveness. Actually, a similar classicism proved a weakness in the other arts, marring now a poetic vein, now an idyllic scene, now a vernacular style. What saves these vast structures from pomposity today is their delightful approaches, their spacious parks, and the softening hand of time. Palladian country houses — indeed, eighteenth-century country houses generally — exert their greatest charm and appeal when medium-sized, neither straining to look impressive nor becoming so impressive as to look like public institutions.

Though long dominant, such classicism was even in its heyday much disputed where disliked, and much modified where approved. Set against this somewhat academic revival, the talented, individualized work of a James Gibbs (1682–1754) proves more engaging. Carrying on from Wren, but adding his own touches of rococo and baroque, Gibbs boasted a varied achievement and a celebrated one: St. Mary-le-Strand and St. Martin's in the Fields in London, the Fellows Building and the Senate House at Cambridge, the Radcliffe Camera at Oxford. Like Jones and Wren, Gibbs did little in the way of country houses; but his small Orleans Octagon (where Louis Philippe lived in exile) is a minor masterpiece, as his Radcliffe Camera is a major one. His famous *Book of Architecture* served builders of all persuasions, and had a decided influence on eighteenth-century church-building in America.

Before Lord Burlington died in 1753, the real vigor of his movement had been sapped. Subsequent Burlingtonians diverged from the Master; other kinds of architects now made themselves felt; and though no important new styles resulted, a sufficient number of fads did. Then, in the same decade as Burlington's death, there blazed forth the name that would stand foremost for a generation and perhaps for the century as well: Adam. If the name is too loosely used, and "the Adam style" too glib an attribution, there is reason for it. For there were four brothers named Adam, partners in what was a business, two of them entirely businessmen; and of the other two who were architects — Robert and James — only Robert (1728–1792) had true imagination and talent. Thus everything of theirs depends on Robert, but not everything of Robert's depends on architecture. He was preeminently a master of decoration and design, ranging from magnificent entrance halls to mere elegant fanlights; accordingly, it is much less houses that he evokes than the interior of houses, much less structures than surfaces. Yet, though he may have been concerned with *building* no great number of country houses, in the architectural development of the century he became one of the supreme creators of whole street façades or "palace façades" — of blocks of town houses combined in a single, often monumental, composition.

The son of a well-to-do Scottish architect, Robert after a sound education spent four years on the Continent, moving about "in notable style" and reaching London in 1758. In him, says John Summerson, "the student, the explorer, the architect and the grand-tourist were united." Already well enough known on his return to be elected to the Royal Society of Arts, he very soon designed the delightful Doric screen which covers the front of the Admiralty, and soon after was designing — actually redesigning — such superior country houses as Castle Ashby, Harewood House, Croome, Compton Verney, and Kedleston. Indeed, within some ten years of setting up in London, Robert had begun work on almost all his best and best-known country houses. The Adam style that emerged, and that stressed "movement," had been variously influenced by English Palladianism, French interior design, Mediterranean ruins, and the Italian Renaissance. Of Robert's work in the country, it is the part rather than the whole, or the minor structure rather than the main house, that oftenest wins the most praise. Thus, at Croome Court, it is the trim elegant Doric orangery and the Garden Room that are triumphantly Adamesque; at Osterley Park, it is the fine Ionic portico; and at Kedleston, which is one of Robert's greatest indoor achievements, there is also the superb South Front, where dome, columns, statuary, and wonderfully curving stairs superimpose a kind of enchanting baroque on a classical façade.

For impressive architectural wholes we must move from the country to the London town houses created in the 1770s and to the street façades done very late in Robert's career. No single façade could better suggest an aristocratic residence than that at 20 St. James's Square or at 20 Portman Square. Of Robert's larger designs, there was the great and financially all-but-ruinous real estate development built on the London Embankment, the Adelphi. And of the long street façades there are (as parts of an unfinished whole) one side of Fitzroy Square in London and of Charlotte Square in Edinburgh. Like Wren, Robert Adam had many thoughts about town planning; and these two very late compositions, along with Edinburgh's Register House and University, prove how real a gift for grand-scale masculine design lay with this master of delicate, often feminine, décor.

It is the master of décor, however — though this means interior architect as well as decorator — who has best survived in artistic fame and physical fact alike. It is Robert's rooms and suites of rooms, and the doors opening out of them, and the decorated ceilings above them, and the pillars supporting them, and the mantels and panels and frequently the furniture adorning them, that most notably bear his signature. Architecturally he introduced nothing altogether new, for where his neoclassicism does not develop from Palladianism, it descends from Wren; and his large street compositions came after those done by other hands at Bath. Even the elegant Adam detail derives from the past: all the motifs and medallions, all that was pillared and coffered, painted and sculptured, marble and alabaster, apical and arched, whispered of Greece and classical Rome, or of Renaissance Rome and rococo Venice. But the Adam stamp on all this, down to the very swags and scrolls and wheat husks, was decidedly individual. The Adam touch was not least a lightness of touch, born of a delicacy imbued with refinement. It consists in an airy charm, a domesticated adventurousness, and we need only observe something like the library at Ken Wood to recognize a style original in the very deployment of its borrowings. In all this, as John Steegman says, the shift from Burlington to Adam is from three dimensions to two, from mass to line, from masculine to feminine — from, we might add, the grand to the graceful.

Robert's treatment, however, could be successfully simpler or could mount above decoration into something ceremonial, even monumental. Thus the magnificent Roman Hall at Kedleston boasts twenty green alabaster statues, two splendid fireplaces, and arabesqued coved ceilings; then, bare of a staircase, it leads directly on to the saloon, its great coffered dome rising to a far grander height. This is Adam at his most dramatic, or heroic; the Adam style generally, if never revolutionary, was for more than a generation the rage. Being light and small-scaled, it could be applied to modest-sized houses; being feminine and sometimes rather too pretty, it could appeal to prosperous middle-class housewives. It lent itself to mass-produced methods, to imitative workmanship, to ill-fitting ensembles, and so could equally wear out its welcome and lose its distinction. But at its best it had lightness, elegance, charm.

English architecture not only remains one of the eighteenth century's great achievements; it also memorializes the period's aspirations and ideals. Like eighteenth-century painting, it is primarily a social art. The century, to be sure, can boast in London impressive public buildings, at Oxford and Cambridge impressive academic ones, and splendid churches all over England. But set against the great religious and secular building from medieval days to the heyday of Wren, and again under Victoria, eighteenth-century architecture is chiefly notable for its private houses, in town and even more in the country. As the country houses might contain two hundred rooms, so might their owners possess twenty thousand acres; as they might win fame for their great hall or gallery, so might they too for a pagoda or a gazebo. Even more important, the country houses served as repositories for art. They are often the very center of the world of Reynolds and Gainsborough — a lustrous pedigreed world, a luxurious moneyed one, something where nature — infinitely oftener than human nature — speaks for discipline and order.

Like the country houses themselves, their owners came in sizes, from what Trevelyan calls the Dukes, "whose manner of life outdid in magnificence the courts of allied monarchs" to the small squires who, by their hunting coats and coats of arms alone, stood socially higher than yeomen. Their kind was actually beginning to dwindle; heavy land taxes and a higher cost of living made for hardships, and with parvenus craving country estates and grandees ambitious for vaster holdings, the small squire was often best advised, in a good selling market, to sell. For a country-house life by now was a matter and proof of status, and could have decided political and Parliamentary value. To begin with, there was the house itself, which could possess magnificence or beauty or both. It could be, uncompetitively, a home; it could be, more declaratively, a kind of museum or palace; one could withdraw from the world, or equally draw the world hither. But almost always it constituted a world in itself: its possessor was lord of all he surveyed, not least of the village close by. He kept the village alive, working and catering for him; and he, or a member of his family, might represent the nearest constituency in Parliament.

But even a fairly modest country house bespoke more than a quite handsome one in town. It bespoke all that was part of an agricultural age and of an Englishman's love of the country, whether bucolic and wild, or idyllic and trim, or rugged and sporting. The English garden is one of the century's most delightful native achievements; so too is the English park, with everything perfectly in place while seeming to be quite accidental. The deepest love of many a squire was his love of outdoor life, his feeling for sport — fishing his own ponds and streams, setting forth with the guns to flush out pheasant and partridge, or riding forth, with the hounds in full cry, in pursuit of the fox. The country gentleman, as Lord David Cecil says, was as often in riding boots as silk stockings. All this for his pleasure; to proclaim his position, his great hall and saloon and eating room were paramount, and not just for their size or height but for their contents. A town house lacked space to exhibit all the family treasures; it was the more affluent country houses that were stocked with Old Masters acquired in Italy, crammed with virtu and ornament from France; and in highborn houses adding to the ancestral Vandykes and Lelys contemporary Reynoldses and Gainsboroughs.

The interiors of these houses, by embodying the century's two great fashions in décor, reintroduce Kent as the earlier dictator, and as the later one, Adam. A failure at painting and not too great a success at architecture, Kent yet displayed a protean talent, ranging from book illustration to royal barges, but centered on furniture. Kent's furniture is at its best in the grandest state rooms of the grandest establishments, as in the Stone Hall and saloon at Houghton or the dining room at Holkham. What can further exalt his furnishings of rooms is his ceilings, as at Holkham; his marble chimney pieces, as at Houghton; his mirrors, again, or his doorcases. Though for a time the massive Kent style pervaded society, reaching down to the middle class, its decidedly unspiritual home was the near-palatial where, with the carved joined to the gilded, and the marbled to the festooned, High Roman grandeur and High Renaissance opulence met.

But far more all-conquering, for being so much more all-purpose, was Adam décor, whose frillier side may have effected a revolution that still persists — the surrender of Adam to Eve, of male strut to feminine elegance, or simply fuss and feathers. The Adam interiors of Sion House and Kedleston still have grandeur; but Adam's "charming" side suggests a shift from oil to watercolor, from swords to sunshades. It could have rather too much pink and pale green, rather too many rosettes and arabesques (known in Adam's own day as "cheese cakes and raspberry tarts"). At other times Adam had more than grace, indeed showed a great feeling for unity. In truth, he designed at every level, using not only fresco painters and muralists like Cipriani and Angelica Kauffmann, but Chippendale for furniture and Wedgwood for medallions.

But talent operated not indoors only; nothing was more essential to the great estates than their gardens and minor structures. England's "man-made humanized landscape" has understandably been called her greatest contribution to the visual arts. So late as the age of Anne the formal French or Dutch garden held sway — the larger and more intricate the better, given to medieval knots, cunning labyrinths, clipped hedges, endless statuary, fantastic topiary work. But with the emergence of a strictly classical architecture, there arose, not least among the Burlingtonians, a desire for romantic landscape. Earlier, Vanbrugh, when building Blenheim, had sought to retain an old ruined manor for its picturesqueness; and indeed, the more direct incentive was the romantically classical landscape painting of the Poussins, Salvator Rosa and Claude. Here again William Kent proved important — "he saw," wrote Horace Walpole, "that all nature was a garden, he felt the delicious contrast of hill and valley." Then a fashionable garden designer named Charles Bridgeman introduced the ha-ha, or sunk fence, which could invisibly separate smooth lawn from rustic park (while also creating a cattle barrier). This did much to produce the look of natural landscape; formal lead statues were replaced by a dead tree looking very Salvator Rosa, or a hermit's cave complete with a hired hermit. In all this, it should be said that flowers played almost no part; they were deemed a hostile element, a subject for botanists rather than gardeners. The century's most famous landscape artist is Lancelot Brown, always referred to as Capability, from his set phrase when called in as an expert remodeler: "I see great capability of improvement here." A visitor from France said that Capability had "so quick and sure an eye" that after riding around for an hour, he had worked out a design for the entire park. He became so much the fashion that his "list of employers read like Debrett." Capability abolished the ha-ha, letting rough park grass advance right up to the house itself. But more often, to achieve parks of great beauty, he went the other way, eschewing the wilder touches of Poussin and Claude, for effects that were patterned and trim. The cedars he planted all over England are many of them today objects of magnificence; today, too, at least eight golf courses "preserve his handiwork."

In the way of improvements, Brown decidedly went in for those small structures which, however toylike, were among the most delightful of eighteenth-century accessories. If the grandest of them, the Hawksmoor Mausoleum, stands austerely alone, such objects as a "Chinese" bridge or a menagerie pavilion, remain elegant rococo reminders of their age. These caprices, the work of many hands, were the children of many fashions, not least the Greek, the Gothic, the Chinese. At their worst such fripperies outdo one another in extravagance: witness some of the sham ruins called follies, or certain towers which, meant to dominate the scene, merely disfigured it. But well conceived and neatly placed — coming as a surprise, or completing a vista — they can still have much appeal. Among the most ambitious, and one of the earliest, is the high-raised temple at Chatsworth, from which descends in great steps the celebrated cascade. This rush of water — rushing still — is remarkable for even a very grand establishment. Of less imposing fountains, there was almost no end. And spanning the streams were decorative bridges; and nestling beside the lakes, chaste Doric temples; and dotting the landscape were garden alcoves and pavilions. Certain of these minor works are among the most justly celebrated creations of the century — Sir William Chambers's lofty pagoda at Kew, or Robert Morris's Palladian bridge at Wilton.

The great establishments entertained vast numbers of relations and friends, and required armies of often odd retainers. There was, for example, the "waiting gentlewoman," a hard-up relative who very often became a genteel drudge; or the Negro page, half pet, half slave, glimpsed in Hogarth's *Marriage à la Mode*. But the staff of a great house went far beyond menials and servitors, gardeners, gamekeepers and grooms; it included governesses and governors (tutors), and very possibly a chaplain, a librarian, a veterinary, and a keeper of an observatory. What with having their own dairies, slaughterhouses, stables, and kennels, making their own soap and candles and ink, the larger country houses had all the activity of a village, and often the population of one.

Among the best intelligencers of the life of country gentlemen is that studiedly casual painting, the conversation piece. It was the least grand and costly of stylish forms of painting, seldom encountered in the great houses where, flanking Old Masters, were large portraits of the owner or even larger panoramas of his estates. But one way or another the conversation piece enjoyed a long and notable vogue and when its scene was well handled, and its people and place seemed well matched, it could have genuine charm. It is the domestic photograph of its age, now assembling its subjects in the drawing room or dining room, now exhibiting them out of doors in a rather got-up classical scene, or gathered on the lawn or even in a paddock or near the stables. Wherever situated, it is today a key to costume. Of the better early conversation painters, Arthur Devis, of a painting family, was the most prolific; later Zoffany came from Germany to achieve tremendous success. He has been damned for making the conversation piece "a machine to record the self-satisfaction of his patrons and his own servility"; but, though he set out to please, he was a gifted, or at any rate a skillful painter. Though perhaps best known for his *Queen Charlotte and Her Children*, he is best represented by less exalted sitters. A particular and superior variant of the conversation piece must not be omitted, the enchanting horses-and-household, family-and-phaeton groups — the Milbanke Family, or the Wedgwoods — of George Stubbs.

There was finally an English watering place frequented in its day by the aristocracy, and still cherished in ours for its architecture: Bath. Its eighteenth-century annals center in Beau Nash, so assured an arbiter and drillmaster as to triumph over duchesses and discipline princesses of the blood. And to Bath under the Beau's regime — to bathe and attend breakfast parties, to dance and drink the waters, to hear music, to shop and promenade, to dine, play cards or go to the theatre — came the ambitious, the illustrious and the very grand — the Prince of Wales or the Prince of Orange — for a routine that was not, truth to tell, very gay. But the surroundings could be delightful. Bath boasted its own famous country house, Prior Park, whose kindly owner, Ralph Allen, entertained Pope and Pitt and Garrick — and Fielding, who immortalized him as Squire Allworthy in *Tom Jones*. But nothing so preserves the face or fame of Bath as the work of the two John Woods, whose architecture transformed it. Beyond the many trim private houses, beyond the exquisite Assembly Rooms, gutted by Nazi bombs, there remains the Circus, and better yet the Queen's Square, and best of all the Royal Crescent. In their time-mellowed brick and stone and their style and sweep, a formal world is still to be discerned — an imposing world, until the sedan chair gave way to the invalid's Bath chair, and fashion slumped into retired-colonel sedateness.

13

THE RISE OF GIBBON AND THE FALL OF ROME

"I was born" — so Gibbon begins his autobiography — "I was born at Putney in the county of Surrey, the 27th of April O.S., in the year 1737." Moreover, the date of his birth had a good deal to do with the tenor of his life — few people have been more the child of their age; while the family he was born into had its eighteenth-century significance also. It was an old family, but one painfully obscure farther back than his grandfather's time: we may conjure up such ancient country gentlemen as we choose; what we can alone be sure of is a grandfather who grew rich as an army contractor and rose to become — as he sank by becoming — a director in the South Sea operations. With what was left to the first Edward Gibbon after the Bubble, he accumulated a second fortune, no vast part of which descended to Gibbon's father. The father — also named Edward — had received a gentleman's education and, both before and after marriage, come to indulge a gentleman's tastes. Capricious and unstable, a Tory M.P., a London alderman, he had of his wife seven children, of whom the third Edward alone survived. Mrs. Gibbon did not herself survive this final childbed; and the orphaned boy, who had been an invalid baby and continued sickly through childhood, was fortunately cared for by a most devoted maiden aunt. Having nursed young Edward at home, she presently followed him to school: when he enrolled at Westminster, Catherine Porten, both to maintain herself and look after her nephew, opened a boardinghouse near by.

At school, Gibbon showed no interest in games nor talent for friendship. He early became a bookworm — "the dynasties of Assyria and Egypt were my top and cricket ball." His aunt was his ally: they read Pope's Homer and the *Arabian Nights* together, while by himself the boy was soon reading volume after volume of the *Universal History*. He was fourteen when, paying a visit with his father, he pitched on a work dealing with the later Roman Empire, and had just become — as he puts it — "immersed in the passage of the Goths over the Danube, when the summons of the dinner bell reluctantly dragged me from my intellectual feast."

We can easily credit his account of his entering Oxford at not quite fifteen: "I arrived . . . with a stock of erudition that might have puzzled a doctor and a degree of ignorance of which a schoolboy would have been ashamed." He arrived at a time when his ignorance consorted with the place far better than his learning did: there existed at Oxford, for gentlemen commoners like himself, the most exceptional facilities for avoiding work. So far from following any regular course of study, certain undergraduates never even met their tutors, and — to judge by the life they led — might rather have been at a spa than a seat of learning. But the young Gibbon was not the less attracted to study for its making him lopsided, and he considered his fourteen months at Oxford the most wasted period of his life. There were things he much wanted to do, such as study Arabic; but his tutor promptly discouraged him, and Gibbon — bound as he was to devour books and think about them — could only, if he wasn't to be guided, explore for himself. He got deep into the Church Fathers, and then into Bossuet and the Elizabethan Jesuit, Parsons; he got in so deep, indeed, that at sixteen, with the help of a London bookseller, he was admitted a proselyte to the Catholic Church.

It was not without a certain satisfaction, an air blending mischievousness with martyrdom, that Gibbon informed his father of what he had done. As a Roman Catholic, he could not continue at Oxford; and his father, acting for once with sagacity and dispatch, decided he had better not remain in England, either. He was packed off to the house of a Protestant clergyman at Lausanne; and the sixteen-year-old boy, who had no friends there and spoke no French, whose very room displayed a strange stove rather than a fireplace, and whose penance included bad cooking, might have pondered the paradox of being cured of Catholicism by being sent to Purgatory. But matters very quickly grew better: the pastor was an understanding man who reclaimed the culprit from Romanism and rebellion by letting him gradually reclaim himself. Moreover, Gibbon soon came to enjoy Lausanne. At first he went about with a group of pleasure-loving young Englishmen: once, indeed, he lost 110 guineas at faro and was sufficiently perturbed to flee the city; though his father, on hearing of such unexpected frivolity, was sufficiently pleased to make good the debt. But inevitably — and all the more as French became his daily language — Gibbon turned toward the native life, and the intellectual life, of Lausanne. There were glimpses of Voltaire acting in one of his own comedies; there were exchanges of letters with Swiss scholars. Thus early in life, Gibbon successfully attempted an emendation in Ovid; thus early, too, he began to respond to the discipline, he began to acquire the balance, of one of the stablest of cultures. How thoroughly he responded he would make plain in the great undertaking of his life; but he perhaps made it plain much sooner, in the matter of his celebrated romance.

Celebrated the romance may surely be called, however special the reasons. When they met, both Gibbon and Suzanne Curchod were extremely young. Suzanne was a Swiss clergyman's daughter, plainly a girl of parts, plainly also one with ambitions: these included marrying outside the clergy and, if possible, above her class. How deeply Suzanne loved the short, gauche, socially desirable enough young Englishman is open to conjecture, though how deeply Gibbon loved Suzanne is open even more. Intrigued he certainly was, and smitten possibly: he swore, at any rate, "an attachment beyond the assaults of time." There is also a story of his stopping strangers at dagger point to compel their praises of Suzanne's superlative charms, a story that can just be believed because it is so out of character — because it reveals a Gibbon who protests too much. Both Gibbon and Suzanne were perhaps, with a certain real intensity, in love with love: in any case, after a num-

ber of meetings and a regular exchange of letters, they got themselves, or judged themselves, or found themselves, engaged.

The matter of getting married, however, was something else:
Suzanne lacked a fortune, Gibbon his own income. And at the
moment there were other complications. Gibbon's father, as it
happened, had just got married himself, and Edward was now, on
the eve of his twenty-first birthday, summoned home. It was an
opportunity for the young lover, who, while saluting his father's
marriage, might try to seal his own. His father greeted him, after
five years, in the friendliest fashion, and his stepmother proved in
every way kind. Between her and her stepson there indeed began a
lifelong relationship of affection and esteem. She was very eager
for such a relationship, and by never having children of her own —
which would have cut sharply into Gibbon's inheritance — she
happily brought it about. Actually his father's main reason for
calling him home was to dock that inheritance himself: he offered Gibbon three hundred a year for life if he would agree to
cutting off the entail. The son consented and then, in respect of
Suzanne, sought his father's consent in turn. He was refused it;
Mr. Gibbon could not approve his son bringing an unknown foreign girl to England, and even less his settling down in a foreign
land. He did not forbid the match: he merely reminded Edward
of his duties, he merely spoke of an action that would bring his
father the earlier to his grave. Highly overwrought, Edward there-
upon — as he wrote to Suzanne — retired for two hours to his
room. When he emerged, it was to do as his father asked. "Fare-
well!" he wound up the letter: "I shall always remember Mlle Curchod as the worthiest and most charming of women. . . . Assure
M. and Mme Curchod of my . . . regrets."

Suzanne's answer mixed self-pity with real feeling, and indignation with both. "You made up your mind in two hours!" she
breaks out; but soon good sense reasserts itself and she wonders
why Gibbon can't marry her with the idea of passing a few months
each year in Switzerland till set free by his father's death. But Gibbon had already lowered their romance into its grave, and would
in due time carve out its monstrous epitaph: "I sighed as a lover,

I obeyed as a son." The result could hardly have been happier: Gibbon achieved the serene bachelor life that suited him so well, and Suzanne in due course married the great French finance minister Necker and became the mother of Mme de Staël; became, too, a notable hostess, with Gibbon among the most famous and favored of her guests.

He, back in England at the age of twenty-one, now set about becoming an Englishman again and mapping out a career. He took rooms in London, but socially — what with a lack of exalted sponsors — things were inclined to be slow. Many of his evenings he spent at dull family parties or with "old Tories of The Cocoa Tree"; many others he passed, "while coaches were rattling through Bond Street," alone with his books. He had his books, as always: but to just what use was he to put them? In the matter of a career, the law — which his stepmother spoke of — did not tempt him in the least, nor did a suggestion of his father's, that since he spoke French like a native, he go in for diplomacy. In the matter of a career, no choice was really necessary: "I know that from my early youth," he wrote in the autobiography, "I aspired to the character of an historian." The real question was what history to write. In the next few years he chose and rejected the crusade of Richard I, the Barons' Wars, the history of the Black Prince, of Sir Philip Sidney, of Sir Walter Raleigh, of Florence under the Medici. He was plainly just glancing about; and between strolls along the corridors of history, he sat down and wrote, in French, an essay on the study of literature. By the time it got published, his quest of a theme had to be put aside. The Seven Years War was on, and largely as a gesture Gibbon and his father had obtained commissions in the South Hampshire Regiment. But in 1760 the regiment, to their surprise, was called up. Gibbon's response was at first good-humored; to be a captain of militia for a season might be rather a lark. But it was quite something else to cease, for two years and more, to be the captain of one's fate, and lead "a wandering life of military servitude." Entry after entry of the journal he kept begins "We marched" or "We paraded" or "We halted"; while the only thing the young scholar learned, beyond how to drill, was how to drink. In time, however, the journal entries tend to start off with "I read . . ."; and before he was finished with soldiering, he had begun to resume a life of scholarship. As an officer Gibbon, though not very effective, was fiercely efficient; and since his superiors were not, he exercised on occasion real authority. But the chief value of peregrinating the South of England, from Alton to Winchester, from Ringwood to Fareham, was best summed up — as so much concerning Gibbon is best summed up — in his own words: "The discipline and evolutions of a modern battalion gave me a clearer notion of the Phalanx and the Legions, and the Captain of the Hampshire Grenadiers . . . has not been useless to the historian of the Roman Empire."

It was not yet to Rome, however, that Gibbon hurried as soon as his regiment was disbanded: it was to Paris. After five years in England, he looked with longing toward the Continent, and his father gave him the money for a tour. In Paris — a Paris that has become peculiarly historical, a Paris of savants and *salonnières*, of *philosophes* and Anglomaniacs — he breathed an atmosphere, he entered into a way of life, that were at least as vital to him as those of London and Lausanne. Moreover, it was the perfect moment for imbibing this new element that his temperament craved, since by now it had quite banished certain other elements it did not want. The spiritual life, early and immaturely embarked on, had been early and unregretfully cast aside: for religion Gibbon would thereafter feel no need. The emotional life, flaring up before Gibbon came of age, produced no second crisis; for romance Gibbon would in future sigh no more. The physical life, the thirty months of camps and countermarches, had ended with the Peace; for action and the out-of-doors Gibbon would not even briefly pine. What now beckoned, without complication or alloy, was intellectual and social life only, the life — in the age that gave the phrase its luster — of the scholar and the gentleman.

Thanks to his French essay, to some letters of introduction, and to the prevailing Anglomania, Gibbon achieved the entrée in Paris: through Mme Geoffrin he got to know Helvétius and d'Holbach; there were morning calls and evening parties; operas, dinners, duchesses, a whole enchanting milieu where the life of the *monde* and the life of the mind were one. "In a fortnight . . . I have heard more conversation worth remembering," he wrote to his stepmother, ". . . than I had done in two or three winters in London." But socially he was, for all that, pretty much an *arriviste*, and in fine company still something of a duffer: besides, if he was to enter society not just as a writer, but as a man of fashion, it would prove highly expensive. Money had to be husbanded for an Italian journey; and Gibbon husbanded it, after fourteen weeks in Paris, by revisiting Lausanne.

He was welcomed back: the scene of his adolescent recantation began ministering to his adult desires. "A holiday resort for all Europe," Lausanne offered much by way of well-bred intellectual intercourse: all sorts of cosmopolites and notabilities stopped over, summered, wintered there; there Gibbon now resumed his friendship with the scholarly young Deyverdun, began his friendship with John Holroyd, the future Lord Sheffield — they were to be the two warmest friendships of his life. There he saw Voltaire act again — "a very ranting, unnatural performance"; and mingled with some pleasant girls who, by banding together into a Société du Printemps, went freely about with young men, unchaperoned and unscathed. He saw Suzanne there, too — a governess now, who might make a most charming friend if she could be dismissed as a fiancée; yet — as things stood — *"fille dangereuse et artificielle,"* to be kept distinctly at arm's length. But the young scholar at Lausanne quite kept pace with the young worldling: thoughts of Italy were uppermost, and the matter of career, of the project that should crown it, was never far away. Burrowing for the one, studying for the other, he read on and on — books, learned journals, the first thirty-five volumes of the *Bibliothèque raisonée*; writing, at the same time, a 214-page treatise on Italian geography. His were detailed preparations indeed; and when the coming of spring "unlocked the mountains," he set forth, like a scholar knight, for Italy.

Turin first — where Gibbon, being presented to the King's daughters, "grew so very free and easy, that I drew my snuff-box, rapped it, took snuff twice" — a scandalous violation of presence-chamber etiquette. Then Milan, Genoa, Bologna, Florence — whose annals he perhaps still toyed with chronicling; then Pisa and Lucca, Leghorn and Siena; and finally, at the beginning of October — with sudden beating pulses — Rome. "From the Silvian Bridge," he wrote in his journal, "I was in a dream of antiquity." "After a sleepless night," he recalled long afterward, "I trod with lofty step the ruins of the Forum; each memorable spot where Romulus stood, or Tully spoke, or Caesar fell, was at once present to my eye." The dream held: avoiding society, neglecting to go kiss the Pope's slipper, Gibbon inhabited the past, talked "with the dead rather than the living." The dream deepened; and suddenly, amid a concourse of images, there came what proved a moment of inspiration:

> It was at Rome, on the fifteenth of October 1764, as I sat musing amidst the ruins of the Capitol, while the barefooted fryars were singing Vespers in the Temple of Jupiter, that the idea of writing the decline and fall of the City first started to my mind.

Commentators are careful to remind us that the friars were singing in the Temple, not of Jupiter, but of Juno: but a man in the moment of encountering his destiny perhaps *ought* not to have a too clear sense of his whereabouts.

The clock had struck; but a good many years were to tick away before Gibbon would read — let alone write — about Rome. In his own opinion, they turned into the least happy years of his life — partly, no doubt, because so little got done where so much was waiting to be; partly because full manhood had not yet brought entire independence, while independence itself, when it came, would at first bring cares. After wintering in Rome and Naples, he started for home, touched at Venice, all "ruined pictures and stinking ditches," paused for "ten delicious days" in Paris, where he encountered Suzanne, now Mme Necker, "as handsome as ever" and full of affection for her former suitor. As for Necker himself, he would each night "go to bed, and leave me alone with his wife." "Could they," Gibbon demanded of Holroyd, "insult me more cruelly?" But now that love had flown out of the window, lifelong friendship might come in at the door.

Back in England, Gibbon made headway of sorts in London society when not condemned to provincial society by visits to his father. There was work to show, too: an essay on the sixth *Aeneid*; and with Deyverdun — who came over each year from Lausanne — a series of critiques, the *Mémoires Littéraires de la Grande Bretagne,* and the beginnings of a book about Switzerland. The chief profit from all this was less how to write history than what language not to write it in. French was now to be abandoned for English — even if an English that had a certain air of Latin. Five more years, in any case, slipped away, during which Gibbon had but very slowly advanced "from the wish to the hope, from the hope to the design, from the design to the execution" of the *Decline and Fall.* Moreover, as his plans matured, his project itself grew larger: what was first envisaged as the decline and fall of a city broadened into that of an empire.

In 1770 when Gibbon — now thirty-three — was at last deep in his subject, his father died. From having to settle a somewhat tangled estate and remove his stepmother from Buriton to Bath, Gibbon was again diverted from his studies; but, these obligations accomplished, he was fully and permanently free. The one thing that had still impeded, that could still becloud, a scholar-worlding's life — his duty toward and dependence on his father — now vanished; and thereafter scholar and gentleman alike made notable progress.

If no vulgar climber, Gibbon had yet had to make a place for himself in London, which he did chiefly through people he met outside it — at Lausanne, in the Militia, in Rome. He became, in his own sedate, pompous, snuffbox-rapping fashion, something of a diner-out and a quite prodigious clubman. There was a Roman Club, dotted with earls and spattered with honorables; there was the old Augustan Cocoa Tree; and Boodle's and Almack's and Brook's; and White's, that great stronghold of Tory rulers; and The Literary Club, where a Tory held forth for posterity and ruled. There was finally what in those days was as much club as legislature, the House of Commons. At his fashionable clubs he could bathe in the atmosphere, however seldom he might share the activities, of the great world. Though he practiced no gallantries, he might hear the gossip about those who did; and while stopping, himself, at shilling whist, might watch others lose their own or their families' fortunes. Despite having very good friends at The Literary Club — Garrick and Sir Joshua in particular — he was not very vocal there. He and Dr. Johnson disliked each other; Johnson — whom no glass house ever deterred from throwing stones — dilated on how ugly Gibbon was; and Gibbon, speaking of Johnson, on how ursine.

In the House of Commons, where he owed his seat to a cousin, Gibbon was less vocal still. He sat, from 1774 on, for almost ten years; but though they were scarcely humdrum years, he was the most silent, as also the most steadfast, of Tories. He not only never spoke, he did not very often listen: the great speakers, he remarked, filled him with despair, the bad ones with terror. On the subject that most agitated the House — the American Revolution — Gibbon, having looked into the facts, took King George's side. He presently confessed, however, that it was easier to approve the justice of that side than the policies; and he eventually murmured that one might be better off humbled than ruined.

To be sure, Gibbon found the year 1776 momentous enough: for on February 17 was published the first volume of the *History of the Decline and Fall of the Roman Empire*. Into it had gone many years of reading and writing and polishing and recasting — the scholarly resolution, really, of a lifetime; and in the course of those years Gibbon had not simply mastered his subject, he had forged a style.

The various modes of worship which prevailed in the Roman world were all considered by the people as equally true; by the philosopher as equally false; and by the magistrate as equally useful.

It was a style that in good time would breast the Bosphorus as well as the Tiber:

The dissolute youth of Constantinople adopted the blue livery of disorder; the laws were silent, and the bonds of society were relaxed; creditors were compelled to resign their obligations; judges to reverse their sentence; masters to enfranchise their slaves; fathers to supply the extravagance of their children; noble matrons were prostituted to the lust of their servants; beautiful boys were torn from the arms of their parents; and wives, unless they preferred a voluntary death, were ravished in the presence of their husbands.

Sentences had learned, as seldom before, to be endowed with majesty while being crammed with violence and overlaid with malice.

The success of the first volume was instantaneous and tremendous. "My book," wrote its author, "was on every table, and almost on every toilette." Horace Walpole hailed it with rapture; Hume's praise recompensed "the labor of ten years"; nor, said Gibbon, "was the general voice disturbed by the barking of any profane critic." Godlier critics were, to be sure, in different case. They violently attacked the even now notorious fifteenth and sixteenth chapters for being attacks, themselves, on Christianity: so much so as for Gibbon to say later that, had he foreseen the effect on "the pious, the timid, and the prudent," he would perhaps have softened the invidious chapters. But as he had not foreseen the effect, he chose instead to rebut an assailant named Davies in a *Vindication* quite as trenchant and almost as pitiless as one of A. E. Housman's floggings of his fellow classical scholars. His other assailants Gibbon took no notice of, beyond sniffing how happy he was to have helped them to worldly rewards: "I dare not boast of making Dr. Watson a Bishop; but I enjoyed the pleasure of giving a royal pension to Mr. Davies, and of collating Dr. Apthorpe to an Archiepiscopal living." Toward the Church itself he showed, in his personal life, no animus; and is said to have kept, during his later years, a Bible at his bedside.

Thereafter he was in any case an extremely famous man. "Charles Fox," he will write from Almack's, "is now at my elbow"; or from Paris: "As soon as I am dressed, I set out to dine with the Duc de Nivernois: shall go from hence to the French comedy,

into the Princess de Beauvau's *loge grillée*, and am not quite determined whether I shall sup at Madame du Deffand's, Madame
Necker's, or the Sardinian Embassadress's." Yet he never ceased
working, though he might interrupt one kind of work for another.
The second and third volumes of the *Decline and Fall* were five
years appearing, partly because of Gibbon's interest in chemistry
and anatomy, and his dive "into the mud of the Arian controversy." When in 1781 the two volumes did appear, there was not
the furor of five years earlier; but there was not, on the other
hand, the need for it. The Duke of Gloucester might respond with
his famous "Another damned thick, square book — always scribble, scribble, scribble — eh! Mr. Gibbon?"; and less highborn
critics might register complaint or disappointment. But the scope
and solidity of Gibbon's *History* were beyond dispute, and the new
books "insensibly rose in sale and reputation to a level with the
first."

Seven years more were to elapse before the three final volumes
appeared, by which time Gibbon would have long since quitted
London for Lausanne. The move, which he never regretted, was
partly a matter of money: with the fall of the North administration, Gibbon lost his seat in Parliament and some £800 a year on
the Board of Trade. The clubman and diner-out who needs must
drastically retrench to squeak through in London could live in perfect comfort by removing to Lausanne. He had a deep affection for
the place: he had been happy there, or at any rate young; he could
live there now with immense prestige; and, most enticingly of all,
could perhaps share the burdens of living with his old friend
Deyverdun. "*Vous me logez, et je vous nouris,*" he wrote, after his
old friend responded with joy to his feelers; and in September,
1783, he returned once more to Lausanne. Thereafter the greatest
historian of the age varied the writing of his history with whist and
chess, strolls or calls on neighbors, and bread and cheese for
supper.

Caught in this serene light, he stands forth to much his best advantage. He is a curious figure: among a few men in history no
less ridiculous than sublime. On the one side, it would be hard to

overpraise Gibbon's achievement, who was equally the architect of a monumentally vast and classic work and of an exquisitely proportioned Georgian existence. To be sure, he had the good judgment to get himself born in the eighteenth century — an age that encouraged its scholars to be men of the world, and that while shielding the better-born from all brusque intrusions, yet did not shut out light and air. Intolerably stilted the age could be, but it was never oppressively stuffy: its complacence was that of statues rather than churchwardens. To Gibbon's ironic temper, to his urbane, dry, skeptical set of mind, England offered much, Paris and the Continent still more. A hundred years later, and scholar and gentleman would not have been so closely or so harmoniously welded: a hundred years later Gibbon would have belonged to the Athenaeum instead of Almack's, been a Regius Professor rather than sat in Parliament, overflowed with neurotic crotchets rather than seignorial airs; the enormous and continuous advance of scholarship would have allowed him far less time for society, the marked deterioration of society would have doomed him to a pundit's role, or a don's. Not his personal experiences only, but his very angle of vision, would have become a great deal more provincial: he would have escaped to the Continent to be caught in the toils of German "method"; or, like his distant kinsman Lord Acton, might have whittled away his brilliance trying to cope with some sixty thousand books.

If Gibbon can't help seeming comic, the wonder is he doesn't seem more so. Extremely short, increasingly fat, extraordinarily ugly, he only stressed his shortcomings by his habit of preening himself. There is the tale of Gibbon getting down on his knees at fifty to pay romantic court to Lady Elizabeth Foster and then being too fat to get up again; servants had to be summoned and an accident invented. He was equally vain where he had more right to be. There is a tale, too, of how, having held forth in his best half-oracular, half-anecdotal style, he rapped the snuffbox and awaited homage, only to be quietly challenged by a mere youth in the company, one William Pitt; who, when Gibbon disdainfully retorted upon him, further argued with such success that Gibbon quit the room in prissy reproof, and at length the house in ill-hidden irri-

tation. Again, there is the pendant to the tremendous compliment
that Sheridan paid Gibbon in his great oration at the opening of
the Warren Hastings trial. No parallel could be found for Hastings's crimes, Sheridan thundered, "in ancient or modern history,
in the correct periods of Tacitus or the luminous page of Gibbon."
Wanting a second portion of praise, Gibbon — who was present
— affected deafness and asked his neighbor what Sheridan had said.
"Oh," he got back, "something about your voluminous pages."
He habitually conducted himself like a prelate and wrote of himself as though he were dead. Yet, having smiled, we must end by
acknowledging how stupendously the man succeeded. In a way,
the comic side only emphasizes his success: in other words, there
is no pathetic side — the few small shadows derive from the sunlight in which he basked. His, moreover, is a serenity that his age,
for all its reputation, seldom attained to — that age which steeped
Johnson and Boswell and Gray in melancholy, which saw Swift
and Smart and Cowper go mad. Gibbon represents the triumph
— however large or limited it may seem in itself — of the eighteenth-century ideal. No doubt, to revive the old fling, he mistook
himself at times for the Roman Empire; but so perhaps did the
eighteenth century mistake itself for Gibbon.

Even that twilit flash of inspiration among the barefoot friars
at Rome had to be long pondered in broad daylight before being
acted upon. It was a real inspiration, moreover, because it told him,
not whom for the moment he loved, but whom he should marry.
The Roman Empire was a *parti* rather than a passion, which is
perhaps why things so magnificently succeeded. No mere callow
infatuation at the outset, it turned with time into a real union, into
twenty years and more of fond, devoted, truly close companionship;
and when on that June night, between the hours of eleven and
twelve, he set down the last words of his *History* in a summerhouse
in his garden, he felt impoverished as well as elated, widowed as
well as set free. It had been an all but unparalleled alliance. To be
married to the Roman Empire, even in its declining years, is a
formidable exertion; but Gibbon proved more, even, than its
worthy mate; he emerged its undoubted master.

On finishing the *Decline and Fall*, Gibbon himself carried the manuscript of the last three volumes to London. It was purchased for the then great sum of £4000, and published — with a dinner to mark the occasion — on Gibbon's fifty-first birthday. All particulars of its reception pale before the fact that it was everywhere received as a full-fledged classic. In the 165 years since, its prestige has hardly diminished and more probably increased. Much has been said and must continue to be said in derogation; but the work remains, at the very least, one of the grandest of all *achievements*. It was most sharply attacked in the generation after it was written — by Romantics who as greatly disliked its style as its tone. To Shelley, Gibbon was "cold and unimpassioned"; to Coleridge, worse even than the language was Gibbon's using "nothing but what may produce an effect. . . . All is scenical and, as it were, exhibited by candlelight." Even more classical-minded critics, even profoundly admiring ones, have deplored Gibbon's habit of sneering and his tendency to snicker. His erudite defender and eulogist, Porson, said what a thousand others have repeated, that Gibbon's humanity never sleeps save "when women are being ravaged or Christians violated." And yet, on this head, there is Cardinal Newman's characterizing Gibbon as "the only Church historian worthy of the name who has written in English."

Doubtless Coleridge put his finger on Gibbon's great limitation — on his being far more interested in creating effects than discovering causes. And though that, in the end, is only to point out his unequaled merit, clearly the *Decline and Fall* is the work of a dramatist rather than a psychologist or philosopher. A true thinker Gibbon was not, or even an acute student of human nature. A scientific historian he certainly was not; nor, had he been, would his *History* have so triumphed over 165 years; for what scientific theory of history, or of very much else, has ever held sway so long? The *Decline and Fall*, being art, is a presentation rather than a reenactment; it stakes its all on a theme — plainly set forth in the title — rather than a theory; it shows no interest in depth, as it possesses no equal for span. As Suzanne said, it projects across chaos a bridge joining the ancient to the modern world. It remains, too, a great feat of erudition, whether in the amassing or the disposing of its materials. If insight was blunted by prejudice or sacrificed to effect, accuracy — an accuracy that Robertson was impelled to verify and Porson was equipped to attest — was not. The inferiority of the second half of the *History* to the first, of the account of the Eastern Empire to that in the West, is partly a matter of inadequate scholarship, but much more so of temperament: to Gibbon what was Byzantine could only seem barbaric or decadent. But his book may call itself history even now when it is more than ever a triumph of literature.

His life's great work behind him, Gibbon, while ruminating new projects, began chronicling that life itself. He wrote no finished version, merely six sketches out of which, after his death, Lord Sheffield wove the autobiography that bears his name and, better than the *Decline and Fall*, asserts and glorifies his manner. Gibbon had, in a sense, not so much a life to record as a way of living it. Even those elements that smack of drama or hint at tragedy — expulsion and exile, stepmother and blighted romance — far from leaving scars, seem almost a vindication of the eighteenth-century precept that "whatever is, is right." Yet if few lives have been, in a way, more undramatic, few have been better dramatized. Gibbon's fateful moment at Rome vibrates almost as memorably as Caesar's a few miles north of it; and not Hector taking leave of his family, or Mary Queen of Scots of the world, catches the light more vividly than Gibbon bidding his *History* adieu.

There is little for any biographer to add beyond where the autobiographer leaves off. Deyverdun died; but Gibbon obtained a life tenure on the house they shared and continued in the old way of living. The Bastille fell; but though the French Revolution shocked Gibbon, it scarcely discommoded him: indeed, by bringing the Neckers and other congenial spirits as refugees to Lausanne, it really brightened his existence. English friends also came to Lausanne, among them the Sheffields. Their sharp-eyed daughter found Gibbon's circle deadly dull, and thought their flattery "the only advantage this place can have over England for him."

He talked much of an English visit; but the Revolution had made travel rather hazardous; and the visit kept being put off. The death, however, of Lady Sheffield in April, 1793, prompted Gibbon to return at once, to bring any comfort he could to his most intimate friend. But it was the friend who must soon think of Gibbon: back in England he took ill. A hypercele, or swelling of the left testicle, that had been diagnosed as far back as his militia days and been totally disregarded ever since, now grew acute. Operations afforded temporary relief; there were even intervals of dining out and of driving to Bath and Apthorp and Sheffield Place. But there could be no cure; and Gibbon died in London on the 16th of January, 1794, at the age of fifty-six.

14

THE REGENCY:
A NINE-YEAR WONDER

The English Regency is a historic fact, or a nostalgic phrase, that evokes certain particular images, or elegances, or events, and certain styles of procedure and modes of behavior — something that stresses a way of life at the expense of life in general, and a primacy of forms that obscure half of life's most familiar functions. If such a conception must be a good deal modified by the Regency's actual makeup, it is yet partly justified by its preeminence in social éclat and in the arts. We speak of Regency houses, Regency sofas, Regency coachwork, Regency waistlines, Regency bowed windows and cast-iron railings; we recall Regency personalities and personages — not just the Prince Regent or the Duke of Wellington, but Canning and Castlereagh, Alvanley and Creevey, Lady Jersey and Princess Lieven; and Regency dandies, and Regency follies, and Regency clubs. That is what, atmospherically, the word connotes, as against what it historically signifies, and as such it is not altogether unprecedented — a comparable atmosphere surrounds the English Restoration, which brings to mind Nell Gwyn and Lord Rochester far sooner than John Bunyan and Judge Jeffreys. For stylishness dusted with wit and splashed with sin leaves its own bright indelible mark, wars and governments notwithstanding.

This aura is the more striking in that the actual Regency lasted for just nine years. George III's periodic, porphyria-induced madness became permanent in 1811, when the Prince of Wales was designated Regent; and the mad, blind, deaf old King died in 1820, when the Regent became George IV. "Regency" has, with some cultural justification, been applied to anything from 1800 to 1830; but J. B. Priestley in his *The Prince of Pleasure and His Regency* restricts himself to the actual nine years, and I would cheerfully follow suit, not because of a pedantic adherence to dates, but because those nine years are a horn of plenty of activities, events, and achievements. More luster has been squeezed into them, and more scandal squeezed out of them, than almost any other nine years of English history. To both elements the Regent himself contributed something; to the latter, indeed, he contributed more than anyone else.

In calling him the Prince of Pleasure Mr. Priestley has undoubtedly nailed his subject's chief object in life. As the son of domestic but despotic "Farmer George," a thrifty and virtuous if pigheaded man, the Regent, born in 1762, was by temperament antithetical to Papa and by Papa's training extremely antipathetic to him. The future George IV and his six brothers, said the Duke of Wellington, were "the damnedest millstones about the neck of any government that can be imagined." Indeed, the seven deadly sons could be, by less than royal standards, frequently loutish, with occasional smidgens of lunacy; several of them went into the Army and the Navy and all of them into debt; they had mistresses and a platoon of illegitimate children, and they also became King of Hanover, or the father of Queen Victoria, or the grandfather of George V's Queen Mary.

As Prince of Wales, George countered his father's viceless habits with a taste for mistresses, his father's frugality with a passion for splurging. The Prince's early liaison with "Perdita" Robinson, a married woman and beautiful actress, he abruptly broke off, with Papa having to pay £5000 to get George's letters back. George flouted his father's Toryism by allying himself with the Whigs, finding a political leader in Charles James Fox and a companion in the witty and worldly Sheridan. Like both these spendthrifts, the Prince in no time was heavily in debt, and soon after madly in love. His relations with Mrs. Fitzherbert, a well-bred, twice-widowed Roman Catholic whom he secretly married and lived with for many years, were the *grande passion* of his life; but the marriage, though sanctioned by Rome, was illegal in England, and George in due course, to placate his father and get his debts paid off, married his first cousin Caroline of Brunswick. The couple loathed each other at sight, had indeed no sooner met than George said, "Harris, I am not well; pray get me a glass of brandy"; and once Caroline had produced a daughter and heir to the throne — who died in childbirth in 1817 — George sent Caroline a message calling it quits, and when she asked for it in writing, received it. Their ruptured marriage was to become, years later, a Regency uproar.

So, to a considerable degree, was the Regent himself. But in the intervening period, along with his endless self-gratifications, monumental debts, and older-than-he-was mistresses, he could display his genuine social gifts, sophisticated tastes, and artistic interests. For clothes he had a dandy's passion if a Falstaff's figure and was constantly designing them; he had a passion for furniture and was regularly installing it; and like all the Georges, he liked music. More valuable was his collecting of pictures; more valuable still, his feeling for architecture: in one way or another he used most of the best architects of the time to create some of its best-known achievements. George's residence, Carlton House, and Carlton House Terrace took years to finish or refinish, but London was the more distinguished for them; and most splendid of all, the work of George's favorite architect, John Nash, were Regent Street and Regent's Park. Nash was also the principal architect for the Brighton Pavilion, the showplace of the little seaside town the Prince turned into a famous resort. Here George's taste for various architectural and decorative styles — Gothic, Chinese, Egyptian — finally took a sort of Muslim Indian form, the array of domes, cupolas, minarets, and pinnacles lending themselves to Sydney Smith's famous jest that "it looked as if St. Paul's Cathedral had come down and littered." Yet the whole effect, however *outré* and fantastic, resembles a sort of fairyland — or Disneyland — marvel.

Appointed Regent, "Prinny" began by dishing the liberal Whigs he had fellowshiped with and retaining his father's Tories. Beyond the disloyalty involved, this revealed a certain irresponsibility, since the nation, rather wormy and rancid under the Regency icing, cried out for reform. But George had no real feeling for politics except as they supported his pleasures, and no real feeling for people, Mrs. Fitzherbert, it would seem, excepted. He could be impulsively kind, and his reckless extravagance could include generosity, but he chiefly, during a troubled decade, conducted a ballroom regime. His public image became as egregious as it was enormous — Charles Lamb dubbed him the Prince of Whales; his debts were so enormous as to antagonize the populace, and he was from all sides caricatured, castigated, denounced. As rulers go, he was possibly overabused: he was weak rather than wicked, vain rather than overbearing, selfish rather than cruel, untrustworthy rather than crafty — in sum, pretty much of a rotter. He had what rotters often have, a feeling for style and art. Despite that feeling, I find him less like the sovereign he is usually bracketed with, Charles II — a witty and perceptive man and a very shrewd monarch — than a royal-style good-time Charlie, rather more akin to Edward VII. He perhaps did more harm to himself as Regent than to his country, and he harmed himself most in his behavior toward his wife.

Caroline, though she has been variously characterized, has chiefly benefited from being ill-treated. She seems to have had no particular virtues or charms, and could be rattlebrained, gossipy, unstable, and indiscreet; but as a displaced consort in a foreign land, suffering from Prinny's edicts, such as how seldom she could see her daughter, and from his virtual campaign to humiliate her, she gained a great deal of sympathy. In 1814 she transferred herself to the Continent, where she had a conspicuous "friendship" with an Italian gentleman. But whatever the extent of her wrongdoing, it paled beside how badly she was wronged; and when, on the Regent's becoming King, she dashed back, as Queen, to England and met with George's rancorous opposition, she became as much England's favorite as he was its favorite butt. Against Caroline he brought charges of "licentious, disgraceful and adulterous intercourse," causing her to be tried by the House of Lords; and .

though a brilliant defense led to the charges' being dropped, she was yet, by her husband's order, refused admittance to his Coronation. He, when appearing in public, was loudly greeted with "God Save the Queen." Caroline died soon after the Coronation; George lived on until 1830. These years saw George install his final *maîtresse en titre*, Lady Conyngham, who came to Court equipped with a husband and departed, as George lay dying, "with sufficient jewellery, plate, etc., to fill two wagons." The monstrous-bellied King ailed during his later years, and his reign lacked both the glitter and the tarnish of his Regency.

In a not particularly long, and loosely integrated but personally pungent, text-and-picture book whose three hundred colored and black-and-white illustrations are part of its content and enhance its attractiveness, Mr. Priestley deals sufficiently with the Regent but wisely devotes more space to "his Regency." These last two words of the book's title we can interpret in two ways: the regime that the Regent gives his name to and the regime that revolved around him. In one very important essential the two meet at times, namely in the achievement between 1811 and 1820 in literature and art. Those nine years saw the publication of Wordsworth's *The Excursion*, Coleridge's *Biographia Literaria*, most of Shelley, almost everything of Keats, all six of Jane Austen's novels, many of Scott's, Peacock's *Headlong Hall* and *Nightmare Abbey*, Byron's *Childe Harold* and the first part of *Don Juan*, and important work by Crabbe, Hazlitt, and Lamb. In painting, besides work by Turner, Constable, and Blake, there were Lawrence and Raeburn, and Crome, Cotman, and the Norwich School; in architecture there were Soane, the Wyatts, Henry Holland, Nash, and chiefly for landscape, Repton. This superb achievement, much of it at odds with Regency tendencies, makes plain how disproportionately prominent those tendencies can be.

They had, however, a decided upper-class impact. The eighteenth century, like an elderly beau, was still offering Regency society its arm; but the French Revolution, the Industrial Revolution, and the Napoleonic Wars had altered society: the minuet now curtsied to the waltz; Bath, set against Prinny's Brighton, was sedate and passé; there was certainly style of a kind, and a lavish party-giving atmosphere — the era fathered Lambton's famous concession that one could "jog along" on £40,000 ($1 million in our money) a year. (After all, the strawberries at a breakfast party cost £150 ($4000 today.) Lady Londonderry went to a ball "so covered with jewels that she could not stand up" and was followed wherever she went with a chair. There was also the dandy, whose appearance was his whole *raison d'être* and whose self was almost the only thing he gave thought to. Indeed, the Regency world was like a fine wine that has begun to go bad, and that in its half-spoiled condition satisfied the Regency palate. The aristocratic too often gave way to the arrogant; elegant clothes were too often worn by vulgar people; Byron spoke of "the would-be wits and the can't-be gentlemen"; bailiffs were disguised as footmen in ducal houses; "It isn't fashionable," proclaimed the Princess Lieven, "where I am not present"; and cheating was an accepted fact. "What would you do," someone was asked, "if you saw a man cheating at cards?" "Bet on him," was the answer. In a sense, the Regency best survives through its headlines, which certainly swathe its three most symbolic figures in scandal.

Beau Brummell, history's most impeccable dandy and fashion's most implacable despot, had attractive qualities and witty bad manners, and amid the excesses of Regency dress ordained for men plain black and white with "fine linen, plenty of it, and country washing." (His boot polish, he gave out, was made from the finest champagne.) He spent an incredible number of hours getting in and out of his clothes and looking critically and no doubt caustically through the privileged bow window of White's Club, and he turned a sort of stylish impudence into an art. By giving a comparative nonentity his arm while crossing the street from Brooks's Club to White's, he wiped out, Brummell felt, a large gambling debt; but in an age of very steep play, many other large gambling debts felled him at last, and very nonchalantly one night he left the opera to flee for good and all across the Channel and escape his creditors, and to die, years after, in senile filth in France.

Lord Byron, having become the romantic hero and social lion of London as the Regency got under way, was by its middle years misbehaving generally and badly mistreating his wife. While she sued for a separation, rumors of incest with his half-sister Augusta were rampant, and smeared with scandal, Byron, like Brummell, left England forever. Our third symbol, the Regent, in exchange for giving the period his name, received its maximum notoriety. The supreme Regency personage was Wellington; around him hovers the period's most famous social event, the Duchess of Richmond's ball — Byron's "sound of revelry by night" — at Brussels on the eve of Waterloo. The greatest pageantry centers in the visits to London after Napoleon had abdicated and gone to Elba, of the crowned and military heads of Europe — among others, Louis XVIII, the Czar of Russia, the King of Prussia, and Blücher. The Russian guest and his Regent host — "the two vainest men alive" — did not get on. The friendly, jaunty, liberal-tyrannical Czar, with the populace falling at his feet, kept Prinny puffing at his heels, now snubbed, now belittled: thus, very ceremoniously introduced to the Regent's current mistress, Lady Hertford, the Czar merely bowed, and turning away, said, "She is mighty old." There were countless less resplendent names and occasions, and a succession of period fashions: Almack's club became the test of social standing, its balls tightly managed by some despotically titled ladies; Watier's, another club, became the gilded road to ruin, where a throw of the dice could overthrow a fortune; prizefights became the rage and the Regency's most popular sport. Under all the social glitter there was a good deal of immoral grime, just as below the ranks of fashion there was a good deal of moral displeasure. While the peerage and its playfellows were sucking the last luscious fruits of the eighteenth century, a well-behaved, well-to-do middle class was sniffing the purer, if stuffier, air of a predawn Victorianism.

But there was the other Regency world, one which reveals something black and unspeakable behind the trim façade; and an outstanding virtue of Mr. Priestley's book is that, within his restricted limits, he does this world justice. Our nine years involve Peterloo as well as Waterloo, and the pinched face of poverty watching pageantry swagger by. Living conditions might be worse than under Victoria, and dying ones more dramatic: women dropped dead from hunger while begging with babies at their breast; and widespread starvation and destitution — and for that matter, almost unprecedented prostitution — infested the country. "An Englishman who can't lay his hands on £25," observed Stendhal, "is an outlaw." A fifteen-hour day was not at all uncommon, and for long perilous working hours miners got less than four dollars a week. And there were the chimney sweeps, children sometimes four years old who were sold by their parents for a few guineas and often forced to beg for their food when not pushed up chimneys, choking from soot, clouted by falling mortar, bigger boys jabbing their bare feet with pins to keep them moving, and occasionally kept moving by "lighting hay or straw below them."

With the end of the Napoleonic Wars the Regency saw the effects of the Industrial Revolution, when new devices and machines were greatly expanding English industries. It was said that the spinning jenny and the steam engine had financed the defeat of Napoleon. Early in the Regency came the trial and harsh punishments of the Luddites, who, though best remembered for smashing machines as the archfoes of human labor, were extremely indignant over shoddy products that made possible bigger profits, and who were chiefly persecuted for attempting to organize. Unhappily, in the year after Waterloo the often hideous working conditions worsened into horrifying unemployment, and the Regency was to culminate in the Peterloo agitation, when possibly 80,000 people came together in Manchester to listen to the well-known "Orator" Hunt and demand reform. There was police intervention, followed by bloodshed and mounds of crushed bodies, producing intense working-class anger, and repercussions for years to come.

In 1817 stones that broke a window of the Regent's coach led, under a Tory administration, to suspending the Habeas Corpus Act; at other times, laws slumbering from the Middle Ages were roused and reapplied, and the miserable unredressed plight of the masses stumbled behind the steadily unreformist nature of those in power. There was of course a Regency England that was well dressed and genteel, or well scrubbed and respectable, or adequately fed and obedient, but set against such domestic candlelight the extremes of selfish pleasure and starveling want are like tremendous flares in the darkness. The vital issues that confronted a nation with a playboy Regent at the helm, a Tory government in the saddle, and a largely frivolous leisure class catching the limelight would continue, but Catholic Emancipation, legalized trade unionism, the full abolition of the slave trade, and the Reform Bill, when at length they came, could boast a kind of connection with the Regency — they helped remedy its evils.

15

IN THE DAYS OF THE BRIC-A-BRAC QUEEN

James Laver, long known for his knowledge of period manners, fashions, décor, has written the opening volume in a projected series of "Manners and Morals" — his covering the Age of Optimism, or 1848 to 1914. The book treats, to begin with, an enjoyably shifting historical climate; and, brightened with numerous illustrations, it abounds in lively and often instructive detail. It not inappropriately opens by scattering things Right and Left, with a lavish display of revolutions, toppling thrones, scurrying monarchs, resonant slogans and manifestos. The book halts at World War I, which, one might add, would also make for a lavish display of revolutions, toppling thrones, scurrying monarchs, manifestos, and slogans. If this evokes that least optimistic of slogans called *plus ça change*, the interval between the topplings and scurryings was yet a momentous one. Though the Year of Revolution guttered out rather than started a blaze, and though a Kossuth as well as a Metternich, and a Louis Blanc as well as a Louis Philippe, fled to England, 1848 left cracks not easily puttied over; sounded a tocsin that both reverberated and would keep sounding again; and hence, for humanity in the mass, did set going an era of optimism. But the optimism that chiefly animates Mr. Laver's book is of an almost opposite, a quite undemonstrative and very English kind, one that affords revolutionaries asylum but deprecates revolutions; that talks not of pie in the sky but of more and more pounds in the bank — one that has bourgeois objectives and goals. This is not just because

Mr. Laver is himself British, but because to an immense degree the subject matter of his book is. When he takes us to France, it is to look at what the English *prefer* should flourish outside England — the sansculotte type, or demimondaine, or avant-garde; and his one visit to America in the book is no more than a short guided, and at moments misguided, tour.

Hence his book, in essence and substance alike, is a survey of Victorian England, with an Edwardian epilogue. But if, as such, it rather fails to bear out its international title, it all the better concentrates on one specific culture, and on one that the title beautifully fits. For Victorian England bulged with manners and morals in every good and bad sense of the words. It also abounded in striking opposites, was both on the march and stuck in the mud, gaudy and drab, bizarre and banal, God-fearing and Mammon-worshiping, humanitarian and heartless, wildly eccentric and servilely conformist. Never perhaps did a culture become so plump and smug, and hence so insistent a target for eventual satire. Mr. Laver, with a proper showman's eye, does not slight the outré or illicit, or scorn the anecdotal bric-a-brac of an age unequaled for bric-a-brac. And his detail does fairly often suggest his period's design.

No juxtaposition could be more telling than that of Victorian poverty and wealth. Not even a Dickens, or a Hogarth earlier, can quite prepare us for how dehumanized the poor could be. Yet it was not the Scrooges who chiefly brought about such conditions as having seven-year-old mill children work fifteen hours a day for two shillings and sixpence a week; it was much more the Manchester school of economics, condemning the masses to such laissez-faire as bitterly fought-over garbage. London, in terms of slum apparel, displayed "what a frock coat could carry in layers of filth"; or, of slum furniture, family "beds" that were piles of soot. A more solid survey, G. M. Young's much esteemed *Victorian England,* gives us even more sordid detail — "drinking water brown with faecal particles," or unburied corpses rotting in midsummer London. Hence theft became the chief trade for boys; and for girls, a prostitution unequaled in all England's history. At twelve-thirty at night, five hundred streetwalkers circulated in an area below Piccadilly Circus, not least directly outside "the chaste portals of the Athenaeum."

Yet the horrors of Victorian poverty somehow reflect less on Victorian wealth than on that tremendously dominant Victorian force, religion (and on its bodyguard, respectability). It was not only that, rather exceptionally, the bishopric of Durham was worth £19,000 (some $300,000 today) a year, but that, not at all exceptionally, "a great Church family could amass an annual £12,000 and have most of the work done by curates for £80." And beyond the fashionable worldliness of the Church of England were the Victorians who turned with the Oxford Movement toward Rome; or, far more numerously, with the Evangelical Movement toward very rigorous faiths. How notably religion triumphed we can gauge from the fact that where in Staffordshire in 1810 only two country gentlemen had family prayers, in 1850 only two did not. The stricter sects endowed the English Sunday with a kind of official gloom that suggested a coffin in every front parlor. High-Church zealots, on the other hand, went incense-wild and stained-glass drunk and vestment-mad with ritual: indeed, said Dickens, the High Churchman of 1850 was the dandy of 1820 in another form.

Religion played a great weekday as well as Sunday role, and gave Lombard Street and Oxford Street a working philosophy. Godly behavior not only constituted a card of admittance to heaven, it augured property and bank accounts on earth. Between the Ten Commandments and the five-percents there was no slightest clash; in fact, it was five percent of another kind — its being the maximum profit the Quakers permitted themselves — that made everybody want to do business with them and made them in turn extremely rich. And the Wesleyans, a century after Wesley, had grown so solidly middle class as to be "as much opposed to Democracy as to Sin." What counted more with the Victorians than any biblical respect for the Sabbath was that workingmen, by resting on Sunday, got much more done on the other six days of the week. And rest on Sunday they did: the proletariat, we are told, never budged from bed "until the public houses opened."

Meanwhile, respectability reached epidemic proportions. The zoo and the panorama, the excursion ticket and the public library vied with one another for thrilling and delighting child and grown-up, matron and maid. Perhaps nothing expresses the period better than its female costume, with its curious notification of bosom and nullification of legs, its orgy of jewels and endlessness of underclothing. Respectability, though it made so many other things, for women, forbidden fruit, was wonderfully permissive about food itself. It is hardly going too far to call Victorian respectability the mother of gluttony, and to equate the menu of a very middle-class English dinner party with that of an old-style American-plan hotel. Still, matrons *might* have managed moderation in the presence, to quote from one menu, of such party food as "mash turnips" (sic), "stewed spinach," "sea cale," "ox rumps," and "macaroni pudding"; all this washed down with champagne during dinner, and claret at the end of it.

Securely immuring middle-class society, respectability no less securely cemented family life. Certainly there was inspiration and to spare for this at Windsor and Balmoral (perhaps, too, what was bourgeois in Victoria and Albert seemed patrician to the bourgeoisie). The usual paterfamilias, though no ogre or Mr. Barrett of Wimpole Street, was sufficiently authoritarian. Indeed, during much of the Victorian era, a wife could own nothing; not only did her dowry and inheritances pass to her husband, but so, even if she was legally separated from him, did her earnings. Respectability in turn condemned her to a conspicuous do-nothing-ism. If motherhood was for her the nearest thing to a vocation, constant "expecting" made of her a homebody as well. At the same time, the new gentility left her all but useless in the home; it insisted on her having — all of them probably underpaid — servants in the kitchen, nannies in the nursery, seamstresses in the sewing room, gardeners in the flower beds. Only a few causes were ladylike enough for her to endorse, only a few diversions unsullied enough for her to indulge in. Sex, as distinct from childbearing, was all too often made odious to her by the proceedings of the wedding night, when the inexperience of the bridegroom had quite matched the ignorance of the bride.

Mr. Laver's Age of Optimism was, in England of course, an Age of Euphemism and Taboo, hence often of Ostracism and Hypocrisy. This could obtain even among the learned and the lineaged. Milman, biblical historian as well as dean of St. Paul's, was virtually ostracized for calling Abraham a sheik; and a member of Parliament, having to refer to a contracted pelvis, had to do so "in a classical language." Where enlightenment reigned, Charles Kingsley characterized Shelley as a "lewd vegetarian"; where morality governed, a council member of the College of Surgeons hoped that syphilis could not be stamped out, for if it was, fornication must become rampant. As for Victorian hypocrisy, a man who published a blackmailing scandal sheet also published a pious religious magazine denouncing the scandal sheet. As for Victorian "audacity," the redoubtable Mrs. Grote, wife of the famous historian of Greece, caused a furore by using the word "disemboweled" at a dinner party.

Mr. Laver, whose researches into American gentility seem rather skimpy, contends that our prudishness was far greater than England's. At its Anthony-Comstock worst, it probably was, but it seems far less pervasive. Mr. Laver concedes that our putting panties on piano legs has been taken too seriously, and cites an English visitor who was told by a wag that the piano's legs were concealed lest "they should give gentlemen ideas." And our puritanism itself could be waggishly combated, as with having poolrooms pose as houses of worship, with the roulette wheel, when the police knocked, hustled out of sight and the "congregation" bursting fervently into "Shall We Gather at the River?" With our immense nineteenth-century regional differences, we clearly ran to extremes — stringent blue laws and roaring red-light districts; even to extremes meeting, with antimacassars in the parlor along with cuspidors.

In England, not surprisingly, an era so prudish and conformist had more than its share of the scandalous and clandestine. Mr. Laver devotes considerable space, textual and pictorial, to both the English and the French demimonde. But despite the allure of the fast-stepping ladies on one side of the Channel, and the *grandes horizontales* on the other, and despite their impressive honorariums, it all, after a while, comes to seem more flyblown and repetitious than glamorous and lustful. Even America's actress-mis-

tress-adventuress-salonnière, Adah Isaacs Menken, though more in
teresting than most and with a more interesting clientele — a huge
corpulent Dumas *père*, a frail tiny Swinburne — has been chronicled too often. One cannot, however, pass over a highborn girl in-
disputably named Miss Horsey de Horsey, who came a social
cropper simply for riding without a groom in the park, and was
thrown for good and all by consorting with married Lord Cardigan.
And though she at length became his Lady, and was greeted by his
six hundred tenants (on horseback), not one soul appeared at the
magnificent country-house ball the Cardigans sent out invitations
for; indeed, she was cut dead till the day she died.

Sexually, the Victorian male is more shadowy and enigmatic,
and hence more interesting. On the one hand, by creating an era of
neurasthenic, frigid, and puritanical wives, he made an institution
of bawds and kept women; on the other hand, thanks to paternal
despotism, public school mishandling, and religious threats of hellfire, he was often, himself, the prey of guilt-ridden lust, a sexual
misfit, a frightened male virgin, a repressed homosexual, a fetishist,
a fantasist, a flagellant. In the world of books alone, Swinburne,
Ruskin, Carlyle, Pater, Edward Fitzgerald, Lewis Carroll, John Ad-
dington Symonds smack of the casebooks as well. Intellectually,
the Victorian male also had the shakes, for behind the sanctities of
family and society were disconcerting theories and ideas. From
Mill, Arnold, George Eliot down, there was decided loss of faith;
Bishop Colenso rejected biblical truth through finding it out of the
question to feed so many in the Ark for so long. From the Victorian hardship to feed so many in the home, by the 1870s contra-
ception had left its mark on the census.

Emotion underwent change no less than thought. Dr. Arnold's
public-school reforms reshaped the public-schoolboy, implanting in
him the seeds of muscular Christianity and new conceptions of
manliness. At schools where "hands, face and perhaps neck" were
washed daily, and feet "once a fortnight," what by all odds commanded the greatest attention was the stiffening of the upper lip.
G. M. Young tells — of a not much earlier generation — how once,
at a great country house, "when Tom Moore was singing, one by

one the audience slipped away in sobs; finally, the poet himself broke down and the old Marquis was left alone." A very few decades later, Tennyson might as easily have written of "tears, shameful tears." The English, one of the most emotional of races — "the Elizabethans," Mr. Laver reminds us, "behaved like a lot of excitable Italians" — were being turned into one of the most stoical. Moreover, a school regimen which featured, for the body's welfare, cold baths and corporal punishment, judged display of intellect almost as unseemly as show of emotion.

The advance of science, the spread of literacy, the growth of a flourishing middle class made increasingly for higher education outside Oxford and Cambridge, and toward more specific and career-minded ends. London University and its successors trained men in medicine, law, engineering, education itself, creating a pattern for the future. (It was said that the classical curriculum long reigned at the Two Universities because they possessed hundreds of people who could teach Latin, Greek, and mathematics, and almost no one who could teach anything else.) Attitudes were changing, time was passing, although Victoria, to be sure, lingered on and was twice jubileed (at the Golden Jubilee, an undertaker was put in charge of decorating the Abbey, and decided to paint and varnish the eight-hundred-year-old Coronation Chair). But much that surrounded Victoria had vanished, and very un-Victorian things like Feminism had arrived; as had the bicycle; as had the American heiress; as had Aestheticism, Beardsley, Wilde, and the *Yellow Book*; and Imperialism, Kipling, Henley, and the Yellow Press; and at length, the Boer War, the birth of a new century, the death of the Queen. The Edwardian era which followed has an aura of chic elegance: on the great Continental trains, for example, everyone dressed for dinner. But there is evidence of inelegance, too; of a King with *nouveaux-riches* friends, a love of display, of publicity, of high living, of gormandizing, who breakfasted off poached eggs, bacon, haddock, chicken, and woodcock, ate a five-course lunch and a seven-course dinner, with midmorning snacks like lobster salad, and quail or a cutlet at midnight. It was an age of optimism indeed as to how long one's digestion, even with Marienbad, would hold out.

Yet with the feeling of progress so widespread, and the evidence of progress so great, a sanguine spirit was inevitable. Between 1815 and 1914 England fought no major war, and none closer to home than the Crimea or the Sudan. The long Victorian age might be unified in name only, and 1840 seem like 1900's antediluvian grandfather; but there was such confidence in the future that progress had been "reduced from an aspiration to a schedule." And how not, what with all the tremendous activity and increment born of the Industrial Revolution, and all that had made ruling a far-flung Empire into the white man's guerdon? Greater Britain had reached its greatest height. Of the large political and economic forces of the era this book, by definition, does not treat. But though Mr. Laver fails to deal with it, surely on his own terms of manners, in his own world of human society, what must have counted most as "progress" proved most personal and near at hand — the sense of ever greater comfort and convenience. A fair while back Macaulay had exulted in the unsurpassable up-to-dateness of England; and unsurpassable up-to-dateness continued, movement accelerated, macadam spread, steel spanned wider, steam hissed louder. The age, while complicating man's thoughts on life, greatly eased his way of living; advanced from the train to the motorcar, the telegraph to the telephone, the electric light to the electric so-much-else; introduced modern plumbing, anesthesia, antitoxins, the penny post, the typewriter, the lift. Much of England remained parched, begrimed, unspeakable, but in bulk things did show progress, a little more milk or soap or sunlight; and there was an honest belief that next year must always be better than this one. There is a good deal more milk and soap and sunlight today, there is an inconceivable up-to-dateness — the pressure cooker symbolizes, indeed, how most men live; nuclear science constantly finds improved methods for how they can die. There is no great feeling, however, that next year must be better than this one; people are even called optimists for thinking it will be no worse.

16

THE SWAY OF THE GRAND SALOON

Though functionally just a form of conveyance, transatlantic ocean travel has long constituted a floating microcosm of human society; a cross section of residential areas, from luxurious subdivisions to loathsome slums; a spectrum of nationalities, personalities, professions, trades, amours, sunsets, cardsharps, bores, and castaways. Plainly such a story, and from fairly far back, deserves to be set down. John Malcolm Brinnin's *The Sway of the Grand Saloon* is a well-documented, well-dramatized and well-written history of transatlantic travel from 1818 to 1968. It is also the work of a cultivated writer, not, as with an enterprising hack, all breeziness and bright paint. Being a history, the book is perhaps longer and more detailed than many readers would ask of it; but, being a history, it seems entitled to its approach.

Discernible almost from the outset, the overwhelming double theme of transatlantic travel has been speed and size, to which the most vital element, safety, has often been sacrificed. In early days, when the risks were numerous and largely uncombatable, and when sail, not steam, was the senior partner, there was less stress on speed, just as there was commercially less call for larger quarters when hordes of steerage passengers were jammed into inhumanly small space — the steerage fare £5 (food self-supplied), the profit "just about £5." But as time and technology went on, and transatlantic travel became a great and growing business need, a considerable social activity, and a corridor to the sights of Europe, the

Blue Riband for breaking speed records would serve as the most eminent figurehead, and the spacious public rooms and promenade decks as the glamour advertisement.

The first of Mr. Brinnin's ships, the *James Monroe*, left New York on January 5, 1818, and its historical claim is not that it used steam — it moved entirely under sail — but that it was the first packet to depart — full or empty, balmy weather or blizzardy — on schedule. It had also its contemporary inducements — a porphyry and mahogany saloon, paneled "sleeping closets," a sizable zoo of live fowl and animals to be consumed en route; and it made the "downhill run" (New York to Liverpool) in twenty-eight days when it might have taken sixty. Within a few years a good many ships would leave, though not necessarily arrive, on schedule, and within a few years a number of ships would join steam to sail. The "uphill run" would be by far the more populous one, bringing, as it did, thousands of emigrants to the Land of Plenty in a hold of horror — beds of rotted straw, filth beyond belief, stench beyond endurance.

The fashionable packet passengers held their noses or looked down them; enjoyed a blend of fake elegance and genuine inconvenience — satinwood and marble, but no bathtubs or running water, and with rat hunts a standard amusement, even for ladies. Various people still known to fame crossed the ocean in packets — Harriet Martineau found it best "not to look into the dishes of dried fruit which formed our dessert"; Emerson complained that "a nimble Indian would have swum as far" as the boat got the first three days out; and Tom Thumb, off to "visit" the crowned heads of Europe, first sat enthroned on a "cut-glass tumbler" and later hopped onto some "*bœuf à la mode*" to sing "Life on the Ocean Wave."

Meanwhile steamships were nosing out packets, though it would be very late in the nineteenth century before a last ocean liner was stripped of its sails. In 1819 the first transatlantic ship "with steam powered machinery," the *Savannah*, had crossed — without a single passenger — largely under sail to England, and had come back using steam only when watched from on land. The early transatlantic "father of steam navigation" was Junius Smith, an affluent American living in England who grew bored and irritated during a fifty-four-day, time-is-money crossing under sail. Championing steamship travel, he tried to enlist well-to-do New York businessmen as investors, but got nowhere. Back in England he sought the approval of the Duke of Wellington, but the Iron Duke, at the moment very hostile to the Iron Horse "because it would encourage the lower classes to move about," cared even less for hulls and funnels. Smith went ahead anyway, working toward a North Atlantic monopoly with his four United States–England steamers. Later, another of his steamers, the *Sirius*, had an England-to-New York challenger in the long-famous, English-owned *Great Western*: the *Sirius*, starting first, did indeed get there first; but the *Great Western* got there a good deal faster. Smith himself, it might be said, also started first and got there first, but got nowhere in the finals.

As steam made headway, British businessmen asked why shouldn't British Halifax, with its fine Nova Scotian harbor, be made the terminus for British shipping. This won the Great Western group's approval, provided a government mail subsidy went with it. The British Post Office and the Admiralty agreed, while stipulating competitive bids; among the bidders was a successful and very knowledgeable Nova Scotian named Samuel Cunard. He went to England and, after many delays and complications, won both mail and shipbuilding subsidies. Meanwhile Bostonians were up in arms at losing terminal status, but sensibly offered inducements for retaining it, with the result that Cunard was awarded runs from Liverpool to Boston for the larger steamships, and an extra subsidy for the extra distance. Thus began the regime of the man whom Fanny Kemble would call "a sort of proprietor of the Atlantic Ocean."

Steam would rise now to the top, even though the *Great Western* would for many years be the only steamship that had a regular England-to-New York run. But if steam tolled the bell for sail, it beat the drum for businessmen and their freight; and when, for example, fast Cunarders docked at Boston and their goods could be loaded right on to the Boston & Albany trains, the drum beat louder. The flagship of the first Cunard fleet, the *Britannia*, suggests an unusually early-to-rise vessel, what with its staterooms often swept at 5 A.M., and its bar open for business at six. Dickens came on it to America and said of his bunk that "nothing smaller for sleeping was ever made," and that his wife's luggage had as much chance of being squeezed into their cabin as "a giraffe could be persuaded . . . into a flower pot." But soon the *Britannia* and her three sisters were making forty successive crossings in one year, Boston's foreign trade doubled, and had Samuel Cunard accepted Boston's dinner invitations, he would have dined out every night for five years.

The United States had its lone big chance to meet the Cunard competition when in 1847 Edward Knightly Collins, who had grown rich off packets, got a government contract which included mail subsidies, and by 1849 had launched his first two steamships, the *Atlantic* and the *Pacific*. The *Atlantic*, exulting in its steam heat, huge ice room, bathrooms, and barbershop, not to speak of its godawful gorgeousness and its stupendous array of mirrors, had a bad maiden voyage to England but returned in record time (ten days, sixteen hours). The *Pacific*, and then the *Arctic* and the *Baltic*, followed, capturing the luxury trade and for years one or another of them breaking the speed records. Collins's quartet ran way ahead of Cunard's, but it forgot about the hare and the tortoise. For, beyond being a drunken sailor about money, Collins drove his liners at a maniacal speed, and was damned rather than saved when his subsidy was doubled. His recklessness led to the fearful destruction of one of his ships and to the never solved disappearance of another. While he was, soon after, building his masterpiece, the *Adriatic*, the government was slicing his subsidy; the masterpiece had a cold-shouldered maiden voyage and a virtually outcast return one; the government revoked what remained of his subsidy; and the dashing Collins Line passed, a mere footnote, into history.

But though the paddle-wheel Cunarders came and went more confidently than ever, there would be considerable new competition for them and considerable technological progress. Thus a young

Englishman, William Inman, built screw-propelled ships that also had iron hulls; specialized in impoverished emigrants; and inside three years had his line carrying a third of all transatlantic passengers. On the lordly side, there was the *Great Eastern,* famous even now for laying the first Atlantic cable, and fabulous in 1859 for being five times bigger than any other ship afloat: "she looked like a fortified town" and indeed had room for four thousand townspeople. Yet on her maiden voyage she carried only thirty-eight, and for all her resplendent boasts failed to score: she rolled "like a drowsy walrus," pitched horribly, got battered to hell in a violent storm, got gouged and stranded off Montauk. Yet, when dismantled in 1889, she was still the largest ship in the world.

With the launching of the *Oceanic* in 1870 we sniff a more modern breeze and sight the White Star Line. The *Oceanic* would have five sister ships and would look "more like an imperial yacht than a passenger steamer"; indeed, her great and lasting innovation was the grand saloon placed amidships rather than, as it had been since medieval days, "in the high rump of the stern." She would also substitute separate armchairs for the long benches at dining-room tables (where, fearing nausea and the need to make for the deck, people had long fought for the end seats). The *Oceanic* caught on at once and within two years all her sister ships made pleasing debuts. Indeed, stressing speed and comfort, the jolly, cheerful White Star Line outshone all its competitors and made Cunard seem dowdy and dull as it went on stressing safety. But in 1873 the White Star's *Atlantic,* racing full steam ahead, smashed to destruction, with huge loss of life — "the century's worst transatlantic disaster" — while not much later Inman's new *City of Berlin* outsped White Star for the Blue Riband and outdid White Star for swank — white marble bathtubs, purple velvet saloons, and great private suites for families of sixteen or twenty-four.

Meanwhile the Cunard Line was finding that, to meet the competition, it needed more than its boast of never losing a life; and now that its great founder was dead, it turned venturesome and built the *Servia,* the biggest ship since the *Great Eastern* and the first to use electric lights. Yet the *Servia* successfully remained true to type in stressing solid comfort rather than glitter. Cunard did eventually buy a very fast and fancy ship, the *Oregon*, which by way of reproving such folly proceeded to collide and sink; but the Company could still boast of never losing a life.

As the century's fashions, innovations, and opulent living were passed along from land to sea, ocean liners not just carried the rich to holiday destinations, they became a very real part of the holiday. First-class travel was Lucullan at mealtimes and gilt-and-marble at all hours: its pseudo-splendors, to which "size" lent a hand, and on which late-Victorian ostentation left its signature, spared neither expense nor the cultivated passenger's sensibilities. Mixed decorative styles had a ball: Louis XIV stepped out with Early Empire, Arabian trod a measure with Old Dutch; and so many were the new trinkets and gadgets that clearly luxury was the mother of invention.

As the nineteenth century limped into old age, the great era of ocean travel entered its youth, Germany energetically entered its competition, technology, with turbines, 24,000 h.p. engines and the like, frequently called the tune, and shipboard Ritz restaurants snubbed mere first-class cuisine. While joining the international competition, Germany had its own internal one — the fierce rivalry between Hamburg-Amerika and Norddeutscher Lloyd. By the 1890s Hamburg-Amerika carried many more passengers to New York than either Cunard or White Star, while Norddeutscher Lloyd built the *Kaiser Wilhelm der Grosse*, which immediately copped the Blue Riband; gained, within a year, 24 percent of all transatlantic passenger revenue; became the first European liner to have wireless; and boasted an interior which looked like a castle except when it looked like a cathedral.

Hamburg-Amerika, under the brilliant direction of industrialist Albert Ballin, had overtaken Norddeutscher Lloyd, for one reason by pitting twin-screws against single ones. Ballin, moreover, had the Kaiser's ear and became part of a transaction ordained by a more awesome Kaiser, Pierpont Morgan. Ocean traffic achieved for the first time the status of the great dry-land industries when

Morgan first bought up five companies and, soon after, the White Star Line. Then Morgan and his satellites, with Ballin mediating between the two Kaisers, reached an agreement which tied the big German lines to the six others, leaving only a hard-pressed Cunard still at large. Morgan almost got it, but lost out by not offering enough. However, should the British government now not pitch in and save it, Morgan would be in a position to seize it; and it was only after a strenuous bout with pride and patriotism — "Should Britannia or Morgan rule the waves?" — that Britannia gave Cunard the loan and annual subsidy it needed. When its nonetheless vast holdings, the Morgan combine, swimming in watered stock, achieved a Morgan-sized fiasco, eventually sold White Star back to the British, and ultimately faded out.

Rehabilitated in the early 1900s, Cunard produced for the great age of ocean luxury its own masterpieces of speed, size, and stateliness, so much so that for many people in after years the *Aquitania* or the *Mauretania* might well have been named the *Nostalgia*. At its Edwardian pinnacle, the great age had yet its interesting contrasts: the magnificence of its maritime architecture and the mishmash of its art; patrician style and plutocratic swagger; famous names and notorious fortunes. Yet, a little like Talleyrand's pre-French Revolution *douceur de vivre*, the pre-World-War I travel era suggests technology's last civilized stopping place. For in retrospect the glittering ostentation seems tempered by the era's unruffled atmosphere: the suave light-opera waltzing, the smart, white-flanneled promenading, the pleasant small formalities, the unmistakable, unapproachable great ladies, and the salubrious, un-price-tagged salt breeze. Yet this halcyon era was to provide the most memorable of disasters: the hull-gashed *Titanic* and the torpedoed *Lusitania*. The *Titanic* remains one of the greatest sea stories and news stories of all time: from the perfection of the ship and the prominence of its passengers to the clockwork of its first four days' navigation and the minute hand that sealed its doom, it bathes the stark and the spectacular in a kind of symbolism: the *hubris* of its boasting it was unsinkable, the high-handedness of paying no attention to stern warnings, the irony that it was sunk by a ten-second contact with an iceberg. The horrifying fate of the

Lusitania in 1915 had greater consequences, turning a largely neutral America into a strongly anti-German one. After World War I three great interned German liners changed their names and nationality: the *Imperator* became the Cunard *Berengaria*, the *Vaterland* the U.S. *Leviathan*, and the *Bismarck* the White Star *Majestic*. Among the new-built elite liners of the 1920s were the *Bremen*, the *Europa*, and the *Ile de France*: the *Bremen* became a great favorite in its day, and the aristocratic *Ile de France* perhaps the greatest favorite of them all. The crack liners of the twenties could come off better bred than many of their passengers in "first": status outran snobbery, plus fours and silver foxes abounded and, by night, the lamps shone o'er jeweled women and bald men. Old and new money were oil and water, but everybody relished the caviar and champagne; and the young, roughing it down in "third" and often popping up elsewhere, had a glorious jazz-age whirl.

The Crash wrought decided change: the gay mid-ocean frivolities vanished; by 1932 Cunard had an operating loss of $20 million, and by 1934 Cunard and White Star had to consolidate. In two cases the way out was to way outdo, in speed and size, the past: the French Line's 80,000-ton *Normandie* broke all Atlantic records, the Cunard Line's *Queen Mary* had the power of "seven million galley slaves all rowing in unison." The *Mary* was to become the last of the long and deeply loved ships, more so than her sister ship — and the biggest ship of all — the *Elizabeth*. Though many splendid ships — the *France*, the *United States*, the great Italian liners, the *Elizabeth II* — would grace the future, and though all kinds of cruises would flourish, transatlantic travel itself had very little future; interrupted by World War II, it would resume to the drone of planes overhead and be done in by jets. When the record-holding *United States* (three days, ten hours) had to stress food rather than speed, the air had eliminated the ocean. By the late 1960s only one of every twenty-four passengers who went to Europe went by sea; and Mr. Brinnin concludes his book with the sister *Queens* passing each other, in the small hours and for the last time, their captains on the bridge doffing their hats — a farewell that was in every sense a funeral.

What chiefly limits *The Sway of the Grand Saloon* is much

more the ocean's fault than the author's: the preeminence of size and speed tends to give our 150 years a certain sameness, somewhat the effect of a long succession of track meets full of record-smashing broad jumps and hundred-yard dashes. I wish Mr. Brinnin had found room for the attractive small French and Dutch ships of the 1920s and '30s, where speed and size were totally unknown words. Mr. Brinnin has, however, very pleasantly introduced incidents concerning a good many famous writers and highborn and high-powered personages. Unfortunately his history comes too late to include pirates and buccaneers and, unlike the variety and villainy of railroad history, boasts no high-seas brigands like Jesse James or robber barons like Jay Gould, no succession of huge grabs, swindles, double crosses; and displays Commodore Vanderbilt and J. P. Morgan at their most ineffective. The truth is that in transatlantic ocean travel the United States has played a minor role. But just so, from lacking the swoop of the wicked oligarchs, *The Sway of the Grand Saloon* retains its nostalgic lure, and even its tasteless full-fig ostentation seems less "commercial" than the endless full-page advertisements of a more recent mode of travel.

IV

WORSHIPERS OF WORLDLINESS

17

HORACE WALPOLE'S LETTERS

Oscar Wilde said of the English aristocracy that it was the best thing the English had done in the way of fiction. Certainly it has provided not only many characters that the most enterprising novelist would have been delighted to invent; it contains many others that no self-respecting novelist would have dared to. Consider that highborn Victorian lady who woke up one night to feel hands moving back and forth, back and forth, over her bed. Too terrified to scream, she held her breath; the motions ceased at last and, too terrified to move, she presently fell asleep. When she woke it was broad daylight and she discovered that her butler had been walking in his sleep and had laid the table for eight on her bed. Could even Dickens have imagined that? Yet people like that dart in and out of Horace Walpole's letters. The English aristocracy, however, is more than a field for anecdote, as the letters of Horace Walpole are more than a fund of it. During the eighteenth century the aristocracy not only ruled Great Britain; it forged, if it sometimes fettered, taste; it commanded a style; it established an attitude; it constituted a way of life. Despite Wilde, it was not fiction but fact: a great fact; a great force; and in its composure, its skepticism, its arrogant freedoms, its tyrannical forms, it was a supreme embodiment of worldliness. And in Horace Walpole it found not at all a simple mirror: were he only that, however great he might be as a social historian, he would have no place in literature. That he has a very marked place is due to his possessing no

less distinctive a temperament than an eye, is due to a certain
ambivalence of approach in him, which must mock at what delights it and satirize what it succumbs to.

If you are the son of a prime minister, you can become many
things yourself. Indeed, if you share some of your father's genius,
like the younger Pitt, you can become prime minister yourself. If,
on the other hand, you are as elegant as your father was bluff, as
waspishly well bred as your father was carelessly open-handed, you
would best use your place in the world to observe rather than participate. Horace Walpole had the entrée; he had, very early, an
eye; and very early, in Horace Mann at Florence and in a number
of other correspondents, he had an attentive ear. Had all his other
correspondents perished, Horace Mann alone would have given
Walpole a posterity. But most of the other correspondents lived
ample lives, while Walpole himself lived on until eighty — so
that he presents us with a just sufficiently altering England under
many rulers and regimes, and a just sufficiently altering Walpole
during many decades.

A conscious artist, he remains detached in much that he ob-
serves, but he is obsessed with observing. He makes light of things,
but he does *not* make light of the business of making light of
things. He is probably the greatest artist in gossip in English literature, yet that does not really characterize him or constitute a
wholly sound unit of measurement. It would be like calling Pope
no more than an artist in abuse. Walpole has a real place, a real
value, from constituting the voice of his age and class, and yet
very much possessing a voice of his own. To us he seems, as he
essentially was, a notable member of the *ancien régime*; yet in his
own time there was something unaccountably avant-garde about
him too, something of the innovator, who invented his own fop-
peries, who adapted his own fiction from the medieval, who translated his own pleasures from the French. In a dilettante way he
constantly adds something to what he embodies; as ultimately, in
his dilettante way, he subtracts something too. Walpole's own
social world, we can feel sure, treated him as a kind of pet eccentric,
regarded him as a kind of privileged sniffer, and consulted him

with a certain faintly contemptuous deference. As we almost always see something flowering in great worldly societies at the cost of something drying up, so within such a society, so with Horace Walpole, there is all the bloom of the hothouse and almost nothing of the fragrance of the field.

He had the eighteenth-century patrician's horror of being a professional, yet could say with much truth, in his amateur fashion, that "no profession comes amiss to me — from tribune of the people to a habit-maker." We, after two centuries, remember him as a printer, an adventurous house builder, an M.P., an antiquary, a historian, a novelist, a playwright, and above all a letter writer; and in his own age he must have seemed one of the very greatest of collectors — of bon mots preeminently, but also of *objets d'art*. And it was important for his role in life that he should have a retinue of intelligencers, of eavesdroppers, of drawing-room spies; it was not enough that the supreme social historian of his age should be able to go everywhere or meet everyone; he had to have, as it were, an eighteenth-century tape recorder in a corner of every room, at each end of every dinner table. In his own high-styled way he ran a kind of factory of anecdote and gossip and news, with duchesses doing piecework and cabinet ministers tying up parcels and ambassadors acting as delivery boys. But it was all handmade, as durably elegant as Sheraton sideboards or Lamerie silver: it was not just transferred, it was transformed in the end into great letter writing.

The letter writing was no accidental virtue, but an almost predestined medium. Though plainly aimed at posterity, it remained in its own time private, offered to an appreciative few. With the secrets of society never peddled to the outside world, there was no need, for the most part, to dot i's. And in all this the point of view has acted as a preservative. The immense amount of mere information which Walpole's letters provide would make them an incomparable source book, but only that. The cultivated reader does not, however, take up the letters for mere information; having taken them up for pleasure, he puts them down having been in contact with perhaps the greatest letter writer of his century and with cer-

tainly one of its most indelible personalities. A fine thing about the
eighteenth century is how beautifully it mingles a form of tradition
and the individual talent; how one eighteenth-century master of
language after another equally evokes his century and leaves his
own signature:

Proud to catch cold at a Venetian door

— that surely can only be Pope;

Solitude is dangerous to reason without being favorable to virtue;

— that can only be Johnson. And so with Walpole:

The first step toward being in fashion is to lose an eye or a
tooth . . . Not that I complain; it is charming to totter into vogue.

"Totter into vogue": part of Walpole's gift for phrase lies in its
conveying a certain temperament, in its imparting a sense of *town*.
Rather than *rus in urbe* he represents *urbs in rure*; he represents
artifice in nature, the hedge that is at once ornament and boundary.
He stands, in a sense, for the greenhouse, the bandbox, Marie-
Antoinette's dairy. He has some of the quality of the best society
verse, in which great things contract into small with wit and grace.
The universe, with Walpole, suddenly turns into a ballroom, the
Trojan War into a hair-pulling match, murals into miniatures. This
small, myopic purview is one way — perhaps the only way — to
see things steadily and see them whole; nor is this just a polite
fancy. Being a century of consolidation, of putting humanity's
house in order after all the discoveries and upheavals of the seven-
teenth century, the eighteenth century in England, by practicing a
bit of sleight of hand, by blinkering its eyes, by slowing down its
pace, could just frame life into something manageable and precise.
But if all this is myopic, it is not *really* blinkered. If it is toylike and
rococo in many of its effects, it is not entirely frivolous. At least it
enables us to see a *way* of life steadily and to see it whole, while
noting a great host of details. Walpole is in one way as thorough
and exact a realist as Defoe is in another, and along similar lines.

Again, because Walpole fights all the century's wars with tin soldiers, or fills England's Parliaments and administrations with puppets and marionettes, it is not to say he is a bad critic of them, or even a bad reporter. His mock-heroic approach must be allowed for, yet remains an offset to the all-too-heroic approach; and, under the aspect of eternity, it comes closer to the truth. Curiously enough, Horace Walpole's father, with just as disenchanted and worldly a view of things, became the greatest and most useful of English administrators. Sir Robert's administrations were decidedly made up of — or turned into — puppets; and tin soldiers or real ones, he would fight no wars at all. There is a certain irony in the fact that Sir Robert was as excessively philistine as Horace could be exquisite, but there is no real contradiction. Common sense governed the father's life as its twin brother, worldliness, governed the son's. And in both men, in the one by way of experience, in the other of temperament, a certain cynicism predominated.

Take from Horace Walpole what makes him an incomparable storehouse of gathered fact and a superb writer of letters, and he emerges a recurrent type of all cultivated societies, someone who is about equally at home in the social world and the artistic one, and who in the final sense is conceivably not *quite* at home in either. Leaving his genius as letter writer and social chronicler aside — or supposing him to have had only a pleasant knack for either — he stands forth a dilettante diner-out, an elegantly fussy bachelor, a delicately feline observer, dainty about food but greedy about gossip; very vain; a connoisseur of wit, and an even greater connoisseur of social oddities and human blemishes. Walpole carefully examined every ointment in hopes of finding a fly; painstakingly tested all available armor in hopes of discovering chinks; and, I venture to suppose, went constantly to parties not so much to have a good time as to unearth a good story. And yet in all this, he is not to be thought unpleasant; in all this there was less malice involved than sense of métier. As Beau Brummell dressed for future ages, or Lucullus dined, so Walpole, we may say, dined out. But he had his more creditable and laborious pursuits. From his house at Twickenham, from Strawberry Hill, we can almost date the Gothic Revival in English architecture; from his novel, *The Castle of Otranto*, we can almost date the Gothic Revival in English fiction. At Strawberry he set up a printing press whose productions are still collected; and his memoirs of the reign of George III, by quite lacking genius, possess very solid virtues of documentation.

At Strawberry, too — it is one reason why Walpole built it — he remained by himself or with a close friend or two for long periods; he rusticated and read, he received tidings by the incoming post and recast them for the outgoing one. It is necessary to note these withdrawals from society, these communings with the self; and as time passed he was, as he said, to find it pleasantest to pay all his visits by letter. He had that bachelor-breed characteristic, a good deal of delicate sensibility, which, when aroused, could make him exceedingly squeamish and, when ruffled, extremely ill-natured. He had also, of course, a good deal of the snob in him. With his taste for special sauces, his snobbery had a certain peculiar flavor of its own — he was rather snobbish about snobs. More to his credit, he had that eighteenth-century ideal of the aristocratic republican; though when the French Revolution threatened to make a republic of England, it vanished. For working people, even for workers on strike, he had much theoretical sympathy and even genuine feeling; on the other hand, for everything bourgeois, or that to him seemed bourgeois, for everyone with the slightest tradesman touch, or with even good professional standing, he had the utmost scorn and contempt.

Walpole runs true to type, again, in being — as a weathercock of taste — more gilded than dependable; in being often the dupe of fashion, the victim of too great a sensibility, and in having in the end no real qualities of *mind*. It is instructive, of course, to glance down the corridors of criticism and see how many responsive, even distinguished, critics lacked — in terms of their great contemporaries — perception or sympathy or even interest. Dr. Johnson thought *Tristram Shandy* would not last long; Matthew Arnold is scarcely inspiring on Tolstoy, nor Emerson on Dickens. And we ourselves always tend to think that our reversals of previous judgments, and our revivals of discarded favorites, end the matter —

only to find that twenty years later it is all reversed again. But about the dislikes of a Horace Walpole we can establish a kind of pattern: it is not just that his tastes are not sufficiently masculine, or his sympathies sufficiently broad. It is that he forever cultivates a lesser thing at the expense of a greater; that his feeling for Gothic is in essence a love of rococo, that his sense of the visionary is in essence a taste for the lurid, that heaven, for him, is hardly more than a garden and hell hardly more than a grotto. He stands at that eighteenth-century point when solid good sense and quick natural feeling are involved in a trial marriage to produce that very eighteenth-century thing, sensibility; just as he stands at that moment when the classical and the romantic elegantly cohabit to produce that very eighteenth-century thing, the picturesque. Walpole was himself a matchmaker in such alliances, in the course of which he could be something of an offender, too — one who worshiped winking idols and followed wandering lights. Strawberry Hill becomes a footnote in the revival of Gothic by virtue of having been a bit of a travesty on it. And that Walpole could not abide Chaucer or Michelangelo, that he sniffed, or sniped, at half the most enduring of his contemporaries — at Johnson, at Sterne, at Boswell, and eventually at Gibbon — if all this is an object lesson in the vagaries of taste, it is, I think, much more pertinently something else. The Walpole type is in the end not so much wrongheaded as wholly unintellectual, not so much intolerant of what is complex as merely uninterested. There was, however, another — and very eighteenth-century — element involved. It was not so much that a Walpole couldn't get inside a Dr. Johnson's mind as that he couldn't get past his manners; not that he couldn't perceive a Gibbon's greatness as a writer, but that he pounced on his small vanities as a man.

Yet, before we come to what lifts Walpole high above mere type, to what he did with genius and a particular grace, we must note what there was of genuine character and feeling in him, and of a kind, moreover, to charm or touch us. When his cousin General Conway lost, for political reasons, his court and army posts, Walpole sat down immediately and wrote him a notably warm and generous letter putting half his fortune at Conway's disposal. Like so many touchy men, Walpole had a great need of friends and a certain gift for friendship. Sometimes his prickliness proved costly, but in the end he would assume the blame. How eighteenth-century a tone hovers over his years-after comment on the quarrel with Gray: "He loved me, and I did not think he did." Early and late, Gray and Bentley, George Montagu and John Chute, General Conway and Horace Mann were the objects of his interest and affection; as were a succession of great ladies, along with Walpole's nieces, who turned into great ladies; and as finally, late in life, were the Miss Berrys. Meanwhile, amid the rewards and consolations of friendship, there was his career — which is to say, his chronicling the life of his times. We pass with him from Ranelagh to the opera, from Houghton to Knole, now to a masquerade, now to a *fête champêtre*; to Oxford, Cambridge, Paris; to a great ball, a midnight fire, a dinner party where dinner is three times brought to the table, awaiting M.P.'s, and three times removed. We accompany Walpole to an auction of pictures, to Charles James Fox losing a fortune at Brooks's, to a conversation with Hogarth, a social call with Gibbon, a visit with Gray; now there is rioting over Wilkes, and now over Catholics; someone resigns, someone else elopes, someone else expires. It resembles a great one-man news chronicle, with a beruffled columnist flavor. Do we want military comment? — take the surrender at Yorktown:

> Well — there ends another volume of the American war. It looks a little as if the history of it would be all we should have for it, except forty millions of debts, and three other wars that have grown out of it.

Do we want theatrical comment? — Walpole went to Drury Lane, the play was *Cymbeline* and seemed, he says, "as long as if everybody in it went really to Italy in every act, and came back again." Do we want political comment? —

> The Duke of Dorset retires with a pension of £4000 a year, to make room for Lord Gower, that he may make room for Lord Temple. Lord Geo. Sackville forces out Lord Barrington from Secretary

at War, who was going to resign with the rest, for fear Mr. Fox *should* . . . Lord Hardwicke, young disinterested creature, waits till something drops.

Do we relish a little comment on décor? — "Blenheim looks like the palace of an auctioneer who has been chosen King of Poland." Or Walpole will write about nothing at all with that touch that proclaims the born letter writer. "If you was dead," he tells Richard Bentley,

> to be sure you have got somebody to tell me so. If you was alive, to be sure in all this time you would have told me so yourself. If you are not dead, I can tell you who is: don't be alarmed, it's only the Queen-Dowager of Prussia.

Or take this, with its suggestion of Congreve:

> Soh! Madam . . . It is very hard one can't come into your house and commend anything, but you must recollect it and send it after one! I will never dine in your house again; and, when I do, I will like nothing; and when I do, I will commend nothing; and when I do, you shan't *remember* it . . . I wonder you are not ashamed — I wonder you are not ashamed. Do you think there is no such thing as gluttony of the memory?

But, in his letters, there are the great scenes too, the epistolary tapestries — the coronation of George II, the events of the Seven Years War or the Gordon Riots, or the beheading of the Jacobite lords:

> Then came old Balmerino, treading with the air of a general. As soon as he mounted the scaffold, he read the inscription on his coffin, as he did again afterwards. He then surveyed the spectators . . . and pulling out his spectacles, read a treasonable speech . . . He said, if he had not taken the sacrament the day before, he would have knocked down Williamson, the lieutenant of the Tower, for his ill usage of him . . . Then he lay down; but being told he was on the wrong side, vaulted round, and immediately gave the sign by tossing up his arm, as if he were giving the signal for battle.

In all this Walpole characterizes, or castigates, or approximates, the tone of his era or the way of his world.

How much of what we call civilization is needed to sum up what, in the end, is so little of what we call culture. For all this raillery or reporting of Walpole's is done *con amore*; is what, temperamentally, he basks in and thrives on and could scarcely live without. "I could not help reflecting," Walpole wrote once, after meeting a countrified baronet, "that living always in the world makes one as unfit for living out of it, as always living out of it does for living in it." Just so, Walpole had already written when still in his twenties: "I am more convinced every day, that there is not only no knowledge of the world out of a great city, but no decency, no practicable society — I had almost said, not a virtue." These two remarks we may regard as classic statements for the Walpole type, for the worldling temperament. For them, *urban* and *urbane* are one; culture and comfort are one; society is more fundamental than humanity. The ennui of the dinner party is for them a pretended affliction, quite unlike that form of solitary confinement called staying at home. Such worldlings as these may yawn over the essential sameness of things, but what a scent they have for novelty — for the new play, the latest witticism, last night's gaffe, this morning's gossip. They may grumble about *plus ça change*, but what they grumble over is largely what they crave. They want the old reassuring faces quite as much as they enjoy the New Look; for them exists that familiar social paradox — life, to be exhilarating, must shift with the speed and color of a kaleidoscope, yet, where one's own comfort and self-assurance are concerned, it must not shift at all. These eighteenth-century people wanted, indeed, old pictures in new frames; wanted what simultaneously could be called the last word but would not have shocked the last generation.

This love of the bravura, of the bagatelle, of the fashionable frisson, this beginning as the jeunesse dorée, this becoming a petit-maître or a connoisseur — you will have noted that every word describing these things is a foreign word — it is in terms of such tastes and cravings and ambitions that we must adduce superior values to pass judgment. If nothing of what these people did pleases one, one has either an extremely lofty or a peculiarly narrow view of things. Walpole, surely, is an artist who depicts and at length defines what is itself a kind of art of living. Here, figuratively, is all but the best of eighteenth-century music, all but the finest of Gluck or Mozart; and, of eighteenth-century painting, all but the finest of Guardi or Watteau. Here is almost everything that we appreciate in eighteenth-century gardens, and domestic architecture, and elegant décor. In other words, here is that sense of style, at once careless and starched, at once frivolous and elegiac, at once formal and intimate that, if it went into curtsies and bows, and compliments and insults, and picknicking and dancing and duels, went also into the arts, and how men wrote and painted, and said good-bye to life. "I shall be quite content," said Walpole himself, by way of good-bye, "I shall be quite content with a sprig of rosemary thrown after me, when the parson of the parish commits my dust to dust."

And with all this, we, up to a point, should be content as well. Beyond that point, however, there are obviously larger and greater things, and even many things we must deprecate. There is more concern for humanity than society, for life itself than for a way of life. This is not simply a matter of different talents, this is not to reject a Horace Walpole for what he never could have written or been. It is to pass judgment on him for never attempting to write, let us say, a *Way of the World*. No, he preferred writing a *Castle of Otranto* and building a Strawberry Hill. But the truth, perhaps, is that he was not only turned into a dilettante by temperament, he was also forced into it by a certain deficiency of mind. Ideas either bored him, or failed to exist for him, or needed to be simplified or personalized. He was not, in either the deep or the jargon sense of the word, at all intellectual; nor was he of large or porous enough mind to assimilate the really new. For all this worldling's craving for new forms and fashions, for the last word in gardens or smart slang, for a new poetic twist or vocal trill or pictorial vista, for all his passion for new types of décor or duplicity, Walpole, to the genuine new voices of the age, in Rousseau or the Encyclopedists, to the new waves of religion that swept over England, or of feeling that swept over Europe, was quite blind, deaf, insensible, uninterested, alien. He cultivated his garden, indeed, and so beautifully that nowhere else, nowhere untidier, did he really feel at ease, or at home, or himself.

18

THE LADY AND THE LION

"Another book about Byron!" began the Author's Note of one of the best writers on him, Peter Quennell, in 1935. "What need is there for another biography of Byron?" began the preface of the definitive biography by Leslie Marchand in 1957. The comments, if relevant, are yet largely rhetorical, for though the literature on the subject is conspicuously great, its lure is understandably greater, for writers as well as for readers, for the scholarly minded hungering after new material as well as the scandal lovers munching the old. Furthermore, beyond being a spectacular hero, Byron also serves as an important hub, as the central figure of an assemblage of people, many of them themselves subjects of fascination, reprobation, controversy, partisanship, none of them more so — despite the Shelleys and Leigh Hunts, the Lady Caroline Lambs and Lady Oxfords, the Trelawneys and Tom Moores, the Claire Claremonts and Countess Guicciolis, the young chorister at Cambridge, the young attendant in Greece — than the figures who at one time or another were seated at the family dinner table. Not least on them — on Byron's father, mother, sister, wife — might be bestowed the phrase that Matthew Arnold applied to the leading family of classical Greek drama: "What a set!"

If there now appears yet another book having to do with Byron, Peter Gunn has also, in *My Dearest Augusta*, written the first book "wholly devoted" to Byron's at once shadowy and calcium-lighted half-sister. Such a book has its points. To begin with, Byron him-

self, like a surefire stage drama, is always good for some form of
revival. In *My Dearest Augusta*, moreover, though less from giving
Augusta the title role than from narrowing the scene, there is the
opportunity to present the once reverberantly hush-hush family
drama, with all its agitations and repercussions, as a more than
sufficient thing in itself.

The Byrons are, like the Borgias, one of those families as well
known for their taints as for their talents, and the story that Mr.
Gunn has recounted here has its forebodings in a good many of
Augusta's both remote and very recent forebears. Said to have come
to England with the Conqueror, the Byrons, after receiving New-
stead Abbey from Henry VIII, lived generation after generation an
unstinted patrician life involving eccentricity, illegitimacy, inebri-
ety. One of them, dubbed the Wicked Lord, always turned up
punctually at orgies and also killed kinsmen in duels; he made
pistols part of the table setting at dinner, and when alone, had
trained crickets run races over his recumbent body. Byron and
Augusta's grandfather was known as Foulweather Jack; Mad Jack,
their spendthrift, profligate father, married, following a scandalous
affair with her, the wife of a future duke. She died in giving Augusta birth; Mad Jack then married an heiress of the great Scottish
Gordon connection, straightway squandered her fortune, and died,
three years after she gave birth to the poet, in 1791. The wastrel,
fleshly heritage that Byron shared with Augusta droops beside his
maternal one: the royally descended Gordons of Gight were for
hundreds of years brutal and lawless lairds; bandits, marauders, and
murderers; and if their blood generally cooled, it still raged in
Byron's mother and himself.

Augusta, brought up very *comme il faut* among her high-seated
and well-off maternal relations, saw nothing of her four-years-
younger half-brother from his earliest days until she was sixteen.
He, handsome but clubfooted, now sullen, now violent, was often
at daggers drawn with his impoverished, embittered, vituperative
mother — he dreaded, he said, the approach of the holidays at
school more than most boys dreaded going back to it. For Augusta

and her "Baby" Byron, their coming together proved remarkably successful: shy, both of them, they could both be tremendously playful, mocking, high-spirited; and the precocious schoolboy-lord and his socially polished sister, from this great affinity of temperament, were united by great affection. When, however, Byron precociously ran into debt and Augusta violated a confidence in trying to help him, he broke with her for something like two years. Though distressed by this, Augusta was deeply in love with her (and Byron's) first cousin George Leigh — the Byrons, among other things, were forever marrying their cousins. Leigh was a young man with no great expectations, even fewer talents, and expensive sporting tastes; but a rather distinguished father's influence got him made an equerry to the Prince of Wales, with the Prince throwing in the gift of a house, Six Mile Bottom, on the strength of which George and Augusta got married. Byron, it seems, did not even send her his good wishes, but within a year they were again on friendly terms. Soon after, Byron came of age, took his seat in the House of Lords, published his first book of any consequence, *English Bards and Scotch Reviewers*, and set forth, without bidding Augusta good-bye, on a two-year grand tour.

She, meanwhile, was having the first two of her seven children while her "exquisite piece of helplessness" husband was piling up debts. Soon after Byron's return to England in 1811 his mother died, and Augusta's letter of condolence set in motion a lively correspondence. By the next spring Byron, with the publication of *Childe Harold*, had become the London lion of the hour, pelted with attentions, besieged by hostesses, and though he had sent Augusta an affectionately inscribed copy of the book, she "receded into the background." Very much in the foreground was Lady Caroline Lamb, the wife of Queen Victoria's future Lord Melbourne, who with her temper fits and histrionics, her brandishing of scissors and knives and her burning of Byron in effigy, constituted the most volcanic and public of his love affairs. It was not till June, 1813, four years after they had last met, that Augusta and Byron came together during a visit of hers to London. Their similar likes and dislikes, their talent for mimicry, and their love of laughter united them when alone or at parties. When Augusta went back to Six Mile Bottom, Byron followed her there, and then to Cambridgeshire, and early in August she was once more in London. Just when their high spirits boiled up into perhaps the most talked-of incestuous liaison of modern times is not known, but already in August, Byron was dropping incriminating innuendos into his letters. If legally the incest must go forever unproved, in every other way it seems irrefutable, not just from all the reported "confessions" of both parties, but from how constantly Byron alluded to it in his talk, his prose, his poetry. Never were there greater proofs of the creative artist's egoistic need to decant — and pour out — his experiences. "All convulsions," Byron once wrote to Tom Moore, "end with me in rhyme." In prose he wrote to others pretty much as he does here to Augusta herself, that he was "utterly incapable of real love for any other human being — for what could they be to me after *you?*" And soon enough he turned to rhyme:

> *I speak not, I trace not, I breathe not thy name,*
> *There is grief in the sound, there is guilt in the fame . . .*
> *Too brief for our passion, too long for our peace*
> *Were those hours . . . Can their joy or their bitterness cease?*
> *We repent, we abjure, we will break from our chain,*
> *We will part, we will fly to — unite it again!*

As for Byron and Augusta themselves, what might seem their natural emotions are to some degree reversed. We might suppose that, however responsive, Augusta felt hers to be a quite sinful role; or, born of her love for Byron, a partly sacrificial one; but, certainly at the time, she seems to have taken it pretty much in stride. She was in fact an unreflective, morally easygoing woman, one of those who "are often lovable," wrote Byron's grandson long after, but "vague about facts, unconscious of duties, impulsive in conduct." On the other hand Byron, whom we might suppose a nonchalant connoisseur of the more unsanctified lusts, may very well, as Peter Quennell suggests, have responded less to a hedonist temptation than to a Calvinist heritage, been allured (beyond Augusta's attractions) by the very sense of sin; the hellfire which should have appalled him being what actually most appealed.

In April, 1814, Augusta gave birth to a daughter, Medora, whom Byron, by several accounts, claimed as his. That summer he went with Augusta and her children to the seaside, but by now the idea of marriage he had been flirting with had taken firmer shape, and Augusta was indeed urging marriage as "the only chance of redemption for *two* persons." She disapproved, however, of his choice of Annabella Milbanke, an earnest, literal-minded bluestocking whom, even during the engagement, Byron himself had grave doubts about. By then, however, Augusta had turned double advocate in their cause; and though the best man said of the wedding that "never was lover less in haste," it took place on schedule. During the honeymoon Byron had devoted moments, but oftener, when not taunting his bride, he was tormenting her. After the wedding dinner, he asked her "with every appearance of aversion" whether she meant to sleep in the same bed with him; on the wedding night he woke up, encountered the reddish light of a taper, and woke *her* up shouting that he was in hell. Thereafter he ranted and raged, talked of a "terrible secret" and an "abnormal, unforgivable sin," promised Annabella to be unfaithful, and glowingly mapped out their future: "I will live with you, *if I can*, until I have got an heir." Two months later, when what Byron called the "treacle moon" was over, he and Annabella visited Augusta, and new taunts and torments were introduced. After dinner Byron would advise his wife to go to bed, saying, "We don't want *you*, my charmer"; or he would say to her, "Now I have *her*, you will find I can do without *you* — in all ways." Other evenings he would lie on a sofa, having Augusta and Annabella kiss him by turns, and indicate a distinct preference for Augusta. "You know," he said, pointing in the presence of both women to Medora, "that is my child." What with trying to stop Byron and solace his wife, Augusta became exhausted, and Annabella saw that she wanted them to leave.

At about the same time Augusta was appointed a lady-in-waiting to Queen Charlotte, a sort of compensation for George Leigh's having just been sacked by the Prince Regent. On getting to London, Augusta stayed for two months, not in her rooms at St. James's Palace but with the debt-soaked Byrons, who were soon to have bailiffs living in the house. Though Annabella was by now apparently very suspicious of Augusta's relations with Byron, the two women were living on the friendliest and most affectionate terms. Byron, on the other hand, had become so uncontrollable, insulting, and blatantly unfaithful that those about him thought he was going mad. In December, 1815, Annabella gave birth to a daughter, Ada, but this changed nothing; indeed, with Augusta once again in the house matters got worse, and in January, Annabella went with her child on a visit to her parents. She never, as it turned out, saw her husband again.

What ensued, much helped along by Annabella's outraged parents, transformed with growing hostility a kind of desperate change-of-air visit into a legal separation and a roaring scandal. The legal grounds for the separation, however, were not Byron's relations with Augusta but his "brutally indecent conduct and language" to his wife. To be sure, Annabella, though by now convinced of it, could not charge incest for lack of eyewitness evidence — though in view of everything else, one could not be much surprised if there had been. And Annabella did decidedly change her very grateful and affectionate attitude toward Augusta, creating for the future a peculiarly barbed situation. Henceforth Byron, who, tarred with scandal, now sailed for Italy and never saw either woman, or England, again, plays in the story only absentee and epistolary roles, or takes to versified revenges. Thus Annabella was to appear in *Don Juan* as Dona Inez:

> *Inez call'd some druggists and physicians*
> *And tried to prove her loving lord was mad,*
> *But as he had some lucid intermissions*
> *She next decided he was only bad;*
> *Yet when they asked her for her depositions*
> *No sort of explanation could be had.*

Henceforth Annabella, humiliated in love — she had cared tremendously for Byron — became dedicated to a sense of duty. She felt that Augusta, whom she refused to see but continued to write to, should not only repent herself but lead Byron to repentance. For Augusta, blackened by a great mass of insinuations, buried under a mountain of domestic debts, and fearful that the Queen would send her packing, it was imperative to remain in Annabella's good books if she was to keep any place in good society. For Augusta, accordingly, the wages of sin was deference. She kowtowed to Annabella, she consulted her, she dutifully sent Byron a prayer book for his sins, she regularly sent Annabella Byron's letters for her injunctions ("they are absolute love letters," the jealousy-pricked wife declared). In time the two women came together again, and Augusta, according to Annabella, confessed to having slept with Byron before his marriage but not after. The gritty story of the two — Augusta befuddled, hard up, and hypocritically compliant on the sinners' bench; Annabella in the pulpit, rich, rectitudinous, emotionally self-barricaded — dragged on long past Byron's death in 1824, until all communication was broken off. But just before Augusta's death in 1852, an ill-starred, weirdly Victorian meeting was arranged at a hotel, Annabella bringing with her a sanctimonious clergyman; later, and what was even more Victorian, an agitated Annabella besought Augusta's daughter Emily to whisper into her dying mother's ear "two words from me" — "Dearest Augusta."

But Augusta's later life was less soppily Victorian than bedraggedly Byronesque. In particular, Medora was seduced at fourteen and had a child by her sister Georgiana's "worthless" husband (he too a cousin); part of Augusta's idea of setting things to rights was that Medora ought to be "confirmed at Easter." Although Medora refused and went back to the *ménage à trois*, two years later she did break it up and enter a convent, only to discover she had again become pregnant, be turned out, and lead a sordid, panhandling, mad-gypsy existence, filled with rancor toward her mother, till she died at thirty-five. Indeed, except Emily, all Augusta's children proved of little or no account.

Mr. Gunn's is not surprisingly the first book "wholly devoted" to Augusta, since she really cannot qualify as a book-length heroine. The book does, however, by detaching its story from the procession of dramas in Byron's life, give it greater continuity and cohesiveness; it also extends the Augusta-Annabella relationship, as biographies of Byron do not, straight on to the end. Even so, even with Augusta sympathetically spotlighted and stage-managed by Mr. Gunn, she is in every sense the weak sister of the story, a trifle faint and blurred when seen in isolation and quickly upstaged when sharing the limelight. Byron has the best speeches and the worst tantrums, all the bravo'd entrances and blackguard exits; Lady Byron holds all the trump cards — the At Home card, the prayer book, the checkbook — and, far from seeming faint, has the distinctness of India ink. Against such demonic wrongdoing and ramrod virtue, Augusta's floppy emotions, frazzled wits, and amoral disarray much more suggest the untidy than the unhallowed.

Mr. Gunn is too hard on Annabella, but it is not difficult to be. She had every right to feel ill-treated — if glaringly wrong for Byron, she was yet harshly wronged by him — and she had every claim to a rather superior woman's role. What she did in return was less to be implacable or vindictive than simply to muff her role, to strip something so painful of almost all sympathetic appeal. At the time of the separation much, besides Byron's misbehavior, can be said in her behalf: she was very young, her parents were very insistent, and she feared that if Byron's hands were not legally tied, he might gain custody of their child. But early and late, despite his tender moments, she riled and alienated him: his valet, acquainted with all Byron's women, remarked, "I never yet knew a lady that could not manage my Lord *except* my Lady." So flagrantly sinned against, she — and her cause — might have been improved by a little sinning, or at any rate some home-style melodramatics. Instead she turned toploftily moral. She had in addition a gift — unhappily a very priggish gift — of phrase: speaking of the brilliant Holland House parties, she confessed to only a limited taste for "the Varnish of Vice"; and late in life, admonishing Augusta for her treatment of Medora, smote the sinning mother with "I would save you, if it be not too late, from adding the guilt of her death to that of her birth." Taken together, the two women accentuate each other's failings, till Annabella seems made wholly of flint, and Augusta of custard. What most harmed Annabella would today be termed her public image.

Set against Byron's romantic image, Byron's panache, Byron's achievement, she was to fare even worse. During many years she confided her "secret," she presented her case, to a number of people, among them a crusadingly sympathetic Harriet Beecher Stowe. When, after Annabella's death, none of her family came forth to "vindicate" her, Mrs. Stowe eventually took over, publishing an article, based on Annabella's by now slightly blurred confidences, in the September, 1869, *Atlantic Monthly* and the English *Macmillan's Magazine*. It was not well received. Beyond inaccuracies small and large, Mrs. Stowe brought forth, in euphemisms but without a shred of evidence, the matter of incest and proceeded to denounce Byron while all but deifying his wife. To charge with incest, however genteelly, the great poet and romantic hero who had died fighting for Greek independence was to incense a vast horde of readers and make Lady Byron the excoriated viper of a scandal-in-reverse. Which proved greater, her loss of reputation or the *Atlantic*'s of readership, is a nice sum to work out; in any case, of the *Atlantic*'s fifty thousand subscribers in 1869, fifteen thousand straightway contrived a separation of their own.

19

THE GREAT WORLD AND GREVILLE

English history is rich in men — Greville is one of the most notable — who from their writing tables looked out upon English history and turned back to chronicle it. Now in letters and dispatches, now in diaries and journals, they set down the eloquent moments that revivify the past, or the scraps of firsthand knowledge or unfiltered gossip that help illuminate it. Thanks to such letters and diaries and memoirs, we know just how one man, or many men, or all of England felt about a prince's marriage or a nobleman's murder, a naval disaster or a maiden speech. Thanks too, we are informed as to what *actually* happened; or why things so abruptly went wrong; or who was behind it all; or on whom the dread decision really rested; or round whom the storm clouds finally broke. For by virtue of such chroniclers we look not only out the window but also behind the door, we not just hear men speak but intercept their nods and glances, we not just marvel at the calm they maintain or the front they put up, but see them crazed with fury or crumpled in despair.

Such men have been invaluable chroniclers of events from being indefatigable connoisseurs of news. What they could not witness themselves they sought accounts of from people who did. And since to be privy to so much that went on in high places, and often behind closed doors, one usually had to be high-placed oneself, it is no accident that almost all these chroniclers were members of the great world, were influential bishops like Burnet or sinuous peers like Hervey or sons of prime ministers like Walpole or adventurous patricians like Scawen Blunt; or were temporarily courted and cosseted like Swift, or annually country-housed and fed like Creevey. You had to be sure of a place in the sun to learn all that went on in the shade and the darkness; had to know the right people to hear all about the wrong deeds. Yours was often a secondary, a so to speak sedentary role, but it meant getting quick tidings of primary matters: if, so to speak, Rothschild was the first man in England with the news of Waterloo, you were to be first with the news of Rothschild.

In that sense Charles Cavendish Fulke Greville was most splendidly placed. We need only pause over his name to see how much history, poetry, aristocracy it encompassed. His remote ancestor was Sir Philip Sidney's friend and fellow poet Fulke Greville, and his Greville relations were the Earls of Warwick. His mother's father, the Duke of Portland, was twice prime minister and almost the grandest of Whig grandees, who had furthermore married the daughter of one equally grand, the Duke of Devonshire. And when Greville was a child, his grandfather obtained for him the reversion of two very pretty posts — the secretaryship of Jamaica, an island he would never set eyes on, and a clerkship of the Privy Council, a politically neutral place where he sat, throughout four decades, with ranking statesmen and reigning ministers. When a young man, Greville, from his interest in racing, came to manage the stables of the Duke of York who, but for dying betimes, would have succeeded his brother George IV as King of England. It was not during working hours alone, however, that Greville met the richest, the royalest, the most powerful and brilliant people in England. During his leisure hours he had the run of the very best clubs and country houses; and, never marrying, he everlastingly dined out, at dinner tables that might in a pinch have converted themselves into Cabinet meetings. But as one side of him diverged from politics to racing, another turned toward letters and intellect. He had, too, a taste for travel; as a young man he paid a lengthy visit to Italy, on other occasions he went to Ireland and Germany, and a number of times to Paris. His access to political affairs at home was not without consequences: he became well acquainted with successive editors of the London *Times*,* feeding them news and occasional articles and in turn being fed by them plums for his diaries. And he is linked to letters as well as to journalism. His Jamaican sinecure bore a certain fruit through Greville's publishing that minor classic of Jamaican life, Monk Lewis's *Journal of a West India Proprietor*.

But Greville's own Journal is his passport to becoming a great minor classic himself, as one of the very few *indispensable* English memoir writers. He is indispensable because no one writing of English (and at times Continental) history between 1820 and 1860 can possibly ignore him or easily not quote from him; he can be disagreed with and occasionally discredited, but as a "source" he simply cannot be done without. His was indeed a privileged place, and during a period of momentous transition when political designs kept tilting with historical forces. Politics was something Greville didn't just *happen* to chronicle; he made it his life's business. His work is not, like Hervey's, primarily a description of life at court; he did not, like Walpole, excel at turning gossip into an art: Greville's is chiefly a concern with the internal and subterranean life of Parliament, with the life (and death) of administrations. From much else he turned away. "If I . . . chose to insert all the trash of diurnal occurrences," he writes, "the squabbles of the Jockey Club, and things which had better be forgotten . . . I might fill books full in no time, but I can't and won't." In general, he disdained gossip for gossip's sake; and though the result, in general, was to save his *Memoirs* from nastiness and triviality, it robbed them at times of lightness and fizz. Gossip usually had to crystallize into scandal (as with the Lady Flora Hastings *crise*) or shed light on events for Greville to grant it entry; and on those scores it gained fairly frequent entry and proves both salt and leaven to the *Memoirs* as a whole. Gossip of a different kind, *political* gossip, with all that it entailed of prognostication and hear-

---

* The second of them, Henry Reeve, became after Greville's death the editor of his *Memoirs*.

say, is of course the very essence of his Journals. Just as Greville disdained repeating boudoir anecdotes and stable-yard squabbling, he refused to repeat what anyone could come upon in the public press. Indeed his object, with regard to posterity, was to supplement the public press; to jot down things that never got into the papers or were designedly kept out of them. And so, for posthumous publication, he queried and harried and "interviewed" statesmen and M.P.s, Cabinet ministers and diplomats, and their sisters and their cousins and their aunts. What resulted was an immense mass of speculation before the event, of discussion at the time of it, and of interpretation afterwards, much of it confidential and extremely revealing, some of it comically wishful or astigmatic, where fears loom large and come to nothing, or prophecies rumble and come to even less.

All this recording of political measures and talk and tactics concerns, as I have said, so great an age of transition as to constitute a period of transformation. Beginning his Journal in 1814, in a highbred Regency world, Greville wound it up in 1860, in a triumphant bourgeois one. Betweenwhiles, along with the clamorous problems of India and Ireland, there were such great issues at home as Catholic Emancipation, the first Reform Bill, Chartism, the Corn Laws and Free Trade, and the agitation over a second Reform Bill. As for men, the list begins with Castlereagh and Canning, embraces Wellington, Liverpool, Grey, Huskisson, Peel, Palmerston, Melbourne, Lord John Russell, Derby, Clarendon, Sidney Herbert, to conclude with Cobden and Bright, Disraeli and Gladstone. In many instances Greville records the chops and changes, the shifts and soundings, over days, weeks, months, and even years. Almost always he records something not found elsewhere, or a version unlike all others, or a version unlike his own of two days before. With its comments on issues and events, and its comments on other commentators, the whole thing approaches a political round game, a hare-and-hounds of opinion, till the chronicle takes on as many voices as changes of key.

The countless footnotes to history that Greville's *Memoirs* supply have provided thousands of actual footnotes for later historians; this side of the *Memoirs* is priceless source material. All the same, it is the side that has chiefly benefited specialists and later writers. It is not, I think, the side that has most nourished Greville's own readers, who will find more engrossing accounts of the Corn Laws agitation or the Crimean War in other books — in books that *drew on* Greville. For often matters are duller, and far more long-winded, behind the scenes than before the footlights. Greville's endless day-by-day entries on, say, the first Reform Bill are such that no single day seems altogether sufficient. We must in any case distinguish between the Greville who chiefly provides others with information and the Greville who constantly provides us with pleasure. The pleasure he gives is of a front-seat view, or of a backstage glimpse, at just the moment when we shall see and hear something vital yet particularly special, historical yet wonderfully human. And in distinguishing between the two Grevilles, we must glance at what distinguishes the man himself: at what he brought to his opportunities and how, at times, he contrived them; at what manner of man he was along with what kind of aristocrat; how perceptive was his eye along with how patient his ear; and, finally, how well he could write up what he wrote down.

Born in 1794 and dying in 1865, he not unnaturally belonged by temperament to the age he came out of. The new order of things he confronted in middle life created an inner conflict for him and a lag in sympathy. He shares, however, the best patrician impulses of the earlier age — he caught and kept what was most enlightened and humane in the great eighteenth-century tradition. He believed in an unobstreperous progress; he deprecated selfish upper-class abuses; he desired a better life for the poor. Indeed, he was for every reform that would not discommode his own welfare. (This is no cynical sneer but only what he half-admitted himself.) As he got older, he grew more set. He remained a Whig when the Whigs themselves had changed their name to Liberals; and what by then he often found most alarming were not the palpable diseases of society but the projected cures. Yet he was never a real fossil as he was never a fool. He had, for one thing, that perhaps best gift in the old Whig heritage, a certain balance and love of balance, a certain fair-mindedness and effort at fair-mindedness, so that it is toward the irresponsible and the intemperate that he seems most severe, and no less when they are ultra-Tory than ultra-radical. He is as outraged, again, by a Palmerston's high-handed methods as by any socialist's beliefs, and as incensed by royalty's attempts to usurp power as by agitators' to undermine it. He shared the old grandee-Whig dislike of the Royal Family, he had the disdain of the great country houses for the court; and though he had a court connection by way of the Duke of York, that never prevented his calling the Duke's elder brother, George IV, a pig and the worst of kings; or his younger brother, William IV, a clown and quite scandalously unroyal; or his niece, Victoria, far more willful than wise. Small wonder that Queen Victoria exploded over the publication of his *Memoirs*, even though they then extended only to William IV's death, even though they then omitted what would have most made her explode.

But toward royal personages, as toward almost everyone else, he was always fair enough to admit his bias or explain his bile; and in the end he did ample justice to their good points, to George's aristocratic tastes or William's democratic ways, and to what was conscientious and judicious in Victoria and Albert. If no brilliant psychologist of men, or notable critic of arts and societies, he was marvelously conversant with the high life of his times, and sagaciously curious about its methods and motive power. As a privileged worldling, he was seldom taken in by noble assertions and professions in high places, he knew every *cui bono* and *sauve qui peut* of the ambitious and the powerful; and anything he knew was always the starting point for finding out what he didn't. There were, to be sure, people about whom he was constantly shifting ground, some even — like the Duke of Wellington — about whom he conspicuously changed his opinion; and about certain people there were things he never apprehended. But as people lived on, or more particularly as they died off, he wrote solid, cogent, perceptive, remarkably unbiased — or admittedly quite biased — summations of their character and summaries of their careers.

These seem to me, indeed, perhaps the best things he did, and among the best things that anyone has done of that sort. He is, to be sure, no Saint-Simon; he seldom summons people to life with a gesture or a phrase, or makes them completely visible, audible, unique. It is rather the opposite: he is a sovereign writer of obituaries, with just enough sense of occasion not to be waspish or petty, but with not so much as to be muzzled by a *De mortuis*. He not just means to tell the truth, he manages to. But, as against composing epitaphs at people's deaths, he is constantly recounting episodes in their lives, portraying his man as bully or buffoon, as taunting the Lords or taming the Commons. As is hardly surprising, he oftener does better with men he dislikes than with men he admires — partly, of course, because he can be more biting, but partly because they themselves are apt to have more bite. Peel and Palmerston are among his decided successes.

In the end, however, Greville wasn't deeply interested in people as people. He was interested, rather, in people as representative figures — the great landowner, the indomitable Tory, the successful whipper-in; or, again, as quite *un*representative figures, whether celebrities like Wellington or prodigies like Macaulay. And he was most of all interested in men of affairs, in those who pulled the strings or ran the show, who established harmony or fomented uproar, who won votes or delivered them. Greville spent his life in clubs and country houses, yet he gives us little, in the end, that mirrors club or country-house life. To his own way of thinking, he misspent his life on the racecourse, and as so great a *bon vivant* that he was forever laid up with gout. Yet of this side of things we are given hardly a pungent anecdote; what we have instead, and in abundance, is self-depreciatory lament and self-recriminatory confession, all of it only saved from being cant by his saying frankly that it is too late for him to reform; and by no means all of it saved from being comic.

But — to resume — his concern with people rests largely on what they know or think, and even then in terms of current issues and crises. Or of what once were issues and crises, for next to inside news Greville most values illuminating reminiscence. And about such things his curiosity is immense. In his own fashion he was a good deal of a Boswell, which is to say a good deal of a busybody. Again and again we get peeps into how industrious he could be: "I had the curiosity," he says of Lord William Russell's murderer, "to go . . . to Tothill Fields prison to see the man"; adding two days later: "Just after writing the above, I went to the house in Norfolk Street, to look at the premises, and the places where the watch and other things were found hidden." And every so often we find him not just examining the premises, but determinedly stalking his prey: "After looking for him for several mornings in the Park, through which he walks in his way to the Courts, I fell in with Thessinger." And the calls he paid on men whose knowledge he sought cannot always, however well he knew the men themselves, have been welcomed. He was forever asking people to talk, as it were, for posthumous publication. And his deafness, at such times, cannot have been very endearing, while his disposition could at moments be "crosser than any pair of tongs." But if a good deal of a busybody, and as hard to escape from in parks as at clubs, he was almost as often Johnson as Boswell, almost as often sought out for his opinions as he sought others out for theirs. If he contrived to meddle, he was yet very frequently asked to mediate; if he panted after leaks, he neatly patched up differences; and by way of his *Times* connection, was often a very valuable go-between. And finally, the examiner of premises and the stalker of prey was laboring so steadily — and dextrously — at his vocation, that on its own terms and for its own time the result remains unparalleled.

Greville's "serious" interests went, however, far beyond political issues, just as his leisure extended far beyond the racecourse and the social round. He came from a world whose commanding figures were cultivated men who delighted in elegance and wit and not least in ideas; a world of lineage that sufficiently prized intellect to constantly break bread with it. Even as the nineteenth century advanced, men of birth continued to be men of background. Matthew Arnold, looking back to the eighteenth century, was moved to cite — as part of its highbred aura — Lord Granville quoting Homer on his deathbed. But in Arnold's own century Melbourne and Disraeli, prime ministers both, are but the best-known of cultivated men of affairs. Lord Derby, also a prime minister, did a famous translation of Homer; Greville's politico brother-in-law, Lord Ellesmere, did a translation of *Faust*; of Lord Harrowby, who refused to be prime minister, Madame de Staël said that he "knows our literature a little better than we ourselves do." In a society that not only made recondite Latin allusions one was expected to identify, but good Latin puns one was expected to laugh at; a society that still went on a version of the Grand Tour, and still paid its visits to the ranking salons; a society that could hold the table at dinner no less than the House at midnight, Greville — to maintain his place — had to be more than a duke's grandson. He had to be, as he was, well read; and well read in fairly backbreaking writers. His Whiggishness, moreover, made him an habitué of Holland House, with its wheelchair Lord and whip-cracking Lady, where fell the showers of Sydney Smith's wit and rolled the torrents of Macaulay's learning, and where too, along with distinguished foreigners, came Melbourne and Palmerston and the ineffable Brougham of whom Macaulay said, "He half-knows everything." On the Continent too, particularly in Paris, Greville encountered the best brains along with the best blood. Birth he could take for granted; and though, when Reform seemed to stride too fast, or his sinecures were endangered, he might dwindle into an aristocrat, he was never a foolish snob and could berate not just his own class but his own cousins. The Bentincks were "insolent, overbearing worshippers of each other, and inflated with notions of their own consequence and right."

At moments Greville might have displayed a more robust comic sense, though his very indignation over Palmerston or the Royal Family helps double the fun. At moments too we might wish for Macaulay's sense of theatre or Walpole's knack for phrase — yet Greville could aptly enough describe Wellington in old age as a kind of "secular Pope" or Holland House as "the house of all Europe." And Macaulay indulged his gift for theatre at some cost to truth, as Walpole achieved his gift for phrase with some help from malice. One of Greville's greatest virtues is his feeling for truth: even his misstatements were never dishonestly actuated and were, as soon as known, avowed. His own definition of what a Journal should be strikes me as notably sound: "To be good, true and interesting, [it] should be written without the slightest reference to publication, but without any fear of it." And it seems to me that he steadfastly followed his rule and richly fulfilled his aim.

20

THE LETTERS AND LIFE
OF HENRY ADAMS

Henry Adams stands so decidedly in the forefront of American historians and autobiographers that it perhaps needs be stressed that he stands decidedly first among American letter writers. Moreover, it is Adams the letter writer who most vividly reveals Henry Adams the man, the possessor of a particular temperament, the product of a particular society — a society that was in one sense to help create his values, in another, to help make them crumble. The *man* is fairly remote from us in the scholar and the historian, the man is posed very formally for us in the autobiographer and the man of thought; on the other hand, the man comes brilliantly alive in the letter writer, where he is constantly the man of the world. If, again, in his letters he makes us think of another man of the world who was also a great social letter writer — Horace Walpole — it is not least because Henry Adams thought so himself. Not only did Adams find Walpole and his eighteenth-century world congenial and absorbing enough to make a dinner companion of them when he dined alone, but, as a young man, Adams could confess that without hoping to become a Walpole, he would like to think that in aftertimes his letters too might be read and quoted as "a memorial of manners and habits," in his case, "of the time of the great Secession of 1860." And "what surprises me most," Adams remarks of Walpole some ten years later, "is that he

is so extremely like ourselves; he might be a letter writer of today
. . . until," Adams adds, "I trip over a sword!"

Now, clearly, what attracted Adams to Walpole was not the
man himself, for in all sorts of important ways they crucially differed — though more than we might imagine, they could be
strangely alike, or allied. What attracted Adams is the world they
both inhabit, and the worldly events they both chronicle, and the
worldly tone they both display in their chronicling. "If we didn't
know these people," Adams says in 1869 of Walpole's cast of
characters, "then we know some one for all the world like them!
How little the world has changed in a century!"

The fact of the matter, of course, is that the world had changed
tremendously in a century. Things are as far apart as *The Vicar
of Wakefield* and Zola; as early Mozart and late Wagner; as the
sedan chair and the transcontinental railroad; as the reign of the
aristocracy and the rule of the middle class; as thirteen discontented colonies and some thirty-odd United States. The world between 1769 and 1869 had passed through momentous revolutions
— American and French, agrarian and industrial, mechanical and
sociological. Malthus and Darwin had invaded the scene; medicine
and science had transformed it. Most people, looking back a century from 1870, would have an all-too-complacent sense of spectacular distance.

And yet one can quite understand how a Henry Adams might
remark, "How little the world has changed in a century!" For the
great point involved is how little the two men's way of looking at
things — and what they looked at — differed. At bottom Adams's
comment is not one of fact but of attitude, of *nil admirari,* and of
encountering nothing that really could surprise one. But in a far
more literal sense, Adams could feel how little the world he encountered in Walpole's letters differed from the world he looked
out on from his Washington window. For what each man means
by "the world" is almost identical, is the world of politics seen
from the inside and the world of society lived at its very center; is
a world of forms and punctilios that conceal much more than they
show and that make, accordingly, for a great hive of gossip, for

looking through keyholes and feeling for cracks; a world of bland treacheries and bizarre alliances and astounding coalitions, a world with moments of fairyland and more frequent moments of farce; a world, above all, of merciless anecdote and mandarin innuendo, its surface all gloss, its underside all grime.

If I so extensively compare two men who lived an eon and an ocean apart, it is to make the essential point that in Adams's case they really didn't — that he was in temperament very much an eighteenth-century man, that he was most often in his sympathies both aristocratic and English. At least two very important qualities distinguish Adams from a social chronicler of genius like Walpole: Adams had a first-rate mind where Walpole, by any significant standards, had no mind at all; and Adams had generally what Walpole wholly lacked, a masculine outlook. But the very fact that Adams far surpassed so distinguished a dilettante worldling is what lends particular interest to his so often resembling him. The magnificence of Adams's letters *as* letters, as light thrown on a whole age and society, remains in the end their high and absolute merit. But they have an additional value, as an accumulative, unwitting self-portrait of someone not just a great letter writer, but of someone who might have been, and in his letters reveals why he failed to be, a great man.

However different the nineteenth century might otherwise seem, it still offered its letter writers decided eighteenth-century opportunities and rewards. If the eighteenth century's Walpole was the son of a tremendous prime minister, the nineteenth century's Adams was the grandson and great-grandson of Presidents. When young, Adams too had his own form of the classic Grand Tour, to become thereafter a member of a wellborn and well-connected circle, and to move very rarely outside it. He professed, as had Walpole, a high-minded Roman-style republicanism, which with him too was a kind of mist-shrouded ideal, a kind of ultrapatrician illusion. Adams took an eighteenth-century pleasure in the company of clever women who possessed the attributes of great ladies; he took an eighteenth-century interest in the minor forms no less than the monuments of culture — in *objets d'art* no less than paintings, in country houses as well as cathedrals. Adams too, within his own constricted social world, became the friend of party politicians as well as of distinguished statesmen, and became, just so, as shruggingly cynical of what his friends were up to as any worldling under the Georges. In high Horatian eighteenth-century strain Adams professed to live apart from society; yet, with eighteenth-century finesse, he contrived to be intimately, indeed confidentially, in touch with it. All this helped imbue his letters with peculiar, particular, delightful eighteenth-century overtones and effects. He shared one thing further with that supreme era of social letter writers: however much he might disparage whom he was writing about, whomever he was writing to he made every effort to please.

Sometimes this was simply by being playful: he wishes, he says, that he could offer news

> either that I was dead, or born again, or had lost my grandmother, or was left an orphan, or was elected King of Manchuria. On the contrary, nothing has happened. Almost every one *else* has died, as usual, or threatened to die, and whole batches of Kings have been *elected* in Manchuria; but I am sitting here in Washington just as you left me ten years ago.

Adams had that quality among great letter writers not only of making something of nothing, but of almost wishing for nothing to show what could be made of it. And he had always a certain sophisticated fancifulness, or whimsicality of phrase. He describes the great Temple of Aesculapius as a sort of "Greek Carlsbad." He writes from his summer home in Massachusetts that "the mosquitoes are so thick that on hot, sunny days they cast an agreeable flickering shade." He speaks of a coming marriage (echoing Lady Mary Montagu) as "meant for wear rather than show." He had also the gift of creating something wild and amusing out of what in itself might be grisly:

> Old Levi P. Morton, who is hovering in or about his nineties, was in the Bernay R.R. accident the other day, and crawled out

from the dead bodies through an upper window; got a cab nearby, drove two hours, caught another train, and got to Paris at 11 o'clock, while his daughters were turning over all the corpses on the field to find him.

And Adams adds by way of postscript:

> The man knew better than to be killed and leave his daughters ten millions apiece. No King Lear about *him!*

In no very different style, Adams describes his fiancée to one of his closest English friends:

> Imprimis, and to begin with, the young woman calls herself Marian Hooper and belongs to a sort of clan, as all Bostonians do. . . . She is 28 years old. She knows her own mind uncommon well. She does not talk *very* American. Her manners are quiet. She reads German — also Latin — also, I fear, a little Greek, but *very* little. She talks garrulously, but on the whole pretty sensibly. She is very open to instruction. *We* shall improve her. She dresses badly. She decidedly has humor and will appreciate *our* wit. She has enough money to be quite independent. She rules me as only American women rule men, and I cower before her.

A little more acidly, indeed with a touch of the snobbish dowager, Adams describes his first White House call on President and Mrs. Grant:

> At last Mrs. Grant strolled in. She squints like an isosceles triangle but is not much more vulgar than some duchesses. Her sense of dignity did not allow her to talk to me, but occasionally she condescended to throw me a constrained remark. . . . I flattered myself that it was I who showed them how they ought to behave. One feels such an irresistible desire . . . to tell this kind of individual to put themselves at their ease and talk just as though they were at home.

Twenty-five years pass, and Adams goes again to the White House, this time to dine with the socially far more acceptable Theodore Roosevelts: they, indeed, are his good friends.

We waited twenty minutes in the hideous red drawing room before Theodore and Edith came down, and we went into dinner immediately with as much chaff and informality as though Theodore
were still a civil service commissioner. . . . Edith was very bright
and gay, but as usual Theodore absorbed the conversation, and if
he *tried* me ten years ago, he crushes me now. To say that I had
enjoyed it would be, to you, a gratuitous piece of deceit. The dinner
was indifferent, very badly served, and, for some reason, nothing to
drink but a glass of sherry and some apollinaris.

It is almost possible to say of Adams, here, that whether or not he
enjoyed the dinner party is beside the point. What is clear is that
he immensely enjoyed *not* enjoying it. After all, to the social
chronicler, the more gaffes and solecisms and contretemps on any
occasion, the better; to a sort of drama critic of the social scene, the
staging, the lighting, the performances of the actors make all the
brighter copy for not being quite right in themselves.

On the public and political side also, even on the side of large
events, Adams can be lightly mocking, can mingle froth with bile.
Though himself keeping, with a certain insistent disdain, outside
the arena, he is decidedly pleased with how well he knows all the
gladiators, and no less pleased with having a commanding view of
the show, which he describes with a kind of cynical gusto.

Mr. J. P. Morgan gets practically the whole loan, and the small
thieves are furious. My view . . . is always to encourage the big
thieves and to force the pace. Let's get there quick! I'm for Morgan, McKinley and the Trusts. They will bring us to ruin quicker
than we could do ourselves.

Like Horace Walpole again, Adams is very wishful of ruin — only
to show considerable fright when anything real starts threatening
him.

But it is time to move on from the eighteenth-century worldling
in Adams to the nineteenth-century man of intellect and the
child of a far more complex age. The nature of the great world may

have changed rather little in a century; but something disenchanting — and democratizing — had intervened. Talleyrand's pre–French Revolution *douceur de vivre,* where it had not vanished, had survived precariously; and where men a century before, with their modishly skeptical minds, were not too often confronted with taxing and vexing new forces and hypotheses, Adams, with his own inquiring nature, was now constantly *assaulted* by them. Where men a century before basked in that short sunny interregnum between the reign of superstition and the reign of smoke, Adams came to manhood in a century whose geology could be as menacing as its munitions, and whose new ways of writing history seemed almost as radical as its new ways of making it. There was also a side of Henry Adams that not just responded to this but went forth to meet it. The ambivalences, the contrarieties, the ironies of life held and fascinated him; and where a mere accomplished worldling could see only the masks and false faces of politics and society, Adams saw into the true, or at any rate trenchant, forces behind them.

The lights of Adams's searching curiosity play all over the letters from the far parts of the world where he went to satisfy it, where, often with considerable discomfort, he went poking and rambling about, and looked into corners and questioned. To grasp their range, we must read the letters from Japan or from Samoa as a whole; short quotations can only garble general reactions, and even pith must be sacrificed, here, to picturesqueness. But let us linger for a moment with Adams in Samoa:

> Another generation will leave behind . . . the finest part of the old Samoan world. The young chiefs are inferior to the old ones. Gunpowder and missionaries have destroyed the life of the nobles. In former times . . . chiefs fought only with chiefs. The idea of being killed by a common man was sacrilege. The introduction of fire-arms has changed all this, and now, as one of the chiefs said with a voice of horror, any hunchback, behind a tree, can kill the greatest chief in Samoa.

He calls the Samoans "the least imaginative people I ever met":

They are pure Greek fauns. Their intellectual existence is made
up of concrete facts. As LaFarge says, they have no thoughts. They
are not in the least voluptuous; they have no longings and very
brief passions; they live a matter-of-fact existence that would scare a
New England spinster. Even their dances — proper or improper —
always represent facts. . . . Old Samasoni, the American pilot here
for many years . . . tells us that the worst dance he ever saw here
was a literal reproduction of the marriage ceremony, and that the
man went through the entire form, which is long and highly peculiar, and ended with the consummation — openly before the
whole village, delighted with the fun — but that neither actors nor
spectators showed a sign of emotion or passion, but went through
it as though it had been a cricket match.

In his earlier days Adams had brought to his letters, as to so
much else, the sense of political and social curiosity, of intellectual
and moral inquiry, that bespeaks the dedicated student of the
world at large rather than the cosmopolitan spectator of a world
of capitals. To the austere, republican, crusading family strain, the
young Henry added a touch of what is good and enriching in
Hamlet. And yet, as the letters — which are the truest index to the
personal life — reveal, there came as time passed, there came increasingly, a touch of what was bad and debilitating in Hamlet,
and hardly anything at all of the old true Adams strain. There
was in Henry Adams on his mother's side — as he was swift to
point out at the very beginning of the *Education* — the Boston
rich mercantile strain, what he called the State Street side. If the
Adamses had put at birth a sword, or a torch, or the tablets of the
law in Henry's hands, the Brookses had put in his mouth a gold
spoon. He spent much of his life pretending to gag on the spoon,
as on so much else; but in truth he was not to suffer from gagging
on it, he was to suffer from being unable to do without it. It was
the golden apple, the apple of *inner* discord, in his life. In terms
of intellectual distinction, in terms of Henry Adams the serious
and great historian, the paternal strain was to prevail. But with
the *man* it did not; with Henry Adams the man, it was the State

Street side, in the sensitive and cultivated forms it had the means
to create, that would predominate.

The tragedy of Henry Adams's marriage — his wife's suicide
when he was forty-seven and at the height of his intellectual career — helps account, perhaps, for the character of his later life,
for what Paul Elmer More called his "sentimental nihilism"; for
what we might call — while saying nothing much different — his
half-rueful, half-malicious pleasure in watching the best-laid plans,
or the world itself, go smash. The great austere Adams tradition
— which he had at the outset cherished, partly because it was a fine
tradition and partly because it was a family product — had lost its
hold on the nation; but in any vital sense it had also lost its hold
on Henry himself. We have no right to demand a militant nature
of someone with a speculative mind. Yet, however much Adams
may have been deterred from the life of the arena by temperament, surely he was drawn *toward* it, for a time, by a consciousness
of his Adams heritage and by an ambition all his own. But something — family pride of a sort, and the very background of family
Presidents — made any rough-and-tumble seeking out of high
office extremely repugnant. Clearly Adams tended to see himself
as an heir apparent; the possessor of the gold spoon expected his
political career to be served up to him on a silver platter. But the
rough-and-tumble political world was not so deferential or oblig-
ing; denied the rewards of office, Henry Adams never, in any crusading sense, endured the rigors of opposition. His were, at first,
privately acidulous avowals, and then disgruntled dissents, and
eventually mere cynical rejections. The world's senates and the
world's stock exchanges, Adams muttered, were dominated by
rascals; and what could any gentleman or any wise man do but sit
back and sniff and shudder? Despite the cultivated voice of Boston
and Henry Adams, we are rather close at times to the tone and
temper of Baltimore and Henry Mencken. They apply to people
the same kind of facetiously derisive epithets; they even inveigh
against the same liberal and labor causes. John Adams and John
Quincy Adams, surveying the triumph of vulgar materialistic
democratic forces, would, in their way, have shuddered as did

Henry Adams in his; but might they not have shuddered a little, too, at what Henry was doing, or not doing, and at what he winked as well as shuddered at?

If Henry Adams was Hamlet in that he lacked the resolution to help avenge the murder of his grandfather's and his great-grandfather's dreams; if he was Hamlet in that he, in the *Education*, like the Prince of Denmark in his soliloquies, had a fine gift for dramatizing himself; if he was Hamlet in possessing a reflective and humorous nature veined with sensibility and streaked with cruelty and disgust, and masculine in its thinking and feminine in its emotions — if he was Hamlet in all these things, he was Hamlet in one thing more: in relishing his place in life, and the privileged, princely atmosphere of courts. Adams might be the retired scholar, but on how high and high-handed a level of retirement: it was not merely as a scholar that he seldom went out in Washington but had everybody come to him; it was as a personage, almost a potentate. That he saw no one in Washington is of course a ridiculous myth: he saw whomever he wanted to, and on his own terms. And elsewhere, any such contention would come close to nonsense; year after year Henry Adams crossed to Europe on luxury liners and for months on end moved about Europe at least as much prince as Hamlet — in a succession of splendid hotels and restaurants and country houses, and in an atmosphere not always so conspicuous for seriousness of thought or loftiness of purpose as for sumptuousness of living and haughtiness of tone; an atmosphere, no doubt, of cultivation and elegance, but also of the great world as it had come to be, and of the new worldlings who had come forth to be part of it.

There was a savor of the English gentry about it, a certain smack of established Boston, but these sureties of aristocratic or republican breeding went hand in hand with the high-mucky-mucks and panjandrums of the Republican party in the age of Mark Hanna, with the enlightened tone of Pennsylvania's ruthless political boss, Senator Cameron. A great many of Adams's companions were very rich. Henry White was to marry a Vanderbilt, John Hay had married a fortune, and his daughter now married a Whitney; and Adams, thanks to his quite handsome inheritance, could always hold up his end. To be sure, even when in 1900 a million-dollar fortune yielded him more than $50,000 a year (perhaps $150,000 in our money), Adams "humorously complained." He had, moreover, as Ernest Samuels tells us in his splendid biography, "an expert knowledge of stocks and bonds." On this head, all the sniffs at vulgar moneymaking from somebody whose money had been made *for* him, and not really very far back, by a merchant grandfather, turn a little tiresome. And in view of his annual London and Paris visits, there is something not just tiresome but a little fraudulent about his remarking — to quote just one of many examples — that "of all parts of the world I know, the rottenest are Paris and London."

It is not that, in all this, one would cut Adams off from the cosmopolitan life and the international scene that he was heir to; but that this cut *him* off from so much else. The drawback to all highbred sensibility is its tendency toward the snobbish and squeamish; the drawback to all traditionary forms and values is their tendency toward petrifaction. At his best Adams was a great individual, and in the letters there is something notably individualizing, too. But more and more in the letters, we begin to encounter, for all their sharp comments and vivid phrases, certain small prejudices and fixed postures; the *tones* of dissent that cloak the gestures of acquiescence, the air of criticism that would diminish the refusal to act. A distinguished intellectual is not to be summarily condemned because so many of his best friends are millionaire pillars of the Republican party during one of its most dubious eras. But it can't help making us wonder how many real artists and intellectuals who lacked social credentials were part of Adams's circle, were the people he saw and not simply people he wrote to. It can't help making us ask how much the worldling Brahmin in him was stopped by surfaces and appearances from appreciating what had decided value and depth. The two American writers whom Adams saw in later years are surely those we might have supposed he did: Henry James and Edith Wharton. This is unexceptionable; but what of other writers? His very first comment on Kipling has nothing to do with his merits as a writer or a man: "I imagine Kipling," Adams wrote to Mrs. Cameron, "to be rather a bohemian and wanderer of the second or third social order." His superbly described meetings with a Robert Louis Stevenson who looked, said Adams, "like an insane stork," acknowledge Stevenson's kindness, but they harp on the messiness of his Samoan ménage, on what Adams calls its "dirt and discomfort." John Jay Chapman was for Adams only "the most ordinary, conventional, simple-minded of cranks," a comment that squares nicely with Adams's brother-in-law assessing Chapman as "just his grand-mother and nothing more." A further drawback to being part of a tight gilded circle is that, with something like the Dreyfus case, Adams becomes an anti-Dreyfusard; moreover, for being pro-Drey-fus, the great scholar Gabriel Monod puts himself beyond the pale and is dubbed by Adams "my idiot friend." And when in 1899 Dreyfus was sent back to France for retrial, Adams writes: "To my regret they have brought Dreifuss [sic] home, and ceased to talk about him, which makes life dull. I hope they soon begin to bait somebody else, to make it lively again." Even accepted as banter, this sounds nasty. In terms, again, of literary taste, Mal-larmé and Verlaine get short shrift; in terms of paintings, Adams could write in 1895, when the Impressionists were still fairly easy to come by, that the Paris dealers "offer no good pictures."

Obviously, a man's personal merits and shortcomings are one thing, and his values as an artist or thinker another. Balzac was not the less truthful delineator of the great world because of his ardent royalism, or Jane Austen less truthful for her personal provincial snobberies, or Proust for a snobbishness almost pathological. An insistence on telling the truth, a compulsive artistic probity, went into all such writers' work. But it seems to me that, over the years, something comparably vital went out of Henry Adams's responses to the life about him. The *History* remains a great monument; both the *Education* and the *Mont-Saint-Michel* have distinction and importance. But the truth is, and the letters are our guide to it, that in the end Henry Adams failed of a certain sense of con-temporary responsibility. Consider his habit, in his letters, of disparaging the powers that be — the cynical tone, the *Schadenfreude* that discolors the criticism, the readiness to blame everything on democratic vulgarians or "Jew bankers" (the anti-Semitism was so intense and rabble-like that when stocks went down, Mr. Samuels tells us, Adams "eagerly gorged himself on the filth of the anti-Semite press"). Such disparagement comes to sound like a glib, mindless justification of his own passivity and withdrawal. Cynicism is always a moral evasion, an inward malaise. In terms of Adams's *personal* emotions, of lostness and perhaps inner deadness and unfulfillment, much that could be ascribed to his wife's death or his frustrating love for Mrs. Cameron can be by so much forgiven. But on that score there is no excusing the callous, irresponsible shoulder shrugs about the public life of the day or the growls that are all too often whines. All this becomes habitual, mechanical — a fixed attitude in Adams, as John Hay described it to Henry Cabot Lodge, of "Whatever is, is wrong." And Hay wrote to Adams himself, in that jocular tone wherewith we maneuver to tell our friends the truth, that his chronic complaints were "the sentiments of a scholar and a gentleman who has had a better time all his life than he deserved, and now whines because it is over." This indeed, and only the more in coming from an intimate friend, is a summary judgment.

The *Education*, unlike the letters, is pretty much a full-dress performance, a careful, skillful, resourceful — and in places rather artful — apologia; a document of disillusionment, a confession of failure. It remains an extremely impressive indictment of the more and more corrupt, and corrupting, forces in the public life in which Adams came to manhood and first sought and later refused to do battle. He had, I think, the right to refuse; with his endowments as a man of thought, it might even have been wrong to become a man of action. But he fought hardly more with the pen than the sword. The mass of cynically disgruntled private letters is surely no offset to the fine public responses to current issues which simply never got written; while, as a kind of monumental abdication speech, the *Education* so laces the sense of futility with a sense of self-pity, so elevates Adams's failure as to suggest something sordid about success, that we may wonder whether he was abdicating the throne of duty from never having occupied the throne of power.

Yet, beyond all their other merits, the letters of Henry Adams constitute an outstanding document of worldliness, revealing the defeat, by a too acute social sense and a too rarefied sensibility, of a final human largeness of spirit. If all this in the great letter writer as worldling induces a final comparison with Horace Walpole, it is to make the point that Walpole found perfect fulfillment in the role. His particular era, his special niche, his temperament and talent — indeed, his decided limitations — blend into something single and whole, never at the expense of anything greater. Walpole was saved a thinker's perturbations; for him, the darker side of things stopped with Gothic dungeons and country-house calamities. In a different way, another eighteenth-century figure with whom Adams was at certain points allied — I mean Gibbon — perfectly fulfilled himself also. Gibbon's reputation, much like Adams's, rests on a voluminous great work of history and on an autobiography. And Gibbon's autobiography is something of a full-dress performance too, and perhaps on one score more acceptable: for being as self-congratulatory about success as is Adams's for being so self-pitying — and, for that matter, self-congratulatory — about failure. What is more important, the scholar in Gibbon had the upper hand over the worldling; whatever his dips and darts into society, Gibbon led a life of supremely unruffled dedication.

Adams, despite superb achievements, can hardly be thought to have fulfilled himself, or even to have altogether nobly failed. I think his failure was on more vulnerable grounds, and from less inevitable causes, and after less determined struggle, than he supposed. It represented a kind of moral valetudinarianism. In the end, what proved harmful to Adams was not despairingly drawing the blinds, but so often peeping gleefully out the window at degrading sights, only to chuckle and turn away. Some of the trouble too must have sprung from his seignorial spurning of favor and acclaim, from his feeling that he was beyond ambition and above contrivance, from such things as making a rather showy ritual of anonymity, with his books to begin with and then with his being buried "without an inscription" — while sharing the most famous cemetery memorial in the United States! About it all there persists a sense of being a kind of law unto oneself, a sacred cow at very luxuriant pasture.

For the whole man, the soundest comparison is perhaps with Matthew Arnold. Arnold had, Adams himself remarked, "the most honest mind I have ever met"; it was a mind, moreover, much concerned with the same cultural, social, political problems as was Adams's own. In moral inheritance, too, Dr. Arnold's son might boast something as sober as could the grandson of John Quincy Adams. And all his life Arnold, like Adams, moved in a world of society and politics, of scholars and public men, and often among the cosmopolitan and wellborn. Nor did tragic death spare Arnold either, who saw son after son taken from him. But, as I have said elsewhere, there was one vital difference between the two men: Arnold had always a living to make. With Arnold, indeed, a *lack* of leisure offers as good a reason for peevishness as any that Adams might put forth. But it was certainly not the pack on his back that made Arnold the finer man; it was that his nature was fed by deeper and purer springs. In Arnold, as in Dr. Johnson, worldliness was always tributary to humanism. And Arnold was not only, like Adams, responsive to the currents of culture, he was roused by them; he again and again spoke out.

Yet, if what is largely absent from Adams's other writings is all too dominant in his letters, it would be quite wrong to put a final emphasis on the letters for what they "reveal." Rather, it is in every way right to conclude with the greatness of the letters as a thing in itself, untouched by the faults in the letter writer. Furthermore, the man of the world is, even late in life, very often absent, replaced by the scholar, the traveler, the thinker, the affectionate uncle or friend. And if the man of the world *is* oftener present, or constantly dancing in and out of the text, or very much its master of ceremonies, he carries us with marvelous verve from country house to country house, from capital to capital, even from crisis to crisis, serving up, with *sauce diable,* what will one day be history; portraying at every season, with its attendant colors and lights, the much changing, never changing way of the world. Doubtless what the letters reveal about Adams is part of the price paid for what they are; but what they are, as I said at the outset, is the best thing of their kind in American literature.

21

DIARY OF A U-MAN

Sir Harold Nicolson has been a small particular adornment of his age, thanks not least to his chameleon way of adorning it. Because of his versatility, he has been a writer whom a dozen sorts of reader could come to know and appreciate. Certainly the reader of belles lettres knows his biographies — of Byron, Tennyson, Swinburne, Verlaine, Sainte-Beuve, Benjamin Constant — and his literary criticism. But the far-from-literary English reader would have encountered Sir Harold too, as a mass-circulation newspaper columnist and a participant on the BBC. The student of cultural history will be aware of *The Age of Reason*. The American businessman may remember Sir Harold's life of Dwight Morrow; the English patriot, his official biography of George V. A student of England's foreign relations would know Sir Harold's life of his diplomatist father, Lord Carnock, or his book on Lord Curzon. For the inquirer into diplomatic niceties there is that distillation of Sir Harold's own Foreign Office years and experience, the informative handbook called *Diplomacy*. The connoisseur of minor literary delights will have cherished *Some People* as a kind of companion volume to Max Beerbohm's *Seven Men*. Even the specialist in gardens will know of Sir Harold by way of his marriage to V. Sackville-West; as, thanks to his inner-circling of society, will the specialist in gossip. From its very beginnings — Sir Harold was born in 1886 in Tehran — his life has been multifaceted, polylingual, cosmopolitan, and at the same time monumentally English, ineradicably upper class.

Accordingly, the publication of the first volume, extending from 1930 to 1939, of Sir Harold's *Diaries and Letters* is the record of an often intimately placed observer, is a kind of tour, during an eventfully unsettled era, of various hives and capitals of political, social, cultural activity. Opening with Nicolson's leaving the Foreign Office to work on the *Evening Standard*, it concludes with England's declaration of war against Hitler. Nicolson — he became Sir Harold in 1953 — was never to find anything less to his liking than his year-and-a-half stretch as a newspaper columnist. He resigned, having joined Oswald Mosley's prefascist New Party and become editor of its political organ, *Action* — only for Mosley to swerve toward fascism, the paper to fold, the party expire, and Nicolson break politically with its leader. Sir Harold's wife had thought it all insane from the outset; and quite fruitless, certainly, were Sir Harold's efforts to divert Mosley from fascism, even on the last-ditch ground of its being altogether unsuited to a nation lacking a military tradition and possessing a sense of humor. Sir Harold's prophecies about Nazism were hardly more successful: by 1932 he thought that Hitler had "missed the boat."

For the next four years, until Sir Harold won a National Labour party seat in Parliament, he led a rather loose-endish, wideranging life. In these earlier years there is much about the Nicolsons buying and turning Sissinghurst, an old Kentish castle already in ruins in the eighteenth century, into a habitable home, which Miss Sackville-West was to endow in time with one of the finest gardens in England. There are, again, the books Sir Harold wrote in the early thirties, among them a novel called *Public Faces*, in which he prophesied, by name and function, the atomic bomb. There are trips abroad on one mission or another, and a first trip for both Nicolsons to America on a double lecture tour; there are later American trips, and there are a great many social occasions, literary encounters, and London sidelights. During these years the *Diaries* is lavish with anecdote.

Thus, on the social side, at a Cliveden weekend: "In order to enliven the party, Lady Astor dons a Victorian hat and a pair of false teeth. It does not enliven the party." On the literary side, A. E. Houseman hated questions about Shropshire, having from

his sketchy knowledge of it pulled several topographical boners in
A *Shropshire Lad*. Or there is the Duchess of Marlborough on
Proust: "His snobbishness was just snobbishness — he would repeat names to himself succulently." When she said she thought
the Duke of Northumberland had a lovely name, Proust "grew
very excited . . . got up, flung the door open and yelled 'Madame
la Duchesse de Northumberland.' This brought on a fit of cough-
ing." D. H. Lawrence, Frieda Lawrence told Sir Harold, said to
her, "If people really knew what you are like, they would strangle
you." "Did he say that," Sir Harold asked, "angrily?" "No," she
answered, "— very quietly, after several moments of deep thought."
Sir Harold had more than one meeting with James Joyce. At a
lunch in his honor, Joyce enters "aloof and blind. . . . My first
impression is of a slightly bearded spinster." At lunch, "I say to
Joyce, hoping to draw him into conversation, 'Are you interested in
murders?' 'Not,' he answers, with the gesture of a governess shut-
ting the piano, 'not in the very least.' " " 'Are you interested,' asks
Desmond MacCarthy a little later, in [Sir Richard] Burton?' 'Not,'
answers Joyce, 'in the very least.' " At a subsequent meeting in
Munich, Joyce reported that someone had taken *Ulysses*, hidden
inside a prayer book, to the Vatican, so that it was blessed by the
Pope. (Joyce pronounced *Ulysses* "Oolissays.")

The Nicolsons' American tour — they visited fifty-three cities,
spending sixty-three nights on trains — included joint appearances,
when they sat on a stage discussing before large audiences
"Changes in English Social Life," "What We Think About Marriage," and "How to Bring Up Children"; they were the lions,
says their son Nigel Nicolson, the able editor of this book, "of the
American lecture-circus." Socially they found the experience very
trying — "the intelligentsia of Springfield, Massachusetts," let
conversation languish, and a Toledo lady remarked that when she
first saw the Grand Canyon, she said, "My, if only Beethoven
could have seen this!" There were compensations to the trip, however. The Grand Canyon was one: Miss Sackville-West, wrote
her husband, "is very much impressed. So am I." Alice Longworth

was another: she "had a sense of background." Mount Vernon was
a third: its ceilings and furniture indicated "a high level of culture
and taste." More endurable were Nicolson's later trips to America
when, at Mrs. Dwight Morrow's invitation, he undertook to write
her husband's life. His being her houseguest coincided with
Hauptmann's arrest and trial, and Sir Harold saw a good deal of
the Lindberghs. At the breakfast table Lindbergh never once
glanced at the papers where he was front-page news. At the height
of his celebrity after flying the Atlantic, Lindbergh got 52,000
telegrams on one day, 63,000 on the next; at the height of the
kidnaping excitement, there were 100,000 letters a day. Anne
Lindbergh told Sir Harold that when she and her husband, bearing one of the most famous names in the world, dined with the
Hoovers at the White House, Mrs. Hoover all through the evening
called them Mr. and Mrs. Lindgrün. What, wondered Nicolson,
"would Freud have said to that?" As for the biography of Dwight
Morrow — who is described in the *Diaries* as having "the mind of
a super-criminal and the character of a saint" — before Sir Harold
was through, the House of Morgan, with whom Morrow had been
connected, created difficulties. Sir Harold, it appeared, showed
them too little awe and reverence. He agreed to make some
changes, so that "the result is soft and flabby." But he felt that
Morrow himself came through, and "I am not really discontented
with the book."

When Sir Harold entered Parliament late in 1935, a political
tension already ominous and formidable during the earlier years
of the *Diaries* was about to become visible in headlines which
are part of history — the Rhineland, Spain, *Anschluss*, Munich,
the invasion of Czechoslovakia, the Soviet-Nazi pact, and then
Poland and war. In England, besides Mrs. Simpson and the King's
abdication, there was an atmosphere of delay, of indecisiveness,
of the ostrich and the unicorn. The *Diaries* abound in political
weather reports. *March 10, 1936:* "Long talk with Ramsay Mac-
Donald. . . . The country will not stand for anything that makes
for war. On all sides one hears sympathy for Germany." *A week
later:* "I found all the lobbies and corridors [of the House] buzzing

with people getting signatures to . . . resolutions, the first to the effect that nothing would make us go to war, the second to the effect that nothing would induce us to break our word." *March 29, 1938:* No administration [says Malcolm MacDonald] "could possibly risk a war when our anti-aircraft defenses are in so farcical a condition. . . . It would mean the massacre of women and children in the Streets of London." *June 30, 1938:* Unity Mitford [a cousin of hers reports] "wants the Jews to be made to eat grass." *September 20, 1938:* The London *Times,* with its wonted magisterial calm, appraises the sellout of the Czechs: "The general character of the terms submitted to the Czechoslovak Government could not, in the nature of things, be expected to make a strong *prima facie* appeal to them." By now Nicolson was vocally against appeasement: he, Winston Churchill, Anthony Eden (who had resigned from the Cabinet), and Duff Cooper were the only government M.P.s who "did not cheer Neville Chamberlain" when he went off to, and came back from, Munich.

As a member of the National Labour party, Sir Harold had a liberal voting record in the House of Commons, and despite gaffes that hurt him politically, he quickly gained a reputation as a speaker. "I have achieved a prominence in the House which is unjustified by my juniority. Thus when I am called, there is a burst of applause and people flock in." He was to keep his seat for ten years.

The many, at times conflicting, sides to Sir Harold's achievement and career cannot but bring into prominence his rather quick-change, man-of-the-world personality, as well as his view of the world and, ultimately, of himself. He was by temperament, says his son, an "aristocrat." I am decidedly ignorant of the distinguishing nuances between the two words, but would myself define him as insuperably upper class, even in its "U" sense, its caste sanctities, its fetishistic enslavements. Sir Harold would seem to have had no *inner* aplomb at all. From the *Diaries* one gets an impression of an encyclopedic knowledge of rules, forms, proprieties, solecisms; of What's Not Done; of choices — between two restaurants, two waistcoats, two words — so crucial as to invoke, socially, the consequences of the Lady or the Tiger. All this, though it conveys an impeccable sense of worldliness, equally suggests a curious sense of worry. The true aristocrat, I would think, is a much more well-bred law unto himself; Miss Sackville-West, one might suppose, was a true aristocrat. Sir Harold is constantly and self-concernedly soliloquizing in his *Diaries*, though far less often like Hamlet than like Prufrock, even the Prufrock of the trousers rolled: at the Eton and Harrow match, he feels "rather out of it" for wearing a trilby hat. It just happens to be T. S. Eliot who once remarked that there is someone more important than the aristocrat, and that is the individual. The individual in Sir Harold seems often blotted out by a stuffy and insular caste consciousness. The statement of the judge in the Hauptmann trial "was one of which even an English judge need not have been ashamed." "Our host," says Sir Harold somewhere, "was the perfect type of the second-rate school and the second-rate college." The smoking room of the House of Commons was "not in the least like the smoking room of the Travellers Club. . . . Shouts and laughter and an almost complete absence of decorum"; and when Churchill and others beckoned to him, "I had to go toward them feeling stared at and conspicuous." Sir Harold could be so put off as to freeze, says his son, on encountering a single false note in people's "conversation or even their pronunciation . . . or a doily under the plate or a grapefruit on it." I keep being reminded of an Englishman from a famous family who, thinking England too stuffy, went to live in Paris, and in a final burst of rebelliousness threw his Old School tie into the wastepaper basket. The next day he saw his valet wearing it and sacked him.

Much of all this clearly qualified Sir Harold to be a diplomatist of merit or an adroit novelist of manners. And Sir Harold could, to be sure, laugh on occasion at himself; his was a sophisticated stuffiness. As a matter of fact, it is perhaps the "outsider" who can come closest to being the complete cosmopolite, the true citizen of the world — he is obliged to cling to so little, he can adapt to so much, he need adhere to no barnacled traditions, no mildewed observances. With Sir Harold the excess of caste feeling was aggravated (at least till his wife came into an inheritance) by the shortage of money. Earlier Sir Harold could only groan, and he and his wife scrape and retrench, even though — it is their son speaking — "they were running three houses . . . and they had two secretaries, a cook, a lady's maid, a chauffeur, a valet and three gardeners." All this keeping up with their ancestors meant putting up with very grubby methods of moneymaking. Grinding out chitchat for the *Evening Standard*, tangling with the House of Morgan, reviewing books in trains, at home, in the House, living through lunch in Springfield, Massachusetts, made for something very abrasive to Sir Harold's French-laundered reflexes.

But there was quite plainly a Harold Nicolson of wit and vivacity, of talent and taste, and of sympathies born of something principled rather than predetermined. And if one bangs away at his snobbish and squeamish side, it is because it so vitally colors, and discolors, his book; so much gives to the annals of an eventful era the accent of a petulantly privileged world. This, to be sure, is not all loss; indeed, it furnishes us, aware already of his many other roles, with one Harold Nicolson the more, with one whose self-avowals have their notably human value. Sir Harold is the first to confess to the hard choice that must be made between principle and ambition. With him, however, the choice does not appear, as it were, so clean-cut; what seems amiss is less the large central conflict between ambition and principle than the jostling of one ambition against another. Yet it is quite understandable: the multiplicity of endowments alone, without regard to the scarcity of money, might conspire to make Sir Harold feel a little bit nowhere from taking him everywhere.

There is certainly in the *Diaries* an element of real self-scrutiny, full of honest insight or self-depreciatory self-commiseration. There are also, at times, bits of moralistic i-dotting, and of I-patting ("I do detest cruelty in any form") as well. But all this constitutes one of the ultimate merits of candid self-portraiture; and we must remember that though we are encountering all this in print, it was set down in privacy. About the whole thing, furthermore, there is a wonderful freedom from cant: unlike a Henry Adams, Sir Harold never pretends to gag over the silver spoon. In the light of his temperament and training, he is doubtless the kind of product that only the very exceptional man will refuse to be. If we must still feel that at his worst Sir Harold is like Emily Post without her capacity to grow, he is no less a kind of born-out-of-season enlightened and civilized Whig. If the era helped turn the man of birth into a diner-out in blatantly smart society, the man of parts into a species of Official Biographer, we can scarcely argue that he should, instead, have invited his soul or cultivated his garden. He was a foreordained man of the world, which he plainly wanted to live in as well as write about; and he is more interesting and rewarding than other "aristocrats" of his age if only because he is more interested and aware. Following her temperament no less, Miss Sackville-West remained at Sissinghurst, to which Sir Harold, who lived in London, came only for weekends. But they wrote constantly to each other; and however unorthodox, their relationship bears all the postmarks of a happy marriage.

Very possibly the *Diaries and Letters*, which will extend to three volumes of selected material, and which Sir Harold insisted to his son were not written for publication, will have a continuing value as a both onstage and behind-the-scenes chronicle of events and occasions, and a continuing interest for the gallery of personages in them, the stream of talk and winds of doctrine. But we must wait for the later volumes to know. In this first volume there are no major revelations or even incisive portraits of major figures; rather, there is much that portrays the confusions of the time, much that was shady in advance of what would prove heroic, and chic and trivial in a decade that has come to signify drabness and want. Diaries and memoirs such as these have been, of course, an upper-class tradition in England from as far back as Bishop Burnet and Lord Hervey; the solidest of them all, and one very relevant to Sir Harold's for its correspondingly large social and political opportunities, is the nineteenth-century Greville's. But it would be quite unsound to bring Sir Harold into comparison with Greville, whose *Memoirs* were indeed his lifework, and who dined out pen rather than fork in hand. The overriding reason, however, is that with Greville what counts most is the history we imbibe, and with Sir Harold the self-history. Yet the self in Sir Harold speaks in many ways for many similar Englishmen, more than one of whom, I venture to think, darts in and out of the pages of this often engrossing book.

DATE DUE

GAYLORD   PRINTED IN U.S.A.